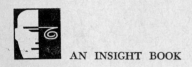

AN INSIGHT BOOK

ROLE PLAYING, REWARD, AND ATTITUDE CHANGE

An Enduring Problem in Psychology

Edited by
ALAN C. ELMS
Department of Psychology
University of California—Davis

VAN NOSTRAND REINHOLD COMPANY
NEW YORK   CINCINNATI   TORONTO
LONDON   MELBOURNE

152.4
E 48 n

Van Nostrand Reinhold Company Regional Offices:
Cincinnati, New York, Chicago, Millbrae, Dallas

Van Nostrand Reinhold Company Foreign Offices:
London, Toronto, Melbourne

Published by Van Nostrand Reinhold Company
450 West 33rd Street, New York, N. Y. 10001

Published simultaneously in Canada by
D. Van Nostrand Company (Canada), Ltd.

70-9941

15   14   13   12   11   10   9   8   7   6   5   4   3   2   1

Preface

Role playing is one of the great natural persuaders. We learn early to mouth opinions which are not our own; and if we express them often enough, they seem almost inexorably to become our own. In many instances this process of self-persuasion appears even more powerful than the direct attempts of others to influence us. As Pascal said, "We are more easily persuaded, in general, by the reasons we ourselves discover than by those which are given to us by others."

The effects of role playing are pervasive. Role playing may well be one of the central processes by which children internalize the attitudes emphasized by their family and their society. Military recruits come to feel more combative, and young executives more businesslike, in part through the outward portrayal of roles assigned to them by their seniors in command. Arguments are still heard that civil rights legislation and Supreme Court decisions may change public behavior, but can't "change the hearts and minds of men." Such arguments ignore substantial evidence that legally enforced changes in the public behavior of Southern whites toward Negroes—role playing in other words—have been followed by significant positive changes in attitudes toward integration.

Psychological practitioners have made frequent use of role playing: to alter patients' self-concepts through psychodrama therapy; to produce faster acceptance of "professional attitudes" by student teachers and student nurses; to promote greater mutual understanding on the part of management and union leaders in collective bargaining sessions. But much of this applied role playing has been done without appreciation of the psychological processes involved. Experimental study of role playing as a source of attitude change began only in the early 1950s (one of the earliest research papers, by Janis and King, is reprinted here); and most of the useful data have been collected during the past decade.

Much of this recent work developed from the realization that role playing is significant not only in itself, but as a means of evaluating general theories of attitude change. Do we shift our attitudes mainly to remain consistent with our behavior or with our publicly stated opinions? Or is attitude change more generally functional, occurring to gain incentives of many types? Do we in fact "discover reasons" to be persuaded, as Pascal suggested; or is attitude change a largely automatic balancing process, a mechanism for psychological homeostasis?

Such alternatives were first raised explicitly in a role-play context when Leon Festinger and Merrill Carlsmith gave volunteers a dollar or twenty dollars to argue publicly that a boring task was genuinely interesting, and found that the volunteers given less money changed their own opinions of the task in a more favorable direction. Festinger fitted these results into the framework of his cognitive dissonance theory, one of the most influential modern approaches to social psychological phenomena. His position has since been repeatedly challenged, supported, and rechallenged on a variety of methodological and theoretical grounds. The controversy over whether Festinger and Carlsmith's large rewards for role playing acted to reduce dissonance, induce disbelief, arouse guilt, or generate resistance has been described by William McGuire as the "Twenty-Dollar Misunderstanding." As in Robert Gover's novel of similar title, part of the argument may have arisen simply from differences in vocabulary; but a large part rests on real divergences in views of human psychology. As research in this area has continued, the apparently simple question of dissonance theory's aptness or ineptness in explaining role-play effects has been replaced by issues of considerably greater depth and complexity. When these issues are finally resolved, our present understanding of attitude formation and change should be substantially expanded.

Meanwhile, this is an exciting area of social psychological research. The central issues are not difficult to grasp, and the implications are of broad importance. Nearly all of the significant research published on the topic to date is reprinted or summarized in this volume, so the reader may follow the controversy throughout and draw his own conclusions (which may be rather different from those of the editor). These certainly will not be the last thoughts or the last data to be printed on the subject. There are variables yet to be studied, inferences yet to be drawn, and role playing effects are likely to figure prominently in attitude change theory and research for years to come.

In preparing this book, I am particularly indebted to Dr. Irving L. Janis, who introduced me to empirical studies of role playing and whose influence on my own thinking in this area has remained strong; to Dr. Clarence Ray Carpenter, who first aroused my interest in attitude change as a serious field of research; and to Dr. John K. Brilhart, who many years ago led me into interscholastic debate, a form of role playing which rarely convinces anyone but the debater himself.

ALAN C. ELMS

Contents

1

The Influence of Role Playing
on Opinion Change[1]

Irving L. Janis and Bert T. King

Though previous researchers had used role playing to explore
other problems, this paper was the first to make role playing itself
the object of careful experimental study. The authors' central
finding, that improvisational role playing is a more effective atti-
tude changer than simply listening to a persuasive speech or even
reading a prepared speech aloud, has been supported repeatedly
in a variety of situations (e.g., Harvey and Beverly, 1961; Janis
and Mann, 1965; Elms, 1966*). The few contradictory studies
appear generally to have involved either unique interacting vari-
ables (e.g., Zimbardo, 1965) or inadequacies in experimental de-
sign (e.g., Stanley and Klausmeier, 1957). Janis and King do not
contend that improvised role playing will prove to be the best
opinion changing process under all circumstances; but that, given
an appropriate setting and a reasonable basis for improvisation, it
is clearly more potent than other persuasive methods involving
similar levels of motivation and information. (Janis and King also
explored, in a section not included here and in a later study
[King and Janis, 1956], the possibility that differences in satis-
faction with one's role-play performance, rather than any direct
effects of improvisation itself, accounted for their results; but that

[1] This study was conducted at Yale University as part of a program
of research on factors influencing changes in attitude and opinion.
The research program is supported by a grant from the Rockefeller
Foundation and is under the general direction of Professor Carl I.
Hovland, to whom the authors wish to express appreciation for helpful
suggestions and criticisms. The authors also wish to thank Professor
Fred D. Sheffield for valuable suggestions during discussions prepara-
tory to designing the experiment.

* All references cited in this book are listed in the bibliography
on pages 225–232.—Ed.

possibility was largely eliminated. Other suggestions as to why *role playing changes attitudes will be found throughout this* book.)

This selection is reprinted with abridgments from the Journal of Abnormal and Social Psychology, *1954, 49, 211–218, with permission of the senior author and the American Psychological Association.*

In many everyday situations, people are induced to play social roles in which they express ideas that are not necessarily in accord with their private convictions. That certain types of role-playing experiences can facilitate changes in personal opinions has been suggested by various impressionistic observations (e.g., Myers, 1921). In recent years, psychodramatic techniques which involve role playing have been developed for use in adult education programs, leadership training, employee counseling, and psychotherapy (Bavelas, 1947; Lippitt, 1943; Maier, 1952; Moreno, 1946; Zander & Lippitt, 1944). The usual procedure consists of having persons in a group play specified roles in a simulated life situation. One of the main values of this role-playing device, according to its proponents, is that it has a corrective influence on various beliefs and attitudes which underlie chronic difficulties in human relations (cf. Maier, 1952).

As yet little is known about the conditions under which role playing leads to actual changes in personal opinions. The present experiment was designed to investigate the effects of one type of demand that is frequently made upon a person when he is induced to play a social role, namely, the requirement that he overtly verbalize to others various opinions which may not correspond to his inner convictions.

As a preliminary step in exploring the effects of role playing, one of the present authors interviewed a group of collegiate debaters who, as members of an organized team, repeatedly were required to play a role in which they publicly expressed views that did not correspond to their personal opinions. Most of the debaters reported that they frequently ended up by accepting the conclusions which they had been arbitrarily assigned to defend. Myers' (1921) impressionistic account of the improvement in morale attitudes produced by participation in an Army public-speaking course points to the same phenomenon and suggests that attitude changes may occur even when role playing is artificially induced. If true, it would appear that "saying is believing"—that overtly expressing an opinion in conformity to social demands will influence the individual's private opinion. Consequently, it seemed worth while to attempt to investigate the effects of this type of role playing in a more controlled laboratory situation where, if the alleged gain from role playing occurs, it might be possible to isolate the critical factors and to explore systematically the mediating mechanisms.

The role-playing effects described above have not as yet been verified by systematic research. If verified, they would still remain open to a variety of alternative explanations. For instance, inducing the individual to play a role in which he must advocate publicly a given position might guarantee exposure to one set of arguments to the exclusion of others. An alternative possibility, however, is that even when exposed to the same persuasive communications, people who are required to verbalize the content to others will tend to be more influenced than those who are only passively exposed. In order to test this hypothesis, the present experiment was designed so that communication exposure would be held constant by comparing the opinion changes of active participants and passive controls who were exposed to the same communications.

METHOD AND PROCEDURES

An initial questionnaire, which was administered as an opinion survey in a large classroom of male college students, contained a series of questions concerning expectations about the future. Included in this "before" questionnaire were the following key opinion items, which dealt with the subject matter of the three communications to which the experimental groups were subsequently exposed:

Item A: During the past year a number of movie theaters were forced to go out of business as result of television competition and other recent developments. At the present time there are about *18,000* movie theaters remaining. How many commercial movie theaters do you think will be in business three years from now?

Item B: What is your personal estimate about the *total supply of meat that will be available for the civilian population* of the United States during the year 1953? (. . . —— per cent of what it is at present.)

Item C: How many years do you think it will be before a *completely effective* cure for the common cold is discovered?

The experimental sessions were held approximately four weeks after the initial questionnaire had been filled out, and were represented as being part of a research project designed to develop a new aptitude test for assessing oral speaking ability. The subjects (*S*s) were asked to give an informal talk based on an outline prepared by the experimenters (*E*s) which stated the conclusion and summarized the main arguments to be presented. The arguments were logically relevant but highly biased in that they played up and interpreted "evidence" supporting only one side of the issue. Each active participant was instructed to play the role of a sincere advocate of the given point of view, while two others, who were present at the same experimental session, listened to his talk and read the prepared outline. Each *S* delivered one of the communications and was passively exposed to the other two. In order to prevent selective attention effects, the active participant was not told what the topic of his talk would be until his turn came to present it. He was given about three minutes to look over the prepared outline, during which time the others (passive controls) also were requested to study duplicate copies of the same outline so as to be prepared for judging the adequacy of the speaker's performance. After the first talk was over, another *S* was selected to present the second communication, and then the remaining *S* presented the third communication, the same procedures being followed in each case.

Immediately after the last talk was finished, *S*s were given the "after" questionnaire, much of which was devoted to rating the performance of each speaker. The key opinion items were included among numerous filler items, all of which were introduced as questions designed to provide information about the student's interests and opinions concerning the three topics so as to enable the investigators to select the most appropriate topic for future applications of the oral speaking test.

In all three communications, the conclusion specified an opinion estimate which was numerically *lower* than that given by any of the students on the "before" test. Thus, all active participants were required to argue in favor of an extreme position which differed from their initial beliefs. The influence of each communication could readily be observed by noting the degree to which the students in each group *lowered* their opinion estimates on the "after" test.

The basic schema of the experiment is shown in Table 1. In

TABLE 1

Schema of the Experimental Conditions

	Group A (N = 31)	Group B (N = 29)	Group C (N = 30)
Communication A: movie theaters	active participants	passive controls	passive controls
Communication B: meat supply	passive controls	active participants	passive controls
Communication C: cold cure	passive controls	passive controls	active participants

each row of the table which represents exposure to a given communication, there is one group of active participants and two contrasting groups which, when combined, form the group of passive controls. In effect, the experimental treatments were repeated with different communication contents, providing three separate instances of active versus passive exposure, although the same Ss were used throughout.

In order to obtain some information for checking on selective attention effects, a variation of the passive control condition (not represented in the table) was introduced into the experiment by using a small supplementary group who listened and took notes on all three talks. In addition, base-line data for assessing the effectiveness of the communications were obtained from a comparable group of "pure" controls who were not exposed to any of the communications.

RESULTS AND DISCUSSION

Effects of Active Participation

Initially, on each of the three key items in the precommunication questionnaire, the difference between the active participation group and the passive control group was nonsignificant. The opinion changes observed after exposure to the three communications are shown in Table 2.[2] The results indicate that in the case of two of the three communications (A and B), the active participants were more influenced than the passive controls. For both communications, the differences in net sizable change are statistically reliable, and the differences in net (slight or sizable) change, although nonreliable, are in the expected direction.

In the case of the third communication (C), the two groups showed approximately the same amount of opinion change. But additional findings (based on confidence ratings given by each S immediately after answering the key opinion questions) indicate that the active participants who presented Communication C, like those who presented the other two communications, expressed a higher level of *confidence* in their postcommunication estimates than did the corresponding passive controls. Table 3 shows the net changes in confidence ratings for each of the three communications in terms of a breakdown that takes account of the direction and magnitude of opinion change. The breakdown was necessary inasmuch as a successful communication would be expected to increase the confidence only of those who changed their opinions in the direction advocated by the communication. The net change in confidence shown for each subgroup is based on a comparison of pre- and postcommunication ratings given by each S, and was computed by subtracting the percentage who showed a decrease in confidence from the percentage who showed an increase in confidence. In general, the findings in Table 3 reveal a consistent pattern for all three communications: in every instance, active participation tended to have at least a

[2] The table does not include the data on the "pure" (unexposed) control group. The net changes for this group were approximately zero in the case of all three key items, and the corresponding net changes for the active participants and the passive controls (shown in the last rows of the table) were significantly greater (p's range from .10 down to $< .01$). Hence, all three communications had a significant effect on the opinions of those who were either actively or passively exposed to them.

The probability values reported throughout this paper are based on one tail of the theoretical distribution. Whenever intergroup comparisons were made with respect to the net percentage who changed by a given amount, the reliability of the difference was tested by the formula presented in Hovland, Lumsdaine, and Sheffield (1949).

TABLE 2

Comparison of Active Participants with Passive Controls on Amount of Change in Opinion Estimates

Changes in Opinion Estimates†	Communication A: (Movie Theaters)		Communication B: (Meat Shortage)		Communication C: (Cold Cure)	
	Active Participants (N = 31)	Passive Controls (N = 57)*	Active Participants (N = 29)	Passive Controls (N = 57)	Active Participants (N = 30)	Passive Controls (N = 53)
Sizable increase	0%	2%	0%	2%	7%	6%
Slight increase	3%	9%	7%	14%	10%	9%
No change	23%	20%	24%	16%	13%	19%
Slight decrease	29%	46%	27½%	49%	23%	15%
Sizable decrease	45%	23%	41½%	19%	47%	51%
TOTAL	100%	100%	100%	100%	100%	100%
Net change (% increase minus % decrease) Slight or sizable change	−71%	−58%	−62%	−52%	−53%	−51%
Sizable change	−45%	−21%	−41½%	−17%	−40%	−45%
p	.01		.01		> .30	

* The number of cases in each passive control group is slightly smaller than expected from the N's shown in Table 1 because the data from a few cases were inadequate and hence were eliminated from the analysis (e.g., the individual failed to give an answer to the particular question).

† The "net change (slight or sizable)" is defined as the percentage changing in the direction advocated by the communication minus the percentage changing in the opposite direction. The "net sizable change" in the case of Communication A refers to the difference in the percentages who lowered and raised their estimate by 5,000 (movie theaters) or more. For Communication B, a sizable change was 25 (per cent) or more; for Communication C it was 5 (years) or more.

slight positive effect with respect to increasing the confidence of those whose opinion estimates were influenced by the communication. The results indicate that active participation resulted in a significant gain in confidence, particularly among those students whose opinion estimates were markedly influenced by Communication C.[3] This finding is especially striking in view of the fact that the opinion change results for Communication C (Table 2) failed to show any gain from active participation.

Insofar as confidence ratings can be regarded as indicators of the degree of conviction with which the new opinions are held, the positive findings based on the opinion change data for Communications A and B are partially confirmed by the confidence change data based on Communication C. Thus, the data based on all three communications contribute evidence that the effectiveness of the communications (as manifested by opinion changes or by confidence changes) tended to be augmented by active participation.

Although Ss were not told what their topic would be until they were about to begin giving the talk, it is possible that the ego-involving task of presenting one of the talks may have given rise to emotional excitement or other interfering reactions which

[3] For the entire group of active participants who were exposed to Communication C, there was a net increase in confidence of 37 per cent; the corresponding net increase for the entire group of passive controls was only 13½ per cent. This difference was due entirely to the marked gain in confidence manifested by those students in the active group who had changed their opinion estimates in the direction advocated by the communication. The results in the first row of the table indicate that, among the students whose opinion estimates were uninfluenced by Communication C, the active participants showed a small net decrease in confidence which was equal to that shown by the passive controls. The next row of Table 3 indicates that, among those students who decreased their opinion estimates by at least one-half year or more after exposure to Communication C, the active participants showed a greater net increase in confidence than the passive controls; the difference of 31 per cent approaches statistical significance ($p = .07$). Finally, the last row of the table shows that an even greater difference in confidence changes emerges when the comparison is limited to those students who decreased their opinion estimates by five years or more. (The 49½ per cent difference is reliable at beyond the .05 confidence level.) Further analysis of the subgroup data indicated that the differences shown in this table could not be attributed to statistical artifacts arising from initial differences between the various subgroups.

TABLE 3

Comparison of Active Participants with Passive Controls on Amount of Change in Confidence

Subgroup Breakdown According to Changes in Opinion Estimates	Net Change in Confidence (Percent increase minus percent decrease)					
	Communication A		Communication B		Communication C	
	Active Participants	Passive Controls	Active Participants	Passive Controls	Active Participants	Passive Controls
1. *Uninfluenced:* opinion estimates increased or unchanged	−12% (N = 8)	−5% (N = 18)	0% (N = 9)	+6% (N = 18)	−11% (N = 9)	−11% (N = 18)
2. *Influenced:* opinion estimates slightly or sizably decreased	+9% (N = 23)	−10% (N = 39)	+20% (N = 20)	+5% (N = 39)	+57% (N = 21)	+26% (N = 35)
Gain from active participation	+19%		+15%		+31%	
3. *Highly Influenced:* opinion estimates sizably decreased	−7% (N = 14)	−38% (N = 13)	+25% (N = 12)	0% (N = 11)	+64½% (N = 14)	+15% (N = 27)
Gain from active participation	+31%		+25%		+49½%	

could have had the effect of reducing the Ss' responsiveness when passively exposed to the other two communications. This possibility appears extremely improbable, however, in the light of supplementary control observations:

1. Some of the passive controls had been exposed to the communications *before* giving their own talk, while others were passively exposed *after* having given their own talk. Nonsignificant differences were found in the amount of opinion change shown under these two conditions.

2. The results from the passive controls were "replicated" by the results from an independent group of 16 students who did not give an oral presentation, but who were asked to follow the prepared outline carefully and to note down the main arguments given by each of the three speakers. Despite the fact that their notes were fairly complete and indicated a relatively high degree of attention to the content of all three communications, these supplementary controls displayed approximately the same amount of opinion change as the original group of passive controls.[4]

Observations Pertinent to Explanatory Hypotheses

Many different types of speculative hypotheses could be put forth to account for the facilitating effects of active participation, postulating a gain in attention and learning from overtly rehearsing the communication, or a gain in comprehension from reformulating the arguments in one's own words, or a gain in motivation from playing the role of communicator, etc. Some supplementary observations were made for the purpose of exploring various factors which might provide leads to the key mediating mechanisms. Although far from conclusive, the evidence derived from these observations provides a preliminary basis for selecting explanatory hypotheses which warrant further experimental analysis.

[4] It is conceivable, of course, that the activity of taking notes on the talks might have interfered with responsiveness to the persuasive content of the communications. While this possibility cannot be excluded, it seems implausible inasmuch as our Ss were college students who had had considerable practice in taking notes during lectures. Educational research on the effects of note taking indicates that this form of activity generally has a beneficial rather than a detrimental effect on the student's ability to absorb the content of an oral communication (Crawford, 1925).

The findings based on the supplementary controls (who were required to take notes on the three talks) suggest that variation in attention level probably was not a crucial factor that could explain the participation effects observed in the present experiment. More promising clues were discovered by taking account of differences in the types of reactions evoked by the three communications. We have seen that in the case of Communications A and B, a clear-cut gain from active participation was manifested by changes in opinion estimates; but, in the case of Communication C, opinion estimates were unaffected, the gain being manifested only in the form of increased confidence. With a view to discovering some differentiating factor, we examined the available evidence bearing on the question of why active participation might be more effective under certain stimulus conditions (represented by Communications A and B) than under other conditions (represented by Communication C).

The first step in this inquiry was to examine E's notes on: (a) the active Ss' behavior while giving their talks, and (b) Ss' statements in the informal interviews conducted at the end of each experimental session. These observations provide two suggestive leads:

1. The active participants who presented Communication C seemed to engage in *less improvisation* than those who presented the other two communications. The Communication C group appeared to adhere much more closely to the prepared outline, making little attempt to reformulate the main points, to insert illustrative examples, or to invent additional arguments.

2. Active participants in the Communication C group seemed to experience much more difficulty than the other groups in presenting their talks. During their performance they appeared to be more hesitant and tense. Afterwards, they expressed many more complaints about the task, claiming that their topic was more difficult to present than either of the other two. In general, these subjects seemed *less satisfied* with their performance than those who presented the other two topics.

The first observation suggests that mere repetition of a persuasive communication may have little or no effect as compared with an improvised restatement. This observation is in line with some suggestive findings from an opinion change study by Kelman (1953) in which seventh-grade students were given a communication, and, immediately afterwards, were offered various incentives to write essays in support of the communicator's position. Kelman observed that the essays written by the group which showed the greatest amount of opinion change tended to be longer, to include more improvisation, and to be of better overall quality (as rated by several judges) than the essays written by the other experimental groups.

Reformulating and elaborating on the communication might be a critical factor in producing the gain from active participation, perhaps because the communicatee is stimulated to think of the kinds of arguments, illustrations, and motivating appeals that he regards as most convincing. The importance of the improvisation factor in relation to participation effects could not be investigated further with the data at hand from the present experiment, but is currently being studied by the present authors in another experiment that is specifically designed to compare the effects of different types of active participation.

With respect to the second observation, it should be noted that there may have been an objective basis for the greater dissatisfaction experienced on Communication C because of the greater amount of unfamiliar technical material it contained. The "cold cure" outline referred to a great many technical details concerning the cold virus, antibiotics, allergic reactions, and antihistamines. Many of these details were probably unfamiliar to Ss, and consequently it may have been difficult for them to "spell out" the implications of the arguments. In contrast, the outlines for the other two topics contained very little technical material, relying mainly on arguments that were likely to be quite familiar to college students. . . .

There is another important problem which arises from the findings in the present experiment and which also requires systematic investigation: Does social role playing facilitate the internalization of externally imposed value judgments, mores, and taboos? The persuasive communications used in this study dealt with relatively impersonal beliefs about the future, and the main findings show that acceptance of opinions of this sort was markedly increased by experimentally induced role playing. It remains problematical, however, whether active participation also influences the acceptance of opinions and attitudes that are more directly tied up with daily life activities, interpersonal relation-ships, and emotionally charged dilemmas.

Obviously, it is unsafe to generalize widely from a single exploratory study based on the opinion changes of college stu-dents produced in a somewhat artificial test situation. Neverthe-less, the present experiment provides preliminary evidence indi-cating that verbal conformity elicited by role playing can signifi-cantly influence the acceptance of new beliefs. Under certain specifiable conditions which await further investigation, it seems to be true that "saying is believing."

2

Attitude Change as a Function of Response Restriction

HERBERT C. KELMAN

This study, published prior to the Janis and King paper, is not primarily concerned with the effectiveness of role playing and does not use that term. Kelman was chiefly interested in the attitudinal consequences of different levels of pressure to make a "desired verbal response." But the verbal response Kelman wanted was a kind of role playing (for the majority of his subjects), and his manipulations of pressure involved variations in the size and certainty of rewards to be given for the response. So this was actually the first study to deal directly with the topic of our book: the effects of varied incentive levels upon attitude change induced by role playing. Though much of the paper involves other matters as well, Kelman's summary and conclusions (the portion of the paper to follow) cogently present issues which remain quite relevant to current role-play research. (Several more recent papers by Kelman [1961, 1967; Kelman and Baron, 1968] contain rewarding discussions of role playing and attitude change generally, but do not deal extensively with variations in pressure or reward level.)

This selection is excerpted from Human Relations, *1953, 6, 185–214, with the permission of the author and Plenum Publishing Company Ltd.*

The present experiment was concerned with the relationship between conformity to social norms and actual changes in attitude. This problem was studied in the specific setting of a fixed verbal communication situation. To induce conformity, the communicator introduced two degrees of response restriction. Response restriction is defined as any action on the part of the communicator which influences his audience in the direction of explicitly making the response which he favors. The experiment investigated the effects of conformity under these two conditions of response restriction on attitude change. It was felt that the amount of change would not be a simple function of the degree of conformity to the communicator's restriction, but would also depend on the conditions under which conformity takes place. It was hypothesized that conformity in the communication situation will increase attitude change to the extent to which implicit *supporting* responses are produced, and decrease attitude change to the extent to which implicit *interfering* responses are produced.

Response restriction was introduced by the use of positive incentives, i.e., the communicator induced conformity by promising his *Ss* a reward. The *Ss* were 246 seventh grade students. The procedure was as follows: 1. *Ss'* attitudes on the relative harmfulness of two types of comic books were ascertained. 2. The next day they heard a communication at variance with most *Ss'* initial attitudes. After the communication they were asked to write essays, presenting their own position. The instructions varied as follows: a—*Control group:* Ss were just asked to write their own opinions. b—*Low Restriction group:* Ss were promised a reward if they agreed with the communicator, but told that only a small percentage of the class would get the reward; it was made clear to them that non-conformity is possible and may have certain advantages. c—*High Restriction group:* Ss were promised a reward and assured that everyone who agreed with the communicator would get the reward; it was made clear that everyone was expected to conform. 3. A week later, the attitude questionnaires were readministered. The differences between the before- and after-questionnaires constitute the measure of change.

The following results were obtained. As expected, the Control group has the lowest, the High Restriction group the highest number of conformists (i.e., *Ss* whose essays agree with the communicator's position). The amount of attitude change is not, however, directly related to the degree of conformity. The greatest amount of change is found in the Low Restriction group. The Low Restriction group changes more than the High Restriction group even though it has fewer conformists; when the proportion of conformists is statistically controlled, this difference becomes significant at the three per cent level of confidence. Also, the Low Restriction group changes significantly more than the Control group, even after there is a correction for the disproportion in number of conformists. There is no significant difference in amount of change between the High Restriction and the Control groups. On the basis of the findings summarized here it can be concluded that attitude change is not a simple function of conformity, but also depends on the conditions under which conformity takes place. The conditions of Low Restriction seem to be more favorable to change than the conditions of High Restriction.

To obtain information on the differences in the conditions of Low and High Restriction which can account for the differences in change, the quality of the Ss' essays was rated and their reactions to the experimental situation were analyzed. These data indicate that Ss in the Low Restriction group make more supporting and fewer interfering responses while writing their essays. Three hypotheses can account for these findings: 1. The more contingent the reward on the quality of performance, the more supporting responses are produced. 2. The greater the indecision, the more supporting responses are produced. 3. The greater the felt pressure, the more interfering responses are produced. Regardless of the specific mechanisms that are involved, however, it can be concluded that conditions favorable to change are those in which conformity is accompanied by implicit supporting responses (as in the Low Restriction group), and conditions unfavorable to change are those in which conformity is accompanied by implicit interfering responses (as in the High Restriction group).

The findings of this experiment have some interesting implications for the study of reference groups and the process of internalization of group norms. They suggest some of the conditions under which internalization would be expected to occur, and some of the conditions which would produce merely overt conformity. There are also some educational implications worth noting. The study provides experimental evidence for two accepted educational principles: The notion that significant learning can occur only if the student has to think through and integrate the material by himself; and the notion that lasting educational results can be achieved only if there is a positive relationship between student and teacher.

It should be stressed that the above implications are merely suggestive, and their validity can only be demonstrated by research in different settings. The generality of the present findings is limited by the kind of setting used in this experiment, i.e., the fixed communication situation. It is further limited by some of the special characteristics of the experimental situation, such as the use of positive incentives to achieve response restriction. To broaden the generality of the findings, it is necessary to study the effects of response restriction under different conditions. For example, it would be important to see if results similar to those of the present experiment are obtained when response restriction is achieved through the use of force, threats, or high-pressure techniques.

3

Cognitive Consequences of Forced Compliance

Leon Festinger and James M. Carlsmith[1]

*This article started the fireworks. Until Festinger appropriated
the work of Kelman and of Janis and King as evidence for his
cognitive dissonance theory, both here and in his book (1957),
most psychologists seemed to accept role playing as involving a
rather straightforward process of self-persuasion. (The role
player thinks up enough good logical arguments and enough good
rational reasons for adoption to convince himself he should believe what he's saying.) When Festinger and Carlsmith set out
to show that the more good rational reasons a person had for
role playing (mainly in the form of cold cash) the less he would
convince himself, their results were so striking and so persuasive
that this paper promptly became the most widely quoted source
of support for dissonance theory.*

*The experiment itself is neatly done and imaginatively con-
ceived. Janis and King's results could apparently be explained
equally well either through their own hypotheses or through dissonance theory. So Festinger's problem was to devise a situation
in which the two approaches clearly predicted different outcomes.
This he did with great success. (An interesting dramatization of
the experimental procedure is available in the film,* Focus on
Behavior: The Social Animal, *produced by the American Psychological Association and National Education Television.)*

This selection is reprinted with slight abridgment from the

[1] The experiment reported here was done as part of a program of
research supported by a grant from the National Science Foundation
to the senior author. We wish to thank Leonard Hommel, Judson
Mills, and Robert Terwilliger for their help in designing and carrying
out the experiment. We would also like to acknowledge the help of
Ruth Smith and Marilyn M. Miller.

Journal of Abnormal and Social Psychology, *1959, 58, 203–210,* *with permission of the senior author and the American Psychological Association.*

What happens to a person's private opinion if he is forced to do or say something contrary to that opinion? Only recently has there been any experimental work related to this question. Two studies reported by Janis and King (1954; 1956) clearly showed that, at least under some conditions, the private opinion changes so as to bring it into closer correspondence with the overt behavior the person was forced to perform. Specifically, they showed that if a person is forced to improvise a speech supporting a point of view with which he disagrees, his private opinion moves toward the position advocated in the speech. The observed opinion change is greater than for persons who only hear the speech or for persons who read a prepared speech with emphasis solely on elocution and manner of delivery. The authors of these two studies explain their results mainly in terms of mental rehearsal and thinking up new arguments. In this way, they propose, the person who is forced to improvise a speech convinces himself. They present some evidence, which is not altogether conclusive, in support of this explanation. We will have more to say concerning this explanation in discussing the results of our experiment.

Kelman (1953) tried to pursue the matter further. He reasoned that if the person is induced to make an overt statement contrary to his private opinion by the offer of some reward, then the greater the reward offered, the greater should be the subsequent opinion change. His data, however, did not support this idea. He found, rather, that a large reward produced less subsequent opinion change than did a smaller reward. Actually, this finding by Kelman is consistent with the theory we will outline below but, for a number of reasons, is not conclusive. One of the major weaknesses of the data is that not all subjects in the experiment made an overt statement contrary to their private opinion in order to obtain the offered reward. What is more, as one might expect, the percentage of subjects who complied increased as the size of the offered reward increased. Thus, with self-selection of who did and who did not make the required overt statement and with varying percentages of subjects in the different conditions who did make the required statement, no interpretation of the data can be unequivocal.

Recently, Festinger (1957) proposed a theory concerning cognitive dissonance from which come a number of derivations about opinion change following forced compliance. Since these derivations are stated in detail by Festinger (1957, Ch. 4), we will here give only a brief outline of the reasoning.

Let us consider a person who privately holds opinion "X" but has, as a result of pressure brought to bear on him, publicly stated that he believes "not X."

1. This person has two cognitions which, psychologically, do not fit together: one of these is the knowledge that he believes "X," the other the knowledge that he has publicly stated that he believes "not X." If no factors other than his private opinion are considered, it would follow, at least in our culture, that if he believes "X" he would publicly state "X." Hence, his cognition of his private belief is dissonant with his cognition concerning his actual public statement.

2. Similarly, the knowledge that he has said "not X" is consonant with (does fit together with) those cognitive elements corresponding to the reasons, pressures, promises of rewards and/or threats of punishment which induced him to say "not X."

3. In evaluating the total magnitude of dissonance, one must take account of both dissonances and consonances. Let us think of the sum of all the dissonances involving some particular cognition as "D" and the sum of all the consonances as "C." Then we might think of the total magnitude of dissonance as being a function of "D" divided by "D" plus "C."

Let us then see what can be said about the total magnitude of dissonance in a person created by the knowledge that he said "not X" and really believes "X." With everything else held constant, this total magnitude of dissonance would decrease as the number and importance of the pressures which induced him to say "not X" increased.

Thus, if the overt behavior was brought about by, say, offers of reward or threats of punishment, the magnitude of dissonance is maximal if these promised rewards or threatened punishments were just barely sufficient to induce the person to say "not X." From this point on, as the promised rewards or threatened punishment become larger, the magnitude of dissonance becomes smaller.

4. One way in which the dissonance can be reduced is for the person to change his private opinion so as to bring it into correspondence with what he has said. One would consequently expect to observe such opinion change after a person has been forced or induced to say something contrary to his private opinion. Furthermore, since the pressure to reduce dissonance will be a function of the magnitude of the dissonance, the observed opinion change should be greatest when the pressure used to elicit the overt behavior is just sufficient to do it.

The present experiment was designed to test this derivation under controlled, laboratory conditions. In the experiment we varied the amount of reward used to force persons to make a statement contrary to their private views. The prediction [from 3 and 4 above] is that the larger the reward given to the subject, the smaller will be the subsequent opinion change.

PROCEDURE

Seventy-one male students in the introductory psychology course at Stanford University were used in the experiment. In this course, students are required to spend a certain number of hours as subjects (Ss) in experiments. They choose among the available experiments by signing their names on a sheet posted on the bulletin board which states the nature of the experiment. The present experiment was listed as a two-hour experiment dealing with "Measures of Performance."

During the first week of the course, when the requirement of serving in experiments was announced and explained to the students, the instructor also told them about a study that the psychology department was conducting. He explained that, since they were required to serve in experiments, the department was conducting a study to evaluate these experiments in order to be able to improve them in the future. They were told that a sample of students would be interviewed after having served as Ss. They were urged to cooperate in these interviews by being completely frank and honest. The importance of this announcement will become clear shortly. It enabled us to measure the opinions of our *S*s in a context not directly connected with our experiment and in which we could reasonably expect frank and honest expressions of opinion.

When the *S* arrived for the experiment on "Measures of Performance" he had to wait for a few minutes in the secretary's office. The experimenter (*E*) then came in, introduced himself to the *S* and, together, they walked into the laboratory room where the *E* said:

This experiment usually takes a little over an hour but, of course, we had to schedule it for two hours. Since we have that extra time, the introductory psychology people asked if they could interview some of our subjects. [Offhand and conversationally.] Did they announce that in class? I gather that they're interviewing some people who have been in experiments. I don't know much about it. Anyhow, they may want to interview you when you're through here.

With no further introduction or explanation the *S* was shown the first task, which involved putting 12 spools onto a tray, emptying the tray, refilling it with spools, and so on. He was told to use one hand and to work at his own speed. He did this for one-half hour. The *E* then removed the tray and spools and placed in front of the *S* a board containing 48 square pegs. His task was to turn each peg a quarter turn clockwise, then another quarter turn, and so on. He was told again to use one hand and to work at his own speed. The *S* worked at this task for another half hour.

While the *S* was working on these tasks, the *E* sat, with a stop watch in his hand, busily making notations on a sheet of paper. He did so in order to make it convincing that this was what the *E* was interested in and that these tasks, and how the *S* worked on them, was the total experiment. From our point of view the experiment had hardly started. The hour which the *S* spent working on the repetitive, monotonous tasks was intended to provide, for each *S* uniformly, an experience about which he would have a somewhat negative opinion.

After the half hour on the second task was over, the *E* conspicuously set the stop watch back to zero, put it away, pushed his chair back, lit a cigarette, and said:

O.K. Well, that's all we have in the experiment itself. I'd like to explain what this has been all about so you'll have some idea of why you were doing this. [*E* pauses.] Well, the way the experiment is set up is this. There are actually two groups in the experiment. In one, the group you were in, we bring the subject in and give him essentially no introduction to the experiment. That is, all we tell him is what he needs to know in order to do the tasks, and he has no idea of what the experiment is all about, or what it's going to be like, or anything like that. But in the other group, we have a student that we've hired that works for us regularly, and what I do is take him into the next room where the subject is waiting —the same room you were waiting in before—and I introduce him as if he had just finished being a subject in the experiment. That is, I say: "This is so-and-so, who's just finished the experiment, and I've asked him to tell you a little of what it's about before you start." The fellow who works for us then, in conversation with the next subject, makes these points: [The *E* then produced a sheet headed "For Group B" which had written on it: It was very enjoyable, I had a lot of fun, I enjoyed myself, it was very interesting, it was intriguing, it was exciting. The *E* showed this to the *S* and then proceeded with his false explanation of the purpose of the experiment.] Now, of course, we have this student do this, because if the experimenter does it, it doesn't look as realistic, and what we're interested in doing is comparing how these two groups do on the experiment—the one with this previous expectation about the experiment, and the other, like yourself, with essentially none.

Up to this point the procedure was identical for *S*s in all conditions. From this point on they diverged somewhat. Three conditions were run, Control, One Dollar, and Twenty Dollars, as follows:

Control Condition

The *E* continued:

Is that fairly clear? [Pause.] Look, that fellow [looks at watch] I was telling you about from the introductory psychology class said he would get here a couple of minutes from now. Would you mind waiting to see if he wants to talk to you? Fine. Why don't we go into the other room to wait? [The *E* left the *S* in the secretary's office for four minutes. He then returned and said:] O.K. Let's check and see if he does want to talk to you.

One and Twenty Dollar Conditions

The *E* continued:

Is that fairly clear how it is set up and what we're trying to do? [Pause.] Now, I also have a sort of strange thing to ask you. The thing is this. [Long pause, some confusion and uncertainty in the following, with a degree of embarrassment on the part of the *E*. The manner of the *E* contrasted strongly with the preceding unhesitant and assured false explanation of the experiment. The point was to make it seem to the *S* that this was the first time the *E* had done this and that he felt unsure of himself.] The fellow who normally does this for us couldn't do it today—he just phoned in, and something or other came up for him—so we've been looking around for someone that we could hire to do it for us. You see, we've got another subject waiting [looks at watch] who is supposed to be in that other condition. Now Professor ———, who is in charge of this experiment, suggested that perhaps we could take a chance on your doing it for us. I'll tell you what we had in mind: the thing is, if you could do it for us now, then of course you would know how to do it, and if something like this should ever come up again, that is, the regular fellow couldn't make it, and we had a subject scheduled, it would be very reassuring to us to know that we had somebody else we could call on who knew how to do it. So, if you would be willing to do this for us, we'd like to hire you to do it now and then be on call in the future, if something like this should ever happen again. We can pay you a dollar (twenty dollars) for doing this for us, that is, for doing it now and then being on call. Do you think you could do that for us?

If the *S* hesitated, the *E* said things like, "It will only take a few minutes," "The regular person is pretty reliable; this is the first time he has missed," or "If we needed you we could phone you a day or two in advance; if you couldn't make it, of course, we wouldn't expect you to come." After the *S* agreed to do it, the *E* gave him the previously mentioned sheet of paper headed "For Group B" and asked him to read it through again. The *E* then paid the *S* one dollar (twenty dollars), made out a handwritten receipt form, and asked the *S* to sign it. He then said:

O.K., the way we'll do it is this. As I said, the next subject should be here by now. I think the next one is a girl. I'll take you into the next room and introduce you to her, saying that you've just finished the experiment and that we've asked you to tell her a little about it. And what we want you to do is just sit down and get into a conversation with her and try to get across the points on that sheet of paper. I'll leave you alone and come back after a couple of minutes. O.K.?

The E then took the S into the secretary's office where he had previously waited and where the next S was waiting. (The secretary had left the office.) He introduced the girl and the S to one another saying that the S had just finished the experiment and would tell her something about it. He then left saying he would return in a couple of minutes. The girl, an undergraduate hired for this role, said little until the S made some positive remarks about the experiment and then said that she was surprised because a friend of hers had taken the experiment the week before and had told her that it was boring and that she ought to try to get out of it. Most Ss responded by saying something like "Oh, no, it's really very interesting. I'm sure you'll enjoy it." The girl, after this listened quietly, accepting and agreeing to everything the S told her. The discussion between the S and the girl was recorded on a hidden tape recorder.

After two minutes the E returned, asked the girl to go into the experimental room, thanked the S for talking to the girl, wrote down his phone number to continue the fiction that we might call on him again in the future and then said: "Look, could we check and see if that fellow from introductory psychology wants to talk to you?"

From this point on, the procedure for all three conditions was once more identical. As the E and the S started to walk to the office where the interviewer was, the E said: "Thanks very much for working on those tasks for us. I hope you did enjoy it. Most of our subjects tell us afterward that they found it quite interesting. You get a chance to see how you react to the tasks and so forth." This short persuasive communication was made in all conditions in exactly the same way. The reason for doing it, theoretically, was to make it easier for anyone who wanted to persuade himself that the tasks had been, indeed, enjoyable.

When they arrived at the interviewer's office, the E asked the interviewer whether or not he wanted to talk to the S. The interviewer said yes, the E shook hands with the S, said good-bye, and left. The interviewer, of course, was always kept in complete ignorance of which condition the *S* was in. The interview consisted of four questions, on each of which the *S* was first encouraged to talk about the matter and was then asked to rate his opinion or reaction on an 11-point scale. The questions are as follows:

1. Were the tasks interesting and enjoyable? In what way? In what way were they not? Would you rate how you feel about them on a scale from −5 to +5 where −5 means they were extremely dull and boring, +5 means they were extremely interesting and enjoyable, and zero means they were neutral, neither interesting nor uninteresting.

2. Did the experiment give you an opportunity to learn about your own ability to perform these tasks? In what way? In what way not? Would you rate how you feel about this on a scale from 0 to 10 where 0 means you learned nothing and 10 means you learned a great deal.

3. From what you know about the experiment and the tasks involved in it, would you say the experiment was measuring anything important? That is, do you think the results may have scientific value? In what way? In what way not? Would you rate your opinion on this matter on a scale from 0 to 10 where 0 means the results have no scientific value or importance and 10 means they have a great deal of value and importance.

4. Would you have any desire to participate in another similar experiment? Why? Why not? Would you rate your desire to participate in a similar experiment again on a scale from −5 to +5, where −5 means you would definitely dislike to participate, +5 means you would definitely like to participate, and 0 means you have no particular feeling about it one way or the other.

As may be seen, the questions varied in how directly relevant they were to what the *S* had told the girl. This point will be discussed further in connection with the results.

At the close of the interview the *S* was asked what he thought the experiment was about and, following this, was asked directly whether or not he was suspicious of anything and, if so, what he was suspicious of. When the interview was over, the interviewer brought the *S* back to the experimental room where the *E* was waiting together with the girl who had posed as the waiting *S*. (In the control condition, of course, the girl was not there.)

The true purpose of the experiment was then explained to the S in detail, and the reasons for each of the various steps in the experiment were explained carefully in relation to the true purpose. All experimental Ss in both One Dollar and Twenty Dollar conditions were asked, after this explanation, to return the money they had been given. All Ss, without exception, were quite willing to return the money.

The data from 11 of the 71 Ss in the experiment had to be discarded for the following reasons:

1. Five Ss (three in the One Dollar and two in the Twenty Dollar condition) indicated in the interview that they were suspicious about having been paid to tell the girl the experiment was fun and suspected that that was the real purpose of the experiment.

2. Two Ss (both in the One Dollar condition) told the girl that they had been hired, that the experiment was really boring but they were supposed to say it was fun.

3. Three Ss (one in the One Dollar and two in the Twenty Dollar condition) refused to take the money and refused to be hired.

4. One S (in the One Dollar condition), immediately after having talked to the girl, demanded her phone number saying he would call her and explain things, and also told the E he wanted to wait until she was finished so he could tell her about it.

These 11 Ss were, of course, run through the total experiment anyhow and the experiment was explained to them afterwards. Their data, however, are not included in the analysis.

Summary of Design

There remain, for analysis, 20 Ss in each of the three conditions. Let us review these briefly: 1. *Control condition.* These Ss were treated identically in all respects to the Ss in the experimental conditions, except that they were never asked to, and never did, tell the waiting girl that the experimental tasks were enjoyable and lots of fun. 2. *One Dollar condition.* These Ss were hired for one dollar to tell a waiting S that tasks, which were really rather dull and boring, were interesting, enjoyable, and lots of fun. 3. *Twenty Dollar condition.* These Ss were hired for twenty dollars to do the same thing.

RESULTS

The major results of the experiment are summarized in Table 1 which lists, separately for each of the three experimental con-

TABLE 1

Average Ratings on Interview Questions for Each Condition

Question on Interview	Experimental Condition		
	Control (N = 20)	One Dollar (N = 20)	Twenty Dollars (N = 20)
How enjoyable tasks were (rated from −5 to +5)	−.45	+1.35	−.05
How much they learned (rated from 0 to 10)	3.08	2.80	3.15
Scientific importance (rated from 0 to 10)	5.60	6.45	5.18
Participate in similar exp. (rated from −5 to +5)	−.62	+1.20	−.25

ditions, the average rating which the Ss gave at the end of each question on the interview. We will discuss each of the questions on the interview separately, because they were intended to measure different things. One other point before we proceed to examine the data. In all the comparisons, the Control condition should be regarded as a baseline from which to evaluate the results in the other two conditions. The Control condition gives us, essentially, the reactions of Ss to the tasks and their opinions about the experiment as falsely explained to them, without the experimental introduction of dissonance. The data from the other conditions may be viewed, in a sense, as changes from this baseline.

How Enjoyable the Tasks Were

The average ratings on this question, presented in the first row of figures in Table 1, are the results most important to the experiment. These results are the ones most directly relevant to the specific dissonance which was experimentally created. It will be recalled that the tasks were purposely arranged to be rather boring and monotonous. And, indeed, in the Control condition the average rating was −.45, somewhat on the negative side of the neutral point.

In the other two conditions, however, the Ss told someone that these tasks were interesting and enjoyable. The resulting dissonance could, of course, most directly be reduced by persuading themselves that the tasks were, indeed, interesting and enjoyable. In the One Dollar condition, since the magnitude of dissonance was high, the pressure to reduce this dissonance would also be high. In this condition, the average rating was +1.35, considerably on the positive side and significantly different from the Control condition at the .02 level [2] ($t = 2.48$).

In the Twenty Dollar condition, where less dissonance was created experimentally because of the greater importance of the consonant relations, there is correspondingly less evidence of dissonance reduction. The average rating in this condition is only −.05, slightly and not significantly higher than the Control condition. The difference between the One Dollar and Twenty Dollar conditions is significant at the .03 level ($t = 2.22$). In short, when an S was induced, by offer of reward, to say something contrary to his private opinion, this private opinion tended to change so as to correspond more closely with what he had said. The greater the reward offered (beyond what was necessary to elicit the behavior) the smaller was the effect.

Desire to Participate in a Similar Experiment

The results from this question are shown in the last row of Table 1. This question is less directly related to the dissonance that was experimentally created for the Ss. Certainly, the more interesting and enjoyable they felt the tasks were, the greater would be their desire to participate in a similar experiment. But other factors would enter also. Hence, one would expect the results on this question to be very similar to the results on "how enjoyable the tasks were" but weaker. Actually, the results, as may be seen in the table, are in exactly the same direction, and the magnitude of the mean differences is fully as large as on the first question. The variability is greater, however, and the differences

[2] All statistical tests referred to in this paper are two-tailed.

do not yield high levels of statistical significance. The difference between the One Dollar condition $(+1.20)$ and the Control condition $(-.62)$ is significant at the .08 level $(t = 1.78)$. The difference between the One Dollar condition and the Twenty Dollar condition $(-.25)$ reaches only the .15 level of significance $(t = 1.46)$.

The Scientific Importance of the Experiment

This question was included because there was a chance that differences might emerge. There are, after all, other ways in which the experimentally created dissonance could be reduced. For example, one way would be for the S to magnify for himself the value of the reward he obtained. This, however, was unlikely in this experiment because money was used for the reward and it is undoubtedly difficult to convince oneself that one dollar is more than it really is. There is another possible way, however. The Ss were given a very good reason, in addition to being paid, for saying what they did to the waiting girl. The Ss were told it was necessary for the experiment. The dissonance could, consequently, be reduced by magnifying the importance of this cognition. The more scientifically important they considered the experiment to be, the less was the total magnitude of dissonance. It is possible, then, that the results on this question, shown in the third row of figures in Table 1, might reflect dissonance reduction.

The results are weakly in line with what one would expect if the dissonance were somewhat reduced in this manner. The One Dollar condition is higher than the other two. The difference between the One and Twenty Dollar conditions reaches the .08 level of significance on a two-tailed test $(t = 1.79)$. The difference between the One Dollar and Control conditions is not impressive at all $(t = 1.21)$. The result that the Twenty Dollar condition is actually lower than the Control condition is undoubtedly a matter of chance $(t = 0.58)$.

How Much They Learned From the Experiment

The results on this question are shown in the second row of figures in Table 1. The question was included because, as far as we could see, it had nothing to do with the dissonance that was experimentally created and could not be used for dissonance reduction. One would then expect no differences at all among the three conditions. We felt it was important to show that the effect was not a completely general one but was specific to the content of the dissonance which was created. As can be readily seen in Table 1, there are only negligible differences among conditions. The highest t value for any of these differences is only 0.48.

DISCUSSION OF A POSSIBLE ALTERNATIVE EXPLANATION

We mentioned in the introduction that Janis and King (1954; 1956) in explaining their findings, proposed an explanation in terms of the self-convincing effect of mental rehearsal and thinking up new arguments by the person who had to improvise a speech. Kelman (1953), in the previously mentioned study, in attempting to explain the unexpected finding that the persons who complied in the moderate reward condition changed their opinion more than in the high reward condition, also proposed the same kind of explanation. If the results of our experiment are to be taken as strong corroboration of the theory of cognitive dissonance, this possible alternative explanation must be dealt with.

Specifically, as applied to our results, this alternative explanation would maintain that perhaps, for some reason, the Ss in the One Dollar condition worked harder at telling the waiting girl that the tasks were fun and enjoyable. That is, in the One Dollar condition they may have rehearsed it more mentally, thought up more ways of saying it, may have said it more convincingly, and so on. Why this might have been the case is, of course, not immediately apparent. One might expect that, in the Twenty Dollar condition, having been paid more, they would try to do a better job of it than in the One Dollar condition. But nevertheless, the possibility exists that the Ss in the One Dollar condition may have improvised more.

Because of the desirability of investigating this possible alternative explanation, we recorded on a tape recorder the conversation between each S and the girl. These recordings were transcribed and then rated, by two independent raters, on five dimensions. The ratings were, of course done in ignorance of which condition each S was in. The reliabilities of these ratings, that is, the correlations between the two independent raters, ranged from .61 to .88, with an average reliability of .71. The five ratings were:

1. The content of what the S said *before* the girl made the remark that her friend told her it was boring. The stronger the S's positive statements about the tasks, and the more ways in which he said they were interesting and enjoyable, the higher the rating.

2. The content of what the S said *after* the girl made the above-mentioned remark. This was rated in the same way as for the content before the remark.

3. A similar rating of the over-all content of what the S said.

4. A rating of how persuasive and convincing the S was in what he said and the way in which he said it.

5. A rating of the amount of time in the discussion that the S spent discussing the tasks as opposed to going off into irrelevant things.

The mean ratings for the One Dollar and Twenty Dollar conditions, averaging the ratings of the two independent raters, are presented in Table 2. It is clear from examining the table that, in

TABLE 2

Average Ratings of Discussion between Subject and Girl

Dimension Rated	Condition		
	One Dollar	Twenty Dollars	Value of t
Content before remark by girl (rated from 0 to 5)	2.26	2.62	1.08
Content after remark by girl (rated from 0 to 5)	1.63	1.75	0.11
Over-all content (rated from 0 to 5)	1.89	2.19	1.08
Persuasiveness and conviction (rated from 0 to 10)	4.79	5.50	0.99
Time spent on topic (rated from 0 to 10)	6.74	8.19	1.80

all cases, the Twenty Dollar condition is slightly higher. The differences are small, however, and only on the rating of "amount of time" does the difference between the two conditions even approach significance. We are certainly justified in concluding that the Ss in the One Dollar condition did not improvise more nor act more convincingly. Hence, the alternative explanation discussed above cannot account for the findings.

4

Attitude Change by Response Reinforcement: Replication and Extension[1]

WILLIAM A. SCOTT

While Festinger studied role playing in terms of dissonance arousal and reduction, William Scott was pursuing an apparently independent line of research. He wanted to apply stimulus-response learning theory to attitude change. Since a response must be performed before it can be reinforced and thereby "learned," according to S-R theory, Scott hit upon the idea of having subjects participate in a debate contest in which they would argue for or against their own opinions, after which some subjects would be rewarded with a substantial cash prize. Of course all this adds up to an experiment very similar in some ways to that by Festinger and Carlsmith: Subjects are asked to role-play a position which, in many instances, they do not hold; and they are given a high or a low (in fact, no) reward for so doing. But McGuire's results were quite the opposite of those in the dissonance study, as we shall see.

This selection is reprinted with slight abridgment from So-ciometry, 1959, 22, 328–335, with the permission of the author and the American Sociological Association.

Within the framework of S-R learning theory an attitude may be regarded, like a habit, as an implicit anticipatory response which mediates overt behaviors, and arises out of them through response reinforcement (Doob, 1947). Such a conception provided the basis for an earlier study (Scott, 1957) of the effect on attitudes of rewarding relevant verbal behaviors. The purposes of the present experiment were to substantiate the earlier results with different operations, to investigate the effects of response

[1] The research reported in this article was supported by a grant from the Foundation for Research on Human Behavior (Ann Arbor, Michigan).

reinforcement on subjects with neutral, as well as extreme, attitudes, and to determine whether or not the induced attitude change were "permanent."

Briefly, the design of the earlier study (Scott, 1957) was as follows: Pairs of students were selected from a number of general psychology classes and asked to debate any of three different issues on which they had previously expressed their opinions. However, both members were required to defend sides of the issue opposite to those which they actually held. The excellence of their presentations was to be judged by class vote, but this vote was falsified so that a predetermined member of each pair won. Posttests of subjects' attitudes showed that the "winners" had changed in the direction of debate significantly more than the "losers" and more than a group of control S's, while the "losers" did not change significantly more than the controls.

This study had used only S's with initially extreme attitudes, and no provision had been made for a second posttest to determine the extent to which the attitude changes persisted. Therefore, a new experiment was designed to fill these gaps. Although the design was conceptually similar to the previous one, the actual operations differed in several respects: different issues were presented, S's debated under different conditions, and the nature of the reinforcing stimuli was different. Given these innovations in operations (not in conceptualization), it was felt that corroborative results would better serve to substantiate the theory on which the experiments were based than would replication by identical operations.

METHOD

Attitudes of students toward three different controversial issues were assessed in several General Psychology classes, by the following open questions:

1. *Curriculum.* If you had the job of laying out a curriculum of required courses for all undergraduates at CU, what kinds of courses would you lay most emphasis on—those related to the study of scientific facts and research methods, or courses dealing with social problems and courses which help the student learn more about people?

2. *Fraternities and sororities.* Some people feel that fraternity and sorority life contributes a great deal to the development of the student during his college career. Others feel that fraternities and sororities work to the detriment of students by taking their attention away from more important academic matters. What do you think about this?

3. *Ideal husband or wife.* If you were thinking of getting married, which kind of a husband or wife would you rather have: One who is mainly interested in people and enjoys being with people, or one who has a wide variety of interests and creative talent in some area?

Immediately after this pretest, a general invitation was addressed to the classes to participate in an elimination debate contest, the winners of which would share a $100 cash prize. The investigator's interest was reported to be "to find out what kinds of people hold what kinds of attitudes." A couple of weeks later volunteers were contacted by phone and asked to take a particular side of one of the three issues for debate. The sides were assigned irrespective of Ss' initial positions, so that some debators defended their own opinions, some the opposite opinions, and some debated "off-neutral" (they expressed no clear opinion on the pretest, but were assigned a definite position in the debate). The only restrictions were to keep these three groups (same, opposite, and off-neutral) approximately equal and to give equal representation to each of the three issues. S's were told that debate positions were being assigned irrespective of actual attitudes, because "the purpose of the study is to see how well people can present opinions they don't actually hold, and how well their opponents can judge their own true attitudes."

The debates took place in a small research room, with the two S's seated at one end of a long table, and three judges at the opposite end. For every debate, two of the judges were professors of psychology, and the third was a mature graduate student; E was one of the judges at every debate, but the other judging professor and the graduate student were changed several times throughout the experiment. Introductions were formal, as was the decorum of the entire procedure. None of the S's had known his opponent prior to that time. It was explained that the winner of this first debate would be contacted for a second debate, and if he won that, as well as a third debate, he would receive a $20 prize. S's presented their initial arguments for five minutes each, followed by two-minute rebuttals in reverse order.

Each judge, in turn, rendered his decision on the relative merits of the two performances. The reasons he offered for his decision were confined to the manner of presentation (style, clarity, convincingness, etc.), rather than to the content of the talk, in order to minimize the possible influences of prestige suggestion which might be entailed if the judgment referred to the substance of the argument (e.g., "that was a good point"). The winner in each case had been predetermined in systematic fashion, so that all the judges had to do during the debate was to jot down plausible reasons for their decisions.

Following the judgment, S's were led to small individual rooms near the debate room, where they filled out questionnaires on the three issues, identical with those from the pretest. E indicated that "we are interested in seeing how you feel about these matters at this time," without explicitly indicating that opinions were expected either to change or to remain constant. In addition there was the question, "How do you think your opponent *really* feels about this issue?" included simply to maintain the pretext previously offered for the study.

Winning S's were called back about ten days later to debate a different issue. Their positions were again assigned irrespective of their true attitudes, and the debating situation was as before, except that judgments of win or lose were based on merit (as the judges saw it).[2] There were no predetermined winners or losers, so occasionally there was a split vote among the three judges; but E always voted last, in order to make the decision as clear and definite as possible. A second posttest of attitudes toward the three issues was obtained. (S's wrote in separate rooms.)

Winners of the second debate were recalled for a third time, to debate the remaining issue of the three. The consequences of this contest were made clear, and S's were given the choice of "winner take all" ($20) or "split the prize" ($15 and $5). Three pairs chose the former division; two, the latter. Again the voting of judges was genuine; a third posttest of attitudes toward all three issues was obtained.

Attitudes expressed in the pretest and on the three posttests

[2] This shift in the basis for determining winners was largely for ethical reasons. Though a random choice of winners was necessary for purposes of experimental control, once this had been achieved on the first round of debates, there appeared to be no reason why virtue should not be rewarded.

were typed on 3″ x 5″ cards, numbered in such a way as to disguise their sources (see Scott, 1957). These were then coded by E on a seven-point attitude scale, representing a neutral position and three degrees of intensity toward each extreme of the issue —e.g.:

1. Greek organizations are very definitely a help.
2. Greek organizations are a help.
3. Greek organizations are mainly a help, but also some hindrance.
4. Don't know; not ascertained; equally a help and a hindrance; depends on the individual.
5. Greek organizations are mainly a hindrance, but also some help.
6. Greek organizations are a hindrance.
7. Greek organizations are very definitely a hindrance.

Check-coding, by an independent judge, of a sample of these attitudes showed their coding reliability to be .87.

RESULTS

Of principal interest is the comparison of winners and losers on the first round of debates, for in that series they were randomly determined. The results are presented in the top part of Table 1, which shows that winners tended to change toward the side debated more than did losers or controls. (The control group was composed of those volunteers who could not be scheduled during the first debate series. Their posttest attitudes were assessed just after the third debate series, approximately one month after the pretest.)

Attitude changes following the second and third debates were comparable to those in the first debate (see bottom of Table 1). It will be recalled that, here, the decisions were not predetermined, but depended on performance as estimated by the judges.

Also of interest are the findings concerning "permanence" of the effects of reinforcement. As previously noted, all 20 S's who participated in the second debate were tested concerning their attitudes toward the issue of the first debate. From their responses it is possible to estimate the degree of "savings" from the first posttest to the second posttest—approximately ten days later. It is clear from the data in Table 1 ("first debate: Winners ten days later") that attitudes expressed on the second posttest are different, both from the pretest attitudes, and from the first posttest

TABLE 1

Mean Attitude Changes of Winners, Losers, and Controls

Group of Subjects	N	Mean Change*	S.D. of Change	Difference in Mean-Changes
First Debate				
(A) Winners	20	+1.67	1.55	A vs. B: t = 2.76; p < .01
(B) Losers	20	+0.15	1.83	A vs. C: t = 3.80; p < .001
(C) Controls	15	+0.24	0.47	B vs. C: t = −0.20; NS
(D) Winners ten				
days later	20	+1.20	1.66	D vs. C: t = 2.40; p < .05
Second Debate				
(A) Winners	10	+1.40	1.80	A vs. B: t = 1.29; NS
(B) Losers	10	+0.36	1.62	
Third Debate				
(A) Winners	5	+2.80	1.72	A vs. B: t = 2.88; p < .05
(B) Losers	5	−0.20	1.17	

* A positive sign indicates a mean change in the direction of debate; or, for control S's, a mean change opposite to their original position. For control S's with initially neutral attitudes the directions of changes were assigned alternatingly positive and negative signs. One-tail tests of significance were used throughout.

attitudes. Thus, there is a significant degree of savings from the first reward experience, even though the reinforcement is not explicitly repeated; but the amount of savings is less than the amount of initial change.

Since S's were assigned debate positions regardless of their own true attitudes, it is possible to see whether or not the response reinforcement was effective when it operated in the same direction as S's initial attitude, or when it aimed at moving him from a neutral position. Table 2 shows the results of the debates, grouped according to the relationship between S's initial attitude and his debate position. When S's debated "opposite sides," the absolute change of winners was largest (2.77 on a seven-point scale). When debating "off-neutral," the mean change was 1.47, and the mean change of winners debating their "own sides" was 0.63 toward a more extreme position in the same direction. A comparison of absolute changes in position is deceptive, however, since S's debating "opposite sides" had the greatest room for movement, and those debating "own sides" had the least. Relative to the amount of movement (in the direction of reinforcement) possible, the three groups showed changes of 55 per cent, 49 per cent, and 63 per cent, respectively. But since there is no way of

TABLE 2

Mean Attitude Change as a Function of the Relationship between S's Pretest Attitude and Debate Position

Group of Subjects	N	Mean Change*	S.D. of Change	Difference in Mean-Changes
Debating Opposite Side				
(A) Winners	10	+2.77	1.97	A vs. B: t = 2.53; p < .05
(B) Losers	10	+0.90	1.05	
Debating Off-neutral				
(A) Winners	11	+1.47	1.25	A vs. B: t = 1.62; p < .10
(B) Losers	13	+0.54	1.44	
Debating Own Side				
(A) Winners	7	+0.63	0.86	A vs. B: t = 2.15; p < .05
(B) Losers	13	−0.77	1.89	

* A positive sign indicates a mean change in the direction of debate. One-tail tests of significance are reported.

comparing scale intervals at various points on the dimension, it would be mere sham to conclude anything about the relative effects of response reinforcement under the three circumstances. All one can say is that winners tended to change in the direction of debate more than losers did, regardless of whether they debated their own positions, opposite positions, or off-neutral.

DISCUSSION

The results of this study suggest, first of all, that the effects of response reinforcement on attitude change are not necessarily transitory, but may be preserved up to periods of at least ten days. On the one hand, this may seem surprising, since, during the interval between tests, S's were presumably living within the same social contexts that had supported their initial attitudes. Thus one might expect them to revert to their old positions as soon as they were removed from the reinforcing situation. On the other hand, the occasion for the second posttest was so nearly identical with that for the first posttest, that the cues present could well have served to reintegrate the former response, even though it did not conform to S's true attitude at that time. In a more imaginative study, one might attempt a follow-up assessment of Ss' attitudes in a completely different context, with someone other than E eliciting the relevant response.

A second result suggests that response reinforcement can be effective either in strengthening previously held attitudes, in changing them, or in creating new ones (if those S's who debated "off-neutral" can be said to have developed "new" attitudes). There was no evidence to indicate that S's with neutral attitudes were more amenable to change than those with more extreme views. Such an outcome might have been expected in the light of the frequently reported finding that people who hold intense attitudes, or who are quite certain of their opinions, are relatively resistant to pressures to change (Birch, 1945; Burdick, 1956; Carlson, 1956; Hochbaum, 1954; Osgood and Tannenbaum, 1955). However, with less than interval-scale measures, it is difficult to compare relative movements at different positions on the attitude scale. Moreover, the status of the initially "neutral" attitudes is by no means clear, since that category included S's who expressed balanced opinions on both sides of the issue as well as those who replied "no opinion." It seems to this writer that neutrality of an attitude as such is probably not the critical feature for predicting susceptibility to change, but rather it is the degree to which the attitude, of whatever direction or strength, is embedded in a cognitive structure of other supporting attitudes and cognitive elements. (This quality of "embeddedness" has been referred to elsewhere as *cognitive consistency* [Scott, 1958, 1959].)

The major significance of the study, however, would seem to lie in its confirmation of previously obtained results (Scott, 1957) not by exact replication, but by "methodological triangulation" (Campbell, 1953). Whereas the earlier experiment required S's to debate in front of their fellow classmates and "rewarded" them by class vote, the present procedure involved debates in a private setting with reinforcement by judges' decisions and monetary reward. Moreover, the issues debated were different from those previously used. Thus one can safely maintain that the hypothesized relationship is not exclusively dependent on the particular methods chosen to assess it. When a number of different sets of empirical operations yield comparable results, it is reasonable to presume that they reflect a valid relationship (i.e., one that is independent of the measuring procedures), rather than just a reliable relationship (one that depends on a particular instrument or experimental design) (c.f., Campbell and Fiske, 1959).

5

An Experiment on Small Rewards for Discrepant Compliance and Attitude Change

ARTHUR R. COHEN

Well before direct criticism of Festinger and Carlsmith's study had reached print, it was sufficiently audible to motivate further research by dissonance theorists. The late Arthur Cohen moved to meet one type of criticism which would soon become central in discussions of role playing: the possibility that large rewards were less important in reducing dissonance than in arousing responses which interfered with role playing effects.

Cohen's study was first published in a book by Jack Brehm and himself, Explorations in Cognitive Dissonance, *which reviews a wide variety of other dissonance studies as well. This selection is excerpted from this book with permission of the publisher and the senior author. Copyright 1962 by John Wiley & Sons, Inc.*

In reviewing the evidence on the manipulation of dissonance through the variation of consonant information, we saw that the data on the effects of rewards and justifications for discrepant commitment are quite consistent with the theory. However, the alternative explanation was raised that the inverse relationship between rewards and attitude change might disappear if rewards were small enough. This alternative explanation assumes that the obtained inverse relationship is due to the fact that large rewards engender suspicion and resistance and that subjects may say something of the order of, "It must be bad if they're paying me so much for it." The fact that high reward subjects show less change than low reward subjects could be due, then, to this resistance effect at the high end of the reward continuum, rather than to a dissonance effect at the low end of the reward scale, where cognitions supporting discrepant commitment are minimal. Therefore, this alternative reasoning goes, if sufficiently small rewards were given, the suspicion and resistance engendered would be reduced and the relationship between reward and attitude change would be a direct function of the magnitude of the incentive determining the response.

In order to explore further the effects of rewards associated with taking a discrepant stand and to gather information relevant to this alternative explanation, Cohen carried out a "forced-compliance" experiment in which rewards were varied at intervals over a wide range. This variation was accomplished by offering college students either $.50, $1.00, $5.00, or $10.00 to *write an essay against their private view on a current issue on campus.* Under the guise of a "general survey," 30 Yale students were asked to write an essay "in favor of the actions of the New Haven police." The attitude issue was chosen because in the spring of 1959, just prior to the study, there had been a student's "riot" at Yale with resulting accusations of police brutality toward the students. There was thus an assurance that (1) motivation and interest on the part of the students were maximal, (2) every student was on one side of the issue, that is, extremely negative toward the police and their actions and sympathetic toward the students, and, therefore, (3) any subject asked to write an essay in favor of the actions of the New Haven police *would be taking a position clearly inconsistent with his own attitudes.*

The students were approached in their dormitory rooms on a random basis; only one subject to a room was selected. The experimenter introduced himself as a fellow student who was a member of a research team from The Institute of Human Relations. He said that the researchers were "interested in and concerned with the recent riots" and that the subject knew that the "university administration and the public are very concerned with the issue." Thus the research group felt that the study had some "relevance and importance, especially in the light of recent events." The experimenter went on to say that, "It has been shown that one of the best ways to get relevant arguments on both sides of an issue is to ask people to write essays favoring only one side. We think we know pretty much how you feel about the students' rights in this matter." Here the experimenter paused for the subject's reaction, and after a usual indication of felt infringement on the part of the subject, the experimenter continued by saying, "What we really need now are some essays favoring the police side. I understand that you have very different views on the matter, but as you can see, it's very interesting to know what kinds of arguments people bring up in their essays if they have very different opinions about it."

The experimenter then went on to say that he would like them to write the "strongest, most forceful, most creative and thoughtful essay you can, unequivocally against your own position and in favor of the police side of the riots." The reward manipulation was then introduced. The experimenter said, "Now as part of our study, we have some funds available, and we are prepared to pay you \$_____ for writing the essay against your own position." All reward groups were told exactly the same thing, except that some were offered \$10.00 ($N = 6$), some were offered \$5.00 ($N = 10$), some were offered \$1.00 ($N = 6$), and some were offered \$.50 ($N = 8$). All groups were told that the decision to write the essay was entirely their own choice. However, in order to prevent their refusing to participate, they were also told that the experimenter *did* need their help in the study since he was a student and this was part of his research paper. Thus, while the latter "constraints" might reduce the absolute amount of dissonance occasioned by compliance, it prevented any considerable differential loss of subjects and therefore any self-selection bias. After the reward manipulations, the subjects were again reminded that they were to take as strong and unequivocal a stand as possible against their own position and in favor of the police.

After each subject wrote his essay on a blank sheet entitled, "Why the New Haven Police Actions Were Justified," the postmeasures were given. Subjects were told, "Now that you have looked at some of the reasons for the actions of the New Haven police, we'd like to get some of your reactions to the issue; you may possibly want to look at the situation in the light of this. So, would you please fill out this questionnaire." Subjects first filled out an opinion scale asking, "Considering the circumstances, how justified do you think the New Haven police actions were in the recent riot?" The scale used was an *a priori* 31-point scale, marked and labeled at every fifth point by the following terms: Completely justified; Very justified; Quite justified; Somewhat justified; Little justified; Very little justified; Not justified at all.

This constituted the major dependent measure of the experiment. Checks were then made of the experimental inductions to clarify the possible effect of differential reward on attitude change. In order to check on the perceived amount of reward offered, the subjects were asked, "How much were you offered to write the essay?" Here the response was in terms of an 11-point scale, graded in tenths of a point, which ran from $0 to $10.00. The last item checked on the subject's perception of the degree of strength of the discrepant essay he agreed to write. On a seven-point *a priori* scale, running from "extremely moderate" to "extremely strong," he was asked, "How strong an essay in favor of the New Haven police did you agree to write?" This completed the experiment. It should also be noted, however, that though there was reasonable assurance that all subjects were extremely opposed to the police and that therefore we could assume some equivalent negative position in their initial attitudes, since the study made use of an "after-only" design, a control group was used. This group, consisting of 14 subjects, was given the attitude measure at the same time as the experimental subjects. The control subjects received none of the manipulations or other measures; they were simply given the attitude questionnaire regarding their opinions of the New Haven police actions. In effect, the control group may be said to have acted as a premeasure in this experiment.

RESULTS

The check on the reward manipulations indicates that the subjects perceived accurately the rewards they were to receive for writing the essay. In all cases they checked the point on the scale reflecting the exact reward they were promised; in no case was there any overlap. It was also found that the subjects, in writing their essays, perceived that they were to take a strong and unequivocal stand against their own attitude position and that this perception was constant and high no matter what rewards they anticipated. On the scale where maximum strength of discrepant essay was seven, the mean for the $10.00 group was 5.72, for the $5.00 group it was 5.80, for the $1.00 group it was 5.58, and for the $.50 group it was 5.82. All of these means indicate strongly discrepant essays, and they do not differ reliably from one another. We may thus assume that the basic conditions for examining the effects of differential incentives in producing dissonance and attitude change have been fulfilled here: The subjects accurately perceived that they would be getting differential rewards, and any differences in attitude change as a function of reward would not be a function of the strength with which the subjects perceived that they had taken the discrepant stand.

The data on attitude change are entirely consistent with the notion that dissonance and consequent attitude change vary inversely with the amount of incentive for taking a stand discrepant with one's cognitions. The data in Table 1 show that as reward

TABLE 1

Mean Attitudes toward the Police Actions

Control condition	2.70*
$10.00 condition	2.32
$ 5.00 condition	3.08
$ 1.00 condition	3.47
$ .50 condition	4.54

* The higher the mean, the more positive the attitudes toward the New Haven police. Highest value equals 7.00, lowest value equals 1.00.

decreases, attitudes toward the police become more positive. Among experimental groups, the rank order of attitudinal effects is exactly what we might expect from the dissonance formulation; the linear trend is significant at less than the .01 level by F test.[1] When the range of scores, including the control group, is tested for differences by the Duncan Multiple Range Test (Edwards, 1960, pp. 136–140), the specific differences between experimental groups emerge. The $10.00 and $5.00 conditions are not significantly different from each other or from the control condition, but the $1.00 condition is different from the control ($p < .10$) as is the $.50 condition ($p < .01$). Furthermore, the $1.00 condition and the $.50 conditions are both different from the $10.00 condition ($p < .05$ and $< .01$ respectively). Finally, the $.50 condition is itself different from the $1.00 condition ($p < .05$) as well as from the $5.00 condition ($p < .01$). These

[1] Significance tests on all original experiments reported in this volume are two-tailed, unless otherwise reported.

results are clearly in line with the derivation from dissonance theory regarding the effects of consonant information.

The alternative explanation for results concerning the effects of differential incentives thus does not appear to gain support from these data. The idea that at high incentive levels, subjects might feel that something is "wrong," and that the suspicion they experience could reflect itself in resistance against changing their attitudes, is not relevant for a comparison between, for example, $1.00 and $.50 conditions. No more suspicion can be attached to a $1.00 offer than to a $.50 offer. The other side of this general alternative explanation asserts that when subjects are given very little reward, they would have very little desire to change and might in fact show a resistance effect. The fact that the results show an inverse monotonic relationship between reward and attitude change over a wide range of rewards does not suggest that such a general alternative explanation is valid.

6

The Influence of Incentive Conditions on the Success of Role Playing in Modifying Attitudes[1]

IRVING L. JANIS AND J. BARNARD GILMORE

Appropriately, Irving Janis was among the first to present an experimental challenge to Festinger's dissonance interpretation of role-play effects. This study elaborates on the account of role playing processes in the Janis and King paper, and attempts to provide experimental support to show not only that the earlier explanation is more appropriate than dissonance theory, but also that Festinger and Carlsmith's own results can be incorporated into an "incentive theory" or "conflict theory" approach to attitude change phenomena.

This selection is reprinted with slight abridgment from the Journal of Personality and Social Psychology, *1965, 1, 17–27, with permission of the senior author and the American Psychological Association.*

Earlier experiments have shown that role playing facilitates the modification of attitudes. Janis and King (1954; King & Janis, 1956) found that when students were required to improvise a speech in support of a position contrary to their private beliefs, they showed an increase in attitude change as contrasted with a passively exposed control group. A similar increment in attitude change was found by Kelman (1953) when a group of school

[1] The experiment described in this paper was carried out under the auspices of the Yale Studies in Attitude and Communication, a research project established by the late Carl I. Hovland and supported by a grant from the Rockefeller Foundation. The present Research Director is Irving L. Janis and the Associate Director is Robert P. Abelson.

children was given a mild incentive to write convincing essays in support of a new attitude position.

In these experiments, and in subsequent ones which have confirmed the positive effects of role playing (for example, Carlson, 1956; Culbertson, 1957; Harvey & Beverly, 1961), the role-playing task was assigned by someone who was himself a highly prestigeful person or the representative of a highly prestigeful organization whose goals were consonant with those of the subjects. It seems quite possible that the success of role playing may partly depend upon positive incentive values attached to conforming with the demands of a benign or prestigeful sponsor. The main purpose of the present experiment is to determine whether favorable versus unfavorable sponsorship conditions influence the success of role playing with respect to inducing attitude changes.

This problem was selected for systematic investigation not only because of the potential importance of sponsorship factors in attitude change, but also because it offers a rare opportunity for testing rival theories concerning the psychological processes that might account for role-playing effects. One theory, which takes account of the "self-persuasion" character of role playing, emphasizes the importance of positive and negative incentives in determining the outcome (see Hovland, Janis, & Kelley, 1953, pp. 223–237). According to this "incentive" theory, when a person accepts the task of improvising arguments in favor of a point of view at variance with his own personal convictions, he becomes temporarily motivated to think up all the good positive arguments he can, and at the same time suppresses thoughts about the negative arguments which are supposedly irrelevant to the assigned task. This "biased scanning" increases the salience of the positive arguments and therefore increases the chances of acceptance of the new attitude position. A gain in attitude change would not be expected, however, if resentment or other interfering affective reactions were aroused by *negative* incentives in the role-playing situation. Among the obvious instances of negative incentives would be information that lowers the prestige of the sponsor or that leads to his being perceived as a manipulative person who is trying to influence people for his own personal aggrandizement or for other alien purposes. Any signs of exploitative intentions in the behavior of the sponsor would also be expected to operate as negative incentives, evoking responses that conflict with the positive incentive value of improvising arguments in support of the conclusion assigned by the sponsor. Thus, incentive theory predicts that role playing will be more successful in inducing attitude change if the sponsor is perceived as someone whose affiliations are benign in character and whose intentions are to promote public welfare than if he is perceived as someone whose affiliations and purposes are commercial or exploitative.

Exactly the opposite prediction would be made by the "dissonance"-theory explanation of role-playing effects, which postulates that "the existence of dissonance [among cognitive elements] gives rise to pressures to reduce the dissonance and to avoid increases in dissonance [Festinger, 1957, p. 31]." According to this theory, the crucial factor in role playing is that it creates dissonance between the person's private opinion and his awareness of what he is overtly saying and doing when he conforms with the sponsor's demands; "the changes in private opinion which ensue are the end result of a process of attempting to reduce or eliminate this dissonance [Festinger, 1957, p. 112]." The total magnitude of dissonance is assumed to decrease as the number and importance of the pressures and justifications which induce the person to say things he does not privately believe are increased (see Brehm & Cohen, 1962, pp. 252–255). Consequently, the prediction would be that more dissonance and therefore more attitude change will result from role playing if the sponsor is perceived as having objectionable affiliations or purposes than if he is perceived as having intentions consonant with the subjects' own goals—provided, of course, that the subjects can be induced to conform to his role-playing instructions.[2] Accordingly, the present experiment was designed to test the opposing predictions from incentive theory and dissonance theory by comparing the effects of a "positive" sponsorship condition that is relatively consonant with the subject's values with a "negative" condition that is relatively dissonant.

[2] Two studies of role playing (Cohen, Brehm, & Fleming, 1958; Rabbie, Brehm, & Cohen, 1959) have attempted to manipulate the *justification* for conformity to the sponsor's demands. But these studies provide ambiguous evidence because in each instance the sponsor was described in terms that were likely to make his status and prestige value dubious. The control condition in each instance was also equivocal in that no information at all was given about the sponsor or his goals.

The experimental design includes a second independent variable —amount of monetary reward—which enables us to test some additional differential predictions from the two theories. Festinger and Carlsmith (1959) claim that the dissonance-theory interpretation of role playing is strongly supported by the findings from an experiment in which they compared the effects of a small and a large monetary reward. They found that when role-playing subjects were given a small monetary reward ($1), more opinion change occurred than when subjects were given a large monetary reward ($20). In this experiment, however, the experimenter presented a justification that had potentially negative as well as positive features and there are grounds for wondering if the extraordinarily large reward of $20 might have unintentionally generated some degree of suspicious wariness about being exploited by the experimenter or some degree of guilt about being "bought" to lie to a fellow student (see pp. 25–26).

Cohen, using more plausible rewards, reported a similar increase in attitude change from small as against large monetary payments when college students were induced to write essays in support of a personally objectionable position (Brehm & Cohen, 1962, pp. 73–78). But Rosenberg (1965) failed to confirm these findings when he carefully repeated Cohen's study, using almost identical procedures except for a methodological refinement that involved having the experimenter who tested the subjects' final attitudes completely independent from the experimenter who administered the role-playing procedure. In fact, Rosenberg's results show exactly the opposite outcome from the two experiments by proponents of dissonance theory, the greatest amount of attitude change occurring among the role players who were paid the largest amount of money.

In view of the controversial evidence concerning the effects of monetary rewards, we used a factorial design that would enable us to obtain additional information about the effects of large versus small monetary rewards under the two different sponsorship conditions.

The third variable introduced into the factorial design involved the degree to which subjects engaged in *overt* role playing by writing essays in which they verbalized arguments in support of the assigned position on the issue. According to a dissonance-theory analysis by Brehm and Cohen (1962), the mere fact that a person commits himself to play any such role, before he executes it, "should be sufficient to produce the attitude-changing dissonance [pp. 254–255]." They cite evidence from a study in which no difference was found between two groups, one of which wrote essays in which the dissonant position was overtly verbalized while the other merely agreed to write the essays (Rabbie, Brehm, & Cohen, 1959).

An incentive-theory analysis would lead us to predict a marked difference in favor of overt role playing: Commitment to play the role could, of course, induce some degree of attitude change (particularly if the subjects engage in implicit role playing in anticipation of executing the task); but actually carrying out the task of verbalizing new arguments in support of the objectionable position would elicit more biased scanning and increase the salience of new incentives, thus increasing the likelihood of attitude change—provided that no strong interfering responses are evoked by unfavorable sponsorship or by other unfavorable conditions.

In order to investigate the effects of overt role playing, we compared two equivalent groups, both of which were given the same information and instructions: overt role players whose attitudes were assessed *after* carrying out the role-playing task, and controls whose attitudes were assessed at a time when they had already agreed to perform the role-playing task but *before* they were given the opportunity to do so.

Thus, the present experiment includes three variables in a $2 \times 2 \times 2$ factorial design: public-welfare sponsorship versus unfavorable (blatantly commercial) sponsorship; small reward ($1) versus very large reward ($20) for agreeing to carry out the role-playing task; overt versus nonovert role-playing conditions. One of the advantages of this type of design, of course, is that it enables us to investigate interaction effects as well as main effects.

METHOD

Procedures

In this experiment, 64 male sophomores and juniors at Yale University were seen in individual sessions at their undergraduate college residences. The experimenter simply knocked at the door of each room and asked the prospective subject to speak with him alone for a short time. Only about 1 out of every 10 prospective subjects refused to participate. All such refusals occurred *before* any information was given about sponsorship or about any of the other conditions and hence there was no differential loss of subjects among the various subgroups. On a stratified random basis, seven subjects were assigned to each of the four control groups and, in order to increase the reliability of the main effect measures, a somewhat larger number (nine) received each of the four different experimental treatments. The experiment was carried out in six steps.

1. The experimenter began with an explanation of his alleged affiliation and purpose. For half of the subjects (decided in advance on a purely random basis) the experimenter conveyed a *public-welfare* sponsorship. Specifically, he explained that he was obtaining information on both sides of the issue, to be used in conducting a survey of college students' attitudes toward science and mathematics courses for a national research organization on behalf of a number of the leading universities in the United States. To the other half of the subjects, the experimenter conveyed an exploitative commercial sponsorship. They were told that he was working for a new publishing company that was trying to build up the market for its science textbooks and would use the information obtained in the interview for preparing an advertising campaign.

2. After the sponsorship information was presented, each subject was given a standard request to engage in a role-playing task. All groups were asked if they would be willing to write a short essay in favor of the proposition that a year of physics and a year of mathematics should be added as a requirement for all college students. Each subject was told that the task required thinking up good arguments that he personally would be inclined to accept.

3. For half the subjects in each sponsorship group, the amount of monetary reward offered for carrying out the task was $20. For the other half, it was $1.

4. The experimenter abstained from putting any special pressure on the subjects when he asked them to decide whether or not

to take on the job assignment, even though a sizable number—especially in the unfavorable sponsorship group—showed some reluctance or hesitation. As soon as each subject announced his decision, he was *paid in advance* and signed a receipt for the payment. Thus, an unambiguous commitment to perform the task was elicited from every subject, whether in a control or experimental group. Those in the latter (overt role playing) groups were given 10 minutes to write their essays. In order to stimulate their thinking, these subjects were given a few general questions (for example, "Considering the type of career you are likely to be in, how might a background in physics and math enable you to function more adequately?"). These questions contained no new information but were found, in a prior pilot study, to serve a "pump-priming" function, without having any direct effects on attitudes. Control subjects were told that they would be asked to write their essays a little later, but that first there was a questionnaire to be filled out. Thus, the controls were given the final questionnaire immediately, without being asked any pump-priming questions and without engaging in any overt role playing.

5. The same questionnaire was given to the role players and to the controls. It contained a series of objective questions and a final open-end question, all of which asked the subjects to express their present attitude toward the proposed new policy.

6. After completing the questionnaire, each subject who had engaged in role playing was asked to rate each of the arguments he had given as "Very good," "Fairly good," or "Inadequate," to indicate his own personal evaluation of each one.

At the end of the session, each of the controls, as well as each of the role players, was given a standard interview to find out how he had perceived the sponsorship and reward conditions, as a check on the adequacy of the experimental manipulations. The subjects were then told the truth concerning the purpose of the study and the experimenter's actual affiliations. At this time the subjects were paid a standard fee of $2 for participating in the experiment. (With only one exception, all subjects given the $20 payment in advance readily returned $18 of their pay without complaint, after the final explanation.)

RESULTS

Assessment of the Experimental Manipulations

By examining certain features of the subjects' performance and their responses to the special interview conducted after the post-test, we were able to assess the adequacy of the manipulations of each of the three main variables.

Sponsorship. The final interview included a series of questions designed to determine whether the information given to the subjects succeeded in conveying the intended perceptions of the sponsor and the purpose of the task. Of the 18 experimental subjects given the information about public-welfare sponsorship, 16 expressed no doubts at all about the authenticity of the benign sponsorship at the end of the session and only 2 subjects said that they thought there might be more to it than was indicated by the experimenter. In both instances, however, the skepticism consisted merely of wondering if perhaps the major universities were conducting the survey because a large industrial organization or foundation was putting up the funds for it. All 18 subjects given the commercial-sponsorship instructions indicated that they accepted the explanation and felt that the primary purpose was to promote the sale of books in order for the publishing company to increase its profits. None of the subjects guessed that the study was intended to investigate the effects of writing the essay on their personal attitudes.

Small versus large monetary incentive. For those paid $1, most subjects asserted in the final interview that the pay was felt to be satisfactory or ample. The comments of those paid $20, however, indicated that this payment was perceived as being so extremely large that it was a highly ambiguous stimulus. Most subjects who received $20 reported feeling puzzled because they could not understand why such a huge overpayment was being made. Every one of these subjects asserted that it was in excess of what he regarded as appropriate for the work involved. Seventeen of the 18 expressed clear-cut surprise (for example, "This I cannot comprehend . . . it was much too much; $5 would be quite sufficient . . . I was rather shocked.") A few subjects reported that despite their puzzlement they responded to the large reward as a strong positive incentive, but a larger number reported having reacted in the opposite way, regarding the unbelievable large payment as a source of vague suspicions, guilt, or conflict (for example, "I feel like a bastard for going against my cause; but for $20, what the hell.")

Thus, it turns out that in repeating the two reward conditions used by Festinger and Carlsmith (1959), we are comparing a small reward that is perceived by our subjects as appropriate for the task at hand with an ambiguous large reward that is perceived by the students as a surprising, *inappropriate* overpayment.

From the standpoint of incentive theory, no clear-cut prediction is possible concerning the immediate effect of the large conflictful reward versus the small appropriate reward, since there is no way of knowing whether the large monetary payment is a stronger or weaker incentive than the low payment. This ambiguity, however, does not affect the opportunity to obtain clear-cut results on the effectiveness of the overt role-playing versus nonovert role-playing condition nor of the public-welfare versus commercial-sponsorship conditions, for which there is evidence that the manipulations were successful.

Overt versus nonovert role-playing conditions. We examined the essays to see if the overt role-playing instructions were carried out and, as expected, the essays were found to be devoted almost exclusively to presenting cogent arguments in support of the assigned position. In order to determine whether the control subjects engaged in implicit role playing, they were asked, just before being dehoaxed, whether they had thought about any arguments in anticipation of writing the essay. Seventeen of the 28 controls (61%) reported having started to plan their essay in advance and 13 controls (46%) were able to mention one or more specific pro arguments that they had thought up. Nevertheless, the amount of role playing in which they could engage was severely curtailed, as compared with the experimental group of *overt* role players, who were given considerably more time to think about the essay, to concentrate on the task, and to write down the arguments. The control condition, therefore, can be regarded as representing a relatively low degree of role-playing activity, characterized by a brief opportunity for implicit role playing with no overt performance at all, as compared with the relatively high degree of overt role-playing activity in the experimental condition.

Effects on Attitudes

Row 1 in Table 1 shows the mean total scores obtained for each of the experimental and control subgroups on a series of five objective items, which asked the subjects to evaluate the proposed educational policy. Comparison of Columns 9 and 12 indicates that for the experimental groups, those who engaged in overt role playing under conditions of public-welfare sponsorship obtained higher scores than those who did so under conditions of commercial sponsorship. For the control group, this trend does not occur and hence it is a characteristic of overt role-playing effects. A series of t tests, based on the error estimate from an overall analysis of variance (Table 2), was applied to the differences in combined scores shown in Columns 9 and 12. For the experimental (overt role playing) groups, the mean for public-welfare sponsorship (10.12) was found to be significantly larger than the mean for commercial sponsorship (6.06). This difference was significant beyond the .01 level. The corresponding difference for the control group (6.94 versus 9.08) was found to be nonsignificant ($p > .25$). Among the control groups, however, there is an unusually low mean score in Column 4, the public-welfare sponsorship-$1 condition, which will be discussed later (see p. 24).

Table 1 also shows the results of a systematic content analysis of the arguments presented by the subjects in their written answers to the open-end question which asked the subjects to state the recommendation they would make to a university committee on the issue of whether their own college should adopt the proposed policy. The answers were rated independently by two judges, each of whom was given typescript copies of the answers without any indication of the group to which any subject belonged. These blind ratings consisted of assessing each argument as favorable, unfavorable, or neutral toward the proposed policy. The mean attitude scores shown in the lower portion of Table 1 are restricted to explicit pro and anti arguments.

The reliability of the blind ratings of the two judges proved to be very high when tested by comparing the frequencies of pro and anti arguments they reported for each subject. The reliability coefficient was above .95 ($N = 64$).

In Table 2, the results of an analysis of variance (corrected for unequal Ns) are shown for each of the two attitude measures

TABLE 1

Mean Attitude Scores of Overt Role Players and Corresponding Controls under Different Conditions of Sponsorship and Reward

Attitude measures	Controls: No overt role playing (N=28)						Experimental conditions: Overt role playing (N=36)					
	Commercial sponsor			Public-welfare sponsor			Commercial sponsor			Public-welfare sponsor		
	(1) $1 reward (N=7)	(2) $20 reward (N=7)	(3) Total (N=14)	(4) $1 reward (N=7)	(5) $20 reward (N=7)	(6) Total (N=14)	(7) $1 reward (N=9)	(8) $20 reward (N=9)	(9) Total (N=18)	(10) $1 reward (N=9)	(11) $20 reward (N=9)	(12) Total (N=19)
1. Combined score for five objective items[a]	8.87	9.29	9.08	4.72	9.15	6.94	5.56	6.56	6.06	10.12	10.12	10.12
2. Responses to an open-end question asking for the subject's personal views												
Explicit pro arguments	0.71	0.71	0.71	0.00	0.14	0.07	0.11	0.00	0.06	0.89	1.56	1.22
Explicit anti arguments	0.57	1.14	0.85	2.14	1.00	1.57	0.44	0.78	0.61	0.22	0.11	0.17
Net attitude score (Σ pro) − (Σ anti)	+0.14	−0.43	−0.14	−2.14	−0.86	−1.50	−0.33	−0.78	−0.55	+0.67	+1.45	+1.05

[a] Based on a 5-point scale of approval-disapproval for each of five questions concerning the proposed educational policy, the maximal score being 25 and the minimal score, 0.

included in Table 1. The main finding is the significant interaction of overt role playing with sponsorship ($p < .03$ on the first measure and $p < .01$ on the second). On both measures, we find that among the subjects who were induced to engage in overt role playing, public-welfare sponsorship produced significantly more attitude change than commercial sponsorship; whereas, among those in the control condition (nonovert role playing), the difference is slight and in the opposite direction.

The analysis of variance of attitude scores based on explicit pro and anti arguments shows a significant main effect for overt role playing, but this is attributable entirely to the large positive scores in the public-welfare-sponsorship condition and hence is merely another reflection of the interaction of overt role playing with sponsorship. For this attitude measure, just as for the first one, the analysis of variance shows that the monetary reward factor has no significant main effect and does not enter into any significant interaction with any other variables.

The pro arguments presented by the four overt role-playing groups in response to the open-end question were found to be very similar to the ones which the subjects had presented earlier in their role-playing essays. On the average, about two-thirds of the pro arguments given by each group were the same as the ones given in their essays, while one-third were new ones. This observation carries an important implication with respect to the differences in the relative frequency of pro arguments shown in Table 1; namely, that favorable sponsorship makes for a greater tendency for the role player to accept the arguments that he previously had presented when he wrote the essay to fulfill the demands of the overt role-playing task.

In order to compare the quality of the essays written by the four experimental subgroups, the judge's blind ratings of the essay arguments were analyzed in the same way as the responses to the final open-end question. As expected, the largest number of explicit pro arguments was given by the subgroup that received the least dissonant treatment ($20 payment under public-welfare-sponsorship conditions) and the smallest number was given by the subgroup that received the most dissonant treatment ($1 payment under commercial-sponsorship conditions). The means are shown in Row 3 of Table 3; the t test results (based on the error estimate from an overall analysis of variance) show a highly significant

TABLE 2

Analysis of Variance of Attitude Scores

Source	df	Combined score for five objective items		Response to open-end question: Net attitude score	
		MS	F	MS	F
Role (experimental condition) (A)	1	0.0	< 1.0	18.1	4.1*
Sponsor (B)	1	29.0	1.1	1.6	< 1.0
Reward (C)	1	29.0	1.1	1.0	< 1.0
A × B	1	151.0	5.7**	34.7	7.8***
A × C	1	14.0	< 1.0	0.1	< 1.0
B × C	1	6.0	< 1.0	9.0	2.0
A × B × C	1	25.0	< 1.0	0.4	< 1.0
Within cells	56	26.7		4.4	
Total	63				

* p = .05.
** p < .03.
*** p < .01.

difference between the subgroups given the most dissonant and the least dissonant treatments. The analysis of variance showed that this measure of the quality of the essays was significantly affected in the positive direction by the favorable versus unfavorable sponsorship variable ($p < .05$) and by the high versus low monetary reward ($p < .05$). Thus, there is some evidence that the positive incentive conditions had a significant effect with respect to inducing a better quality of performance of the role-playing task.

Additional but inconclusive evidence was also obtained from the subjects' own self-ratings of the arguments in their essays. The highest frequency of good quality arguments (those rated by the subjects as "very good") was again found in the subgroup paid $20 under favorable sponsorship conditions and the lowest frequency in the subgroup paid $1 under unfavorable sponsorship conditions; but an analysis of variance showed that these subgroup differences were not large enough to be statistically significant.

DISCUSSION

The finding of a significant interaction between sponsorship and role-playing conditions suggests that the psychological processes operating when a person engages in overt role playing may be somewhat different from those operating at the stage when the person has decided to play the role but has not yet executed it. The findings for the nonovert role-playing condition seem to point in the direction of dissonance-theory predictions in that favorable sponsorship gave rise to somewhat less acceptance of the new position than unfavorable sponsorship, although the differences are not large enough to be statistically significant. But it is noteworthy that the relatively low degree of acceptance of the new position among the nonovert role players who were exposed to the unfavorable sponsorship condition is entirely attributable to the subgroup that received the small monetary payment. According to the dissonance-theory analysis, under favorable sponsorship conditions (as well as under unfavorable sponsorship conditions) a large reward should decrease dissonance and, therefore, should evoke less attitude change than a small reward. Our control group

TABLE 3

Subgroup Comparisons Showing the Influence of Extreme Dissonant
and Consonant Conditions on the Effectiveness of Overt Role Playing

Effect measure	Role players in the most dissonant condition ($1 reward, commercial sponsor) (N = 9)	Role players in the least dissonant condition ($20 reward, public-welfare sponsor) (N = 9)	Difference (most-least dissonant)	t
1. Total approval score on five objective questionnaire items (From Table 1)	5.56	10.12	−4.56	1.87**
2. Responses to final open-end question (Net attitude scores based on explicit arguments; from Table 1)	−0.33	+1.45	−1.78	1.79*
3. Quality of role-playing essays: Explicit pro — explicit anti arguments[a]	−0.22	+1.45	−1.67	4.38***

Note.—Higher scores on the two attitude measures indicate more attitude change following role playing.
[a] For the other two subgroups, the corresponding mean was 1.0 in both instances.
* $p = .08$.
** $p = .07$.
*** $p < .01$.

findings, however, show the reverse outcome (see Columns 4 versus 5 in Table 1).

In any case, since the differences among the control groups are not statistically significant, we would not expect to find that in replications of our study the group of nonovert role players in the favorable sponsorship condition will consistently show less attitude change than those in the unfavorable sponsorship condition. This expectation is borne out in a study by Elms and Janis (1965), which replicated and extended the present research. In the Elms and Janis experiment, the *nonovert* role-playing groups again yielded no significant differences (but this time those in the unfavorable sponsorship condition showed somewhat less attitude change than those in the favorable sponsorship condition, the lowest scores occurring in the control subgroup that was given low payment and unfavorable sponsorship); the data from the *overt* role-playing groups, however, again showed that a significantly greater amount of attitude change was produced by favorable incentive conditions.

The results in Tables 1 and 2 show that overt role playing proved to be significantly more effective than nonovert when sponsorship was favorable, but not when sponsorship was unfavorable. This interaction outcome supports one of the assumptions of an incentive-theory analysis: Overt verbalization of one's own improvised arguments in favor of an initially unaccepted attitude position will facilitate biased scanning of the positive incentives and therefore will lead to more attitude change—provided that there are no strong interfering responses engendered by feelings of suspicion, guilt, or other negative reactions of the type elicited by unfavorable situational conditions.

The results in Tables 1 and 2, together with the subsidiary *t* test data presented in the text, support the hypothesis that the effectiveness of overt role playing depends upon *favorable* sponsorship conditions. Unfavorable sponsorship (as represented by a commercial company, which was hiring the subjects to help them prepare advertising copy) resulted in significantly less personal approval of the induced position than consonant sponsorship (as represented by a public-welfare organization, which was hiring the subjects to help prepare for a nationwide opinion survey). Thus, the overt role players were more influenced when the sponsor's affiliations and goals were presented to them as being consonant with their own values then when they were presented as being more dissonant.

According to dissonance theory, if a person complies with a role-playing demand, the less the reward or justification he has been offered for arguing in favor of a position that is contrary to his own personal opinion, the greater the dissonance and the stronger the motivation to reduce the dissonance by changing his personal opinion (Festinger, 1959, p. 95). Dissonance theory asserts that the effectiveness of role playing will be decreased by any factor that makes the role-playing task more rewarding, more justifiable, or more compatible with the subject's pre-existing values and attitudes. If this theory were correct, we should have found that among the overt role players the commercial sponsor was more effective than the public-welfare sponsor; but the data show the opposite outcome. We should also have found that the low-reward condition ($1) was more effective than the large-reward condition ($20); whereas the data show no significant difference. Our results on the effects of $20 versus $1 payments fail to confirm the findings of the Festinger and Carlsmith (1959) experiment, in which the same amounts were compared. There is no reason to expect that with larger samples the differences predicted by dissonance theory would have emerged because, with the present sample ($N = 18$ in each reward condition), the trend is in the opposite direction from that predicted by dissonance theory. The nine overt role players given the most dissonant conditions ($1 reward with commercial sponsorhip) obtained lower approval scores on the attitude measures than the nine given the least dissonant conditions ($20 reward with public-welfare sponsorship). The pertinent results, extracted from Tables 1 and 2, together with t test data based on the error estimates obtained from the corresponding analyses of variance, are summarized in Table 3. It will be noted that on both attitude indicators, the differences are large enough to approach statistical significance ($p < .10$, two-tailed test). These findings parallel those obtained from the blind ratings of the quality of the essays, shown in Row 3 of Table 3. Thus, our results fail to bear out the prediction from dissonance theory that the most dissonant condition of role playing will produce the most attitude change; in fact, the outcome tends to be the opposite.

Our findings call into question the generality of those reported by the adherents of dissonance theory (Brehm & Cohen, 1962; Festinger & Carlsmith, 1959) with respect to the way in which small versus large amounts of money paid in advance will influence the effectiveness of role playing. Their results are subject to a number of alternative interpretations. For example, in the Festinger and Carlsmith experiment, the students were informed by the experimenter that he regularly does not tell the truth to his subjects about the purpose of his study and the role-playing task consisted of helping to perpetrate this type of deceit by lying to a fellow student who would be the next subject. Under these rather unfavorable conditions, the finding that a $20 reward resulted in less attitude change than a $1 reward might well have been the consequence of a predominance of negative incentive effects over whatever positive effects accrued to the higher monetary value. Blatant lying to a fellow student may be felt by college students to be even more objectionable than writing down some arguments to be used in the future as advertising copy in a commercial sales campaign that will try to promote an educational policy with which one disagrees, as in our present experiment. If we are correct in surmising that the context for the role-playing activity in the Festinger and Carlsmith situation was likely to evoke suspicion or guilt, we would expect an inordinately large reward to stimulate a considerable increase in suspiciousness, guilt, or other negative feelings to such an extent that the positive incentive value accruing to the increased financial reward could be outweighed and thus produce less attitude change than a lower amount of reward.

In order to assess the effects of monetary rewards in relation to incentive theory, it is necessary to take account of the way in which the different amounts of reward were perceived by the subjects. No information about this is provided either by Festinger and Carlsmith or by Cohen for the role-playing situations they investigated. In the present experiment, the final interviews indicated that the large monetary reward was an ambiguous incentive. While the $1 reward was regarded by the subjects as a satisfactory payment, the $20 reward evoked diverse and often highly conflictual anticipations, apparently functioning as a predominantly positive incentive for some subjects, as a negative one for others, and as a source of puzzlement for everyone who received it. Hence no specific predictions about the monetary reward effects can be made from incentive theory, since clear-cut predictions are possible only when the larger incentive can be considered as a predominantly positive one that evokes relatively little guilt, suspicion, or other negative affects.

According to incentive theory, if a very large reward generates negative affect, it will tend to interfere with acceptance of the conclusions advocated in the role-playing performance; but if the monetary reward elicits positive feelings of gratitude and satisfaction, we would expect it to facilitate acceptance. Thus, the possibility arises of an interaction between sponsorship and reward: With positive sponsorship, the very large monetary reward would be expected to have a predominantly positive incentive effect and thus make for an increase in the amount of attitude change; whereas, with negative sponsorship a very large reward would be more likely to induce negative affects that would tend to make for less attitude change. No such interaction trend emerged in the present study, perhaps because it was obscured by the mixed reaction evoked by the overpayment for the high-reward condition, or because the less favorable sponsor was still regarded as a socially acceptable business enterprise that was preparing for a legitimate advertising campaign. In order to test the interaction hypothesis, it is essential to carry out another experiment that replicates the design of the present one except that: the effects of a plausible large reward should be compared with the effects of a small reward; and the role-playing task, when carried out under unfavorable sponsorship conditions, should be perceived as a *counternorm* action (as might have been the case in the Festinger and Carlsmith, 1959, experiment). The evidence from the present experiment, however, suggests that when the overt role-playing activity does not violate any dominant norms of our society: (*a*) the payment of a large versus small monetary reward has no effect on the amount of attitude change; and (*b*) favorable sponsorship is markedly more effective than unfavorable sponsorship, irrespective of whether the accompanying monetary reward is large or small.

7

When Dissonance Fails: On Eliminating Evaluation Apprehension from Attitude Measurement[1]

MILTON J. ROSENBERG

Approaches to attitude change which stress the response-strengthening effects of rewards or incentives (such as those offered by Janis, Kelman, and Scott) are not the only alternatives to dissonance theory. Nor is dissonance theory the only approach emphasizing psychological consistency. In his theory of affective-cognitive consistency, for example, Milton Rosenberg's assumptions about consistency needs are similar to Festinger's. But his hypotheses concerning the influence of these needs on attitude processes lead sometimes to distinctly different conclusions—for instance, with regard to role playing. (Rosenberg has expanded upon the position presented here, in chapters for two recent books on consistency theories [Rosenberg, 1966, 1968]. A dissonance-oriented criticism of Rosenberg's and other approaches to role playing is presented by Aronson, 1966.)

This selection is reprinted with abridgments from the Journal of Personality and Social Psychology, *1965, 1, 28–42, with permission of the author and the American Psychological Association.*

---

[1] This study was carried out while the author was a member of the Psychology Department at Ohio State University. It was supported by Contract 495 (24) with the Group Psychology Branch of the Office of Naval Research. The author is indebted to Frederick Weizmann for his assistance in executing the experiment and to David Glass and Irving Janis who raised a number of useful questions.

EVALUATION APPREHENSION AS A RESEARCH CONTAMINANT

It is proposed that the typical human subject approaches the typical psychological experiment with a preliminary expectation that the psychologist may undertake to evaluate his (the subject's) emotional adequacy, his mental health or lack of it. Members of the general public, including students in introductory psychology courses, have usually learned (despite our occasional efforts to persuade them otherwise) to attribute special abilities along these lines to those whose work is perceived as involving psychological interests and skills.[2] Even when the subject is convinced that his adjustment is not being directly studied he is likely to think that the experimenter is nevertheless bound to be sensitive to any behavior that bespeaks poor adjustment or immaturity.

In experiments the subject's initial suspicion that he may be exposing himself to evaluation will usually be confirmed or disconfirmed (as he perceives it) in the early stages of his encounter with the experimenter. Whenever it *is* confirmed, or to the extent that it is, the typical subject will be likely to experience *evaluation apprehension;* that is, an active, anxiety-toned concern that he win a positive evaluation from the experimenter, or at least that he provide no grounds for a negative one. Personality variables will have some bearing upon the extent to which this pattern of apprehension develops. But equally important are various aspects of the experimental design such as the experimenter's explanatory "pitch," the types of measures used, and the experimental manipulations themselves.

Such factors may operate with equal potency across all cells of an experiment; but we shall focus upon the more troublesome situation in which treatment differences between experimental groups make for differential arousal and confirmation of evalua-

[2] As used in this paper the term "psychologist" is merely a convenient categorical simplification. It denotes anyone who "runs" subjects through an experimental or interview procedure and is perceived as being at least somewhat skilled at, and professionally interested in, figuring people out. For example, this is certainly the case when undergraduate subjects participate in a study conducted by an advanced psychology major or graduate student.

tion apprehension. The particular difficulty with this state of affairs is that subjects in groups experiencing comparatively high levels of evaluation apprehension will be more prone than subjects in other groups to interpret the experimenter's instructions, explanations, and measures for what they may convey about the kinds of responses that will be considered healthy or unhealthy, mature or immature. In other words, they will develop *hypotheeses* about how to win positive evaluation or to avoid negative evaluation. And usually the subjects in such an experimental group are enough alike in their perceptual reactions to the situation so that there will be considerable similarity in the hypotheses at which they separately arrive. This similarity may, in turn, operate to systematically influence experimental responding in ways that foster false confirmation of the experimenter's predictions.

Let us consider one example of a situation in which some well-known findings might be accounted for in these terms. It seems quite conceivable that in certain dissonance experiments the use of surprisingly large monetary rewards for eliciting counterattitudinal arguments may seem quite strange to the subject, may suggest that he is being treated disingenuously. This in turn is likely to confirm initial expectations that evaluation is somehow being undertaken. As a result the typical subject, once exposed to this manipulation, may be aroused to a comparatively high level of evaluation apprehension; and, guided by the figural fact that an excessive reward has been offered, he may be led to hypothesize that the experimental situation is one in which his autonomy, his honesty, his resoluteness in resisting a special kind of bribe, are being tested. Thus, given the patterning of their initial expectations and the routinized cultural meanings of some of the main features of the experimental situation, most low-dissonance subjects may come to reason somewhat as follows: "they probably want to see whether getting paid so much will affect my own attitude, whether it will influence me, whether I am the kind of person whose views can be changed by buying him off."

The subject who has formulated such a subjective hypothesis about the real purpose of the experimental situation will be prone to resist giving evidence of attitude change; for to do so would, as he perceives it, convey something unattractive about himself, would lead to his being negatively evaluated by the experimenter. On the other hand, a similar hypothesis would be less likely to occur to the subject who is offered a smaller monetary reward and thus he would be less likely to resist giving evidence of attitude change.

AFFECT TOWARD THE EXPERIMENTER AS A RESEARCH CONTAMINANT

Yet another and even simpler type of possible systematic bias should be noted. This involves the unsuspected affective consequences of designs which call for the experimenter to behave differently toward persons in different conditions of an experiment. Under certain circumstances such differences may generate further differences in how subjects feel toward the experimenter or toward his experiment; and these intercell affective differences too may have the final consequence of influencing experimental responses in ways which make for false confirmation of hypotheses. Thus, turning again to dissonance studies in which subjects are offered large rewards for the writing of counterattitudinal essays, this manipulation, instead of creating low dissonance, may establish comparatively high arousal of the suspicion that one is being deceived; and this in turn may generate anger. A possible consequence is that the low-dissonance subject, provoked to hostility by the suspected duplicity, may find emotional release in refusing to show the response (attitude change) that he perceives the experimenter to be after.

CONTAMINANT CONTROL BY ALTERED REPLICATION

One way of checking upon the presence of these types of contamination is to ask the subject how he interpreted the purpose and meaning of the experiment. This will often be possible but it may sometimes involve one major hazard: such interviewing in itself can be open to the very kinds of contamination it seeks to disclose. Another approach is to conduct an altered replication of the original experiment, one in which we redesign those of its aspects that are presumed to have fostered the contaminating processes. Not only does such an approach enable application of the law of parsimony in interpreting the relation of data to theoretical claims, it also facilitates further study of the social psychology of the psychological experiment.[3] . . .

The study upon which the present paper is focused was conducted by Cohen and is one of the many recently reported by Brehm and Cohen (1962). Its general design was similar to earlier dissonance studies except that it used four levels of monetary reward, instead of the usual two. The prediction was that with this graded range of monetary rewards the resulting attitude change would be monotonically and inversely related to the size of the reward.

The subjects were Yale undergraduates. The issue concerned the actions of the New Haven police in a campus riot that had occurred a few weeks earlier. The experimenter, appearing at randomly chosen dormitory rooms, introduced himself as a "member of an Institute of Human Relations research team," ascertained by verbal inquiry that the subject disapproved of the actions of the police and asked him to write an essay in support of the actions of the police.[4] The request for the counterattitudinal essay was explained in this way:

It has been shown that one of the best ways to get relevant arguments, on both sides of an issue, is to ask people to write essays favoring only one side. . . . What we really need now are some essays favoring the police side. I understand that you have very

[3] Footnote deleted.—ED.

[4] It is not clear from the research report whether the experimenter actually referred to himself as a psychologist. But belonging to an "Institute of Human Relations research team" would have been sufficient to establish that he was some sort of psychologist or advanced psychological trainee who would be reporting back to a more senior colleague. This was because the "Institute of Human Relations" was the name of the building that housed the Yale psychology department; no other department that gave undergraduate courses was located there and the research organization for which it was named had long since ceased to exist. The experimenter also described himself as a "fellow student." This may have worked to further heighten the arousal of evaluation apprehension, since the Yale undergraduate culture places great emphasis upon the competitive show of maturity, sophistication, and "all around balance." It would probably be particularly important to the subject that the evaluation of him formed by a psychologically trained "fellow student" be a positive one.

different views on the matter, but as you can see it's very interesting to know what kinds of arguments people bring up in their essays if they have different opinions about it.

The reward manipulation was then introduced by telling the subject that he would receive a particular sum for "writing the essay against your own position." Eight subjects were offered $.50, 6 were offered $1, 10 others were offered $5, 6 others were offered $10. The subject wrote his essay on a blank sheet headed "Why the New Haven Police Actions Were Justified." He was then told:

Now that you have looked at some of the reasons for the actions of the New Haven police, we would like to get some of your reactions to the issue: *you may possibly want to look at the situation in the light of this.* So, would you please fill out this questionnaire.

The questionnaire on which the subject was invited to indicate approval of the New Haven police, if so inclined, began with this query: "Considering the circumstances, how justified do you think the New Haven police actions were in the recent riot?" An a priori 31-point scale was used with labels at every fifth point and ranging from "completely justified" to "not at all justified." Additional questionnaire items were used to check that the subject correctly perceived the amount of payment that he had been promised and that he had understood that he was to write a strong essay opposite to his own attitude. A control group was given the attitude questionnaire but received neither the manipulation nor the other measures.

It was found that the $5 and $10 groups did not differ significantly from the control group in expressed attitude toward the New Haven police. However, the subjects in the $.50 group were less negative toward the New Haven police than the $1 subjects ($p < .05$) who in turn were less negative than the $10 subjects ($p < .05$); and both the $.50 and $1 groups differed significantly from the control group.

Thus in the main the data appeared to confirm the original prediction. However, the point of view outlined above would suggest that in this study, as in others of similar design, the low-dissonance (high-reward) subjects would be more likely to suspect that the experimenter had some unrevealed purpose. The gross discrepancy between spending a few minutes writing an essay and the large sum offered, the fact that this large sum had not yet been delivered by the time the subject was handed the attitude questionnaire, the fact that he was virtually invited to show that he had become more positive toward the New Haven police: all these could have served to engender suspicion and thus to arouse evaluation apprehension and negative affect toward the experimenter. Either or both of these motivating states could probably be most efficiently reduced by the subject refusing to show anything but fairly strong disapproval of the New Haven police; for the subject who had come to believe that his autonomy in the face of a monetary lure was being assessed, remaining "antipolice" would demonstrate that he *had* autonomy; for the subject who perceived an indirect and disingenuous attempt to change his attitude and felt some reactive anger, holding fast to his original attitude could appear to be a relevant way of frustrating the experimenter.[5] Furthermore, with each *step* of increase in reward we could expect an increase in the proportion of subjects who had been brought to a motivating level of evaluation apprehension or affect arousal.

How can such an interpretation be tested? If it is correct it

[5] Some other reasons (see Footnote 4 for the first) why the experimenter calling himself a "fellow student" might have increased the potency of these biasing processes are worth noting here. Given the fact that the antipolice attitude was highly normative among Yale undergraduates at this time many subjects would have been likely to assume that the experimenter was also antipolice. Thus among the high-reward subjects who made this attribution to the experimenter any tendency to inhibit showing themselves capable of being "bought off" would be further strengthened by the expectation that the experimenter would personally disapprove of the subject's new attitude. On the other hand if the experimenter was perceived, as he might have been by some subjects, to actually be propolice, the fact that he was a "fellow student" would lead to his being seen as violating an important group standard; and this, particularly for high-reward subjects who might interpret the experimenter as trying to "buy them off" for the propolice side, would have engendered even more anger toward the experimenter than would otherwise be the case. In turn this would have increased the likelihood that the high-reward subject would resist showing any change in the propolice direction. Thus both the evaluation apprehension and affect arousal patterns of contamination might well have been intensified by the experimenter being perceived as a fellow student.

points to the importance of the fact that the experimenter conducts both the dissonance arousal and the attitude measurement. Evaluation apprehension and negative affect, if they exist, have been focused upon the experimenter; and it would be either to avoid his negative evaluation or to frustrate him, or both, that the high-reward subject would hold back (from the experimenter and possibly even from himself) any evidence of having been influenced by the essay he has just completed.

The most effective way then to eliminate the influence of the biasing factors would be to separate the dissonance arousal phase of the experiment from the attitude measurement phase. The experiment should be organized so that it appears to the subject to be two separate, unrelated studies, conducted by investigators who have little or no relationship with each other and who are pursuing different research interests. In such a situation the evaluation apprehension and negative affect that are focused upon the dissonance-arousing experimenter would probably be lessened and, more important, they would not govern the subject's responses to the attitude-measuring experimenter and to the information that he seeks from the subject.

This was the main change introduced into the original design.[6] A second change was that the reward manipulation involved not only telling the subject that he would be paid a certain amount, but also the actual delivery of that amount to him immediately after he completed the essay. It was assumed that this change too would work to reduce the likelihood that the high-reward subjects would develop suspicions concerning the experimenter's possible duplicity and unrevealed purposes.

Adherence to the dissonance view would suggest that under these altered conditions the results would still show an inverse relationship between magnitude of reward and extent of attitude

[6] The author is aware of only one dissonance study in which some attempt was made to separate counterattitudinal advocacy from subsequent attitude measurement; this is the experiment by Festinger and Carlsmith (1959). However, the degree of separation may well have been insufficient. That experiment did not involve, as did the present one, disguising the two phases as two different studies conducted in two different departments. Furthermore the dependent variable was not change in a previously stable social attitude but rather a momentary rating of how much the subject liked or disliked an experiment just completed.

change. Indeed the significance of the dissonance-confirming relationship might be expected to increase; for now with each subject having actually received a monetary reward the cognitions concerning reasons for undertaking the counterattitudinal performance would be less variable within experimental groups than could have been the case in the original experiment.

However, the consistency theory developed by the present author (Rosenberg, 1956, 1960) suggests the opposite prediction. It holds that the most usual basis for attitude change is the establishment of new beliefs about the attitude object, beliefs that are inconsistent with the original affective orientation toward that object. In this view the significance of a reward received for writing a counterattitudinal essay (that is, for improvising or rehearsing inconsistency-generating cognitions) would be different from that claimed in dissonance theory: such a reward would, in proportion to its magnitude, be likely to have a positive effect both upon the development and the stabilization of the new cognitions. From this it would be predicted that with the removal of the biasing factors the degree of attitude change obtained after the subjects have written counterattitudinal essays will vary directly, rather than inversely, with the amount of reward. Thus the altered design outlined here may afford something approximating a critical test between this approach and the dissonance approach as regards their applicability to predicting the attitude-change effects of counterattitudinal advocacy.

METHOD

Attitude Issue and Subjects

To replicate as closely as possible, except for the major changes that distinguish the present study from its model, the author sought an issue comparable to "the actions of the New Haven police." Late in 1961 the Ohio State University football team, having won the Big Ten championship, received an invitation to the Rose Bowl. Concerned with the extent to which its reputation as the "football capital of the world" weakened OSU's academic reputation and performance, the faculty council of the University voted to reject the invitation and thereby engendered, both in the student body and the surrounding community, a sense of incredulous outrage. This, through the promptings of local news media, was rapidly turned toward active protest. The immediate result was a riot in which a large crowd of undergraduates (estimates varied between one to three thousand) stormed through University buildings shouting pro-Rose-Bowl and antifaculty slogans. The more longlasting result was the stabilization among the undergraduates of an attitude of disapproval toward any limitation upon Rose Bowl participation. This attitude remained salient during the following year and even in the face of the fact that during that year the faculty council, by a close vote, reversed its original decision. In general interested students felt that future faculty interference with participation in bowl games continued to be a real possibility.

With a pilot questionnaire administered early in 1963 it was confirmed that opposition to a Rose Bowl ban remained a consensual position among the undergraduate body; more than 94% of the sample indicated strong disapproval toward any restoration of the ban in the future. Upon completion of this pilot study a new group of male subjects was recruited from sections of introductory psychology for participation in the present study. In all 51 subjects were finally used. Ten were randomly assigned to each of three experimental conditions and 21 to a control condition.

Dissonance Arousal

As each experimental subject arrived at the author's office he found him busily engaged either in writing or in a conversation with another "student." The experimenter then told the subject:

I'm sorry but I'm running late on my schedule today and I'll have to keep you waiting for about 15 or 20 minutes. Is that all right?

Most subjects simply said it was though a few expressed concern about getting to their next class on time. All of the latter, when assured that the work the experimenter wanted them to do would take no more than 20 minutes, accepted the situation with equanimity. The experimenter then said:

Oh, I've just thought of something; while you are waiting you could participate in another little experiment that some graduate student in education is doing.

The experimenter explained that he had had a call the previous day from the "graduate student" who needed volunteers in a hurry for

some sort of study he's doing—I don't know what it's about exactly except that it has to do with attitudes and that's why he called me, because my research is in a similar area as you'll see later. [The experimenter went on to say] Of course he can't give you any credit [the usual research credit point used to keep up experimental participation rates in introductory psychology courses] but I gather they have some research funds and that they are paying people instead. So if you care to go down there you can.

All but three subjects indicated that they did want to participate in the other study. (The three who did not were eliminated from the experiment.) With some show of effort and uncertainty the experimenter then recalled the name of the education graduate student and the room, actually located in the education department, where he could be found.

Upon reporting to the "education graduate student" the subject received an explanation modeled word-for-word upon that used in the earlier experiment reported by Brehm and Cohen. Also, as in that experiment, it was determined by verbal inquiry that the subject held an attitude position opposite to the one he was to argue for in the essay. Subjects were randomly assigned to one of three reward conditions ($.50, $1, $5), and the amount that each subject was to receive was made clear to him before he undertook to write an essay on why the OSU football team should not be allowed to participate in the Rose Bowl. After the subject had completed the essay he was *paid* the amount that he had been promised, then thanked for his participation and dismissed. He then returned to the experimenter's office and, under the guise of participating in another study, his attitudes toward the Rose Bowl ban and toward various other issues were ascertained.

Attitude Measurement

This phase of the study began by the experimenter telling the subject that the study for which his participation had originally been solicited was a continuing survey on student attitudes "that I run every semester as a sort of Gallup poll to keep a check on opinion patterns on different University issues." (The experimenter, of course, did not know at this point which of the three magnitudes of reward the subject had received for writing the essay.) The subject then filled out an attitude questionnaire dealing with eight different issues. One of these read, "How would you feel if it were decided that from now on the OSU football team would not be allowed to participate in the Rose Bowl?" Following the procedure in the earlier study the subject responded on a 31-point graphic scale, marked at every fifth point by these labels: I think this decision would be not justified at all; very little justified; little justified; slightly justified; rather justified (instead of "quite justified" as in the earlier study); very justified; completely justified.

The same scale form was used with the other seven issues. One of these dealt with the area of varsity athletics and read, "How would you feel if it were decided that the University would no longer give any athletic scholarships?" This issue was included to provide another and more indirect test of the attitude-change consequences of writing the anti-Rose-Bowl essay under varying conditions of reward. The other six issues dealt with nonathletic matters such as dormitory regulations, University admission policies, library rules, etc.

When the subject had completed this questionnaire he was asked what he thought the experiment was really about. His responses during a period of subsequent inquiry were transcribed and these were to be analyzed for the extent to which they reflected any suspicion that the two experiments were actually related to one another. The subject then filled out a follow-up questionnaire. The first item asked, "while you were filling out the opinion questionnaire did it occur to you that there might be some connection between this experiment and the one you worked on in the education department?" After he had answered this item the subject was told that in fact there had been "a connection between the two experiments" and that it would all be explained after he completed the questionnaire. The subject then proceeded to answer the other questions which asked how strong an essay he had agreed to write, how strong an essay he did write, how free he had felt in his decision to write the essay, how getting paid for the essay had made him feel, etc. Each of the questions was answered by choosing one of a number of alternative positions.

The experimenter then told the subject about the nature (but not the purpose) of the deception that had been used and proceeded to engage him in an interview designed to elicit further evidence of any doubts or suspicions that the subject might have felt during the experiment. The experimenter then explained the actual purpose of the experiment, commenting both upon its basic hypothesis and its design, and then answered all of the subject's questions. Before the subject was thanked and dismissed he was urged not to speak of the experiment to any fellow students during the remainder of the academic semester. All subjects promised to comply with this request.

In distinction to the experimental subjects each of the control subjects, upon reporting for his appointment, was merely told that the experimenter was conducting "a sort of Gallup poll on University issues" and then filled out the attitude questionnaire.

RESULTS

In all 62 subjects were originally run through the experiment. Eleven were discarded from the final analysis because on one basis or another they failed to meet necessary conditions that had been specified in advance. Six subjects (two originally assigned to the control condition and four to the experimental conditions) were rejected because postexperimental questioning revealed that they were members of varsity athletic teams. It had been decided that persons in this category would not be used since their pro-Rose-Bowl attitudes could be assumed to be considerably stronger, more firmly anchored, than those of other students. Two other subjects, originally assigned to experimental groups, were discarded from the analysis because they evidenced virtually complete and spontaneous insight into the deception that had been employed. One other subject was discarded because he reported, on the postexperimental questionnaire, that he had been asked to write a "weak" rather than a "strong" essay. Two additional experimental subjects were discarded because they impressed both the experimenter and his assistant as showing psychotic tendencies. However, when the analysis reported below is repeated with the last three rejected subjects *included* the findings are in no wise altered.

Except for the manipulated independent variable other factors that might influence attitudinal response appear to have remained constant across experimental groups. Thus on the postexperimental questionnaire the subjects in the three experimental groups do not differ in their perceptions as to how strong an essay they were asked to write or actually did write; nor do they differ in their self-reports on how free they felt to refuse. From the postexperimental interview data it appears that though a few subjects were surprised to find the Rose Bowl situation featured in the "two different experiments," the groups were equally lacking in insight both as regards the deception that was used and as regards the real purpose of the experiment.[7]

[7] It has been already suggested that in interviews, as in experiments, subjects' responses may often be influenced by their private interpretations of the situation. Thus the postexperimental data collected in this study cannot necessarily be taken at simple face value. But there is at least one important consideration (probably relevant whenever the credibility of an experimental deception is being assessed) that suggests that the subjects were not holding back evidence of having discerned the true design of the experiment or of having doubted the explanations that were given them. Experienced experimenters will probably agree that college student subjects usually desire to represent themselves as sophisticated and as not easily misled. Thus when the postexperimental interview situation is a permissive one the subjects are likely to disclose, rather than withhold, promptings toward insight. *Yet none of the present subjects revealed any such insights when, after completion of the experiment, they were asked "what do you think the experiment was really about?"* Later on when *told* by the experimenter that the "two experiments" were really one or still later when the full explanation was given, only a few subjects (two or three per group) claimed to have had suspicions suggestive of what had now been revealed. However, in their attitudinal responses on the two athletic issues these subjects do not differ from others in their groups (that is, they are not clustered in the low, middle, or high portions of the within-group attitude score rankings). Thus it seems likely that most of these particular subjects were exaggerating, and

It will be remembered that the measurement phase of the present study consisted of a questionnaire concerned with eight different University issues. On the six issues concerning matters unrelated to athletic policy, and thus not subjected to manipulation through the essay-writing procedure, statistical analysis reveals no overall differences and no differences between any specific groups taken two at a time.

On the main matter of experimental interest, whether attitude change on the Rose Bowl and athletic-scholarship issues varies directly or inversely with the magnitude of monetary reward, the data reviewed below reveal that the former is the case; that is, the prediction drawn from a consistency-theory interpretation appears to be confirmed and the opposite prediction based upon dissonance theory appears thereby to be disconfirmed.

Scoring the 31-point attitude scale from 1.0 (for the banning of Rose Bowl participation would be "not justified at all") through 1.2, 1.4 . . . to 6.8, 7.0 (banning Rose Bowl participation would be "completely justified") we find the following mean scores: 1.45 for the control group, 2.24 for the $.50 reward group, 2.32 for the $1 reward group, and 3.24 for the $5 reward group. The attitude score ranges are 1–3 for the control group, 1–4 for the $.50 group, 1–5 for the $1 group, and 2–6 for the $5 group.

The significance of the reward variable in its influence upon attitude toward a Rose Bowl ban was assessed by computing the Kruskal-Wallis one-way analysis of variance from the ranked scores of all groups. H, which is distributed as chi square, equals 17.89 and has a chance probability of less than .001 (see Table 1). In addition to this overall confirmation of the original prediction it is desirable to test the significance of differences between the specific groups.

Analysis by the Mann-Whitney rank sum test (computing z; see Mosteller & Bush, 1954) reveals that there is no significant difference between the $.50 and $1 groups. Accordingly in some

some perhaps were even imagining, their earlier doubts and in so doing were seeking positive evaluation from the experimenter after they had been shown capable of being "taken in." As intended, then, the procedures of the present experiment seem to have achieved their basic purpose which was to avoid, or at least to minimize, the kind of suspicion and disturbing confusion that tends to activate such biasing processes as affect arousal and evaluation apprehension.

TABLE 1

Group Means and Differences between Groups on Attitude toward the Rose Bowl Ban

Group	M	Group differences[a]			
		$.50	$1	$.50 and $1	$5
Control	1.45	$z = 1.97$, $p < .03$	$z = 1.80$, $p < .04$	$z = 2.31$, $p < .015$	$z = 3.93$, $p < .00$
$.50	2.24		$z = .11$		$z = 1.77$, $p < .04$
$1	2.32				$z = 1.81$, $p < .04$
$.50 and $1	2.28				$z = 2.11$, $p < .02$
$5	3.24				

Note.—Overall difference between groups as assessed by Kruskal-Wallis test: $H = 17.89$, $p < .001$.
[a] Tested by Mann-Whitney z, one-tailed.

of the additional analyses these two groups were combined. As Table 1 indicates the combined $.50–$1 group is significantly more favorable toward banning Rose Bowl participation than is the control group ($p < .015$) and significantly less favorable than the $5 group ($p < .02$). When the $.50 and $1 groups are analyzed separately each is found to be significantly different from both the control and $5 conditions (see Table 1). As would be expected the difference between the control and $5 groups is of very large significance ($p < .0001$).

Thus the only deviation from the original prediction in this set of findings is the absence of a significant difference between the $.50 and $1 groups. Since these groups do differ as predicted from both the control and $5 groups, respectively, it might be conjectured that the $.50 difference between them does not generate a large enough *subjective* difference in the magnitude of payment. However, the alternative possibility that even this small magnitude of difference in reward does have some subtler influence upon attitude is suggested by the additional data regarding the issue of abandoning the policy of giving athletic scholarships.

This issue was used as a second test of the basic hypothesis. The expectation was that attitude change on the Rose Bowl issue should tend to *generalize* toward a similar issue, one that suggests another way of deemphasizing the role of varsity sports in university life. It would of course be expected that the group differences would be of lesser magnitude on this issue than on the Rose Bowl issue since the latter served as the actual topic for the counterattitudinal essay.

Analysis of the subjects' responses on the athletic-scholarship issue reveals again a pattern of findings that supports the original hypothesis. Responding on a 31-point scale from 1.0 to 7.0 (with higher scores indicating greater approval for "abandoning athletic scholarships") the groups yield the following mean scores: 2.28 for the control group, 2.26 for the $.50 group, 3.04 for the $1 group, and 3.88 for the $5 group. The score ranges are 1–7 for the control group, 1–4.8 for the $.50 group, 1–6 for the $1 group, and 1.2–7 for the $5 group.

Application of the Kruskal-Wallis test indicates a significant main effect ($H = 14.50$, $p < .005$); thus the extent to which the writing of the essay affects an attitude *related* to the topic of the essay is shown to be a positive monotonic function of the amount of reward.

Analysis of the differences between the specific groups as reported in Table 2 clarifies certain interesting details. While the mean attitude scores of the control and $.50 groups are virtually identical there is a slight and insignificant trend ($p < .20$) toward a greater concentration of extreme negative scores in the control group. The difference between the control and $1 groups comes closer to an acceptable probability level ($p < .10$) reflecting the greater differences in means (control $= 2.28$, $1 = 3.04$) reported above.

As predicted, the control and $.50 groups do show significantly less approval of abandoning athletic scholarships than does the $5 group; $p < .01$ in both cases. When the control and $.50 groups are combined the difference from the $5 group has a probability of less than .005 as compared to less than .08 when the difference between the combined group and the $1 group is assessed. The $1 group clearly stands in an intermediate position. While its mean attitude score reflects greater endorsement of the antiathletic scholarship view than does the $.50 group and less endorsement than the $5 group, neither of these differences ($p < .15$ and $p < .12$, respectively) reaches significance.

Thus in comparison to the $.50 group the $1 group is less

clearly differentiated from the $5 group and more clearly differentiated from the control group. From this it is apparent that the difference in size of reward between the $.50 and $1 groups

TABLE 2

Group Means and Differences between Groups on Attitude toward Ending Athletic Scholarships

Group	M	Group differences[a]		
		$.50	$1	$5
Control	2.28	$z=.95,$ $p<.20$	$z=1.33,$ $p<.10$	$z=2.45,$ $p<.01$
$.50	2.26		$z=1.09,$ $p<.15$	$z=2.36,$ $p<.01$
Control and $.50	2.27		$z=1.44,$ $p<.08$	$z=2.67,$ $p<.005$
$1	3.04			$z=1.24,$ $p<.12$
$5	3.88			

Note.—Overall difference between groups as assessed by Kruskal-Wallis test: $H = 14.50, p < .005$
[a] Tested by Mann-Whitney z, one-tailed.

does have some influence upon the extent to which the writing of the essay affected the subjects' attitudes on a related issue; and that influence too is consistent with the prediction that attitude change following counterattitudinal performance will be a *positive* function of the degree of reward received for such performance.

A question of considerable interest is why the difference between the $.50 and $1 groups shows up more clearly on a related issue rather than on the issue with which the essay was directly concerned. One possible interpretation emerges when we recall that the $.50 group does differ significantly from the control group on the Rose Bowl issue but does not show such a difference on the athletic-scholarship issue. With this small amount of reward there may be a minimal likelihood that the induced attitude change will generalize to a similar issue; with the somewhat larger reward of $1 a somewhat stronger tendency toward generalization may be operative.

On the basis of the findings that have so far been presented, the following conclusion seems warranted: when the design of the original study reported by Brehm and Cohen is altered so as to eliminate aspects that were likely to have generated evaluation apprehension and unsuspected affect arousal, the prediction that guided the present study is confirmed and the original dissonance prediction is disconfirmed.

DISCUSSION

This paper has combined two purposes: to present some propositions about how subjects' perceptions of experimental situations may affect their experimental performances; and, on this basis, to report an experimental reexamination of the dissonance-theory interpretation of attitude change due to counterattitudinal advocacy.

As regards the first purpose, the confirmation of the predictions in the present study lends support to the original propositions about evaluation apprehension and affect arousal; for it was in part on the basis of those propositions that the experimental predictions were formulated. However, more direct investigation of these contaminating processes is possible and desirable. For example, in two recent studies the author has, by intention rather than by inadvertence, supplied cues to the subjects about types of responding that might connote maturity and immaturity. In one of these studies some subjects were led to believe that mature persons like strangers more than immature people do while other subjects were led to believe the opposite. In a second study some subjects were led to believe that mature people perform well on dull arithmetic tasks while others were led to believe that immature people do better at such tasks. The results of these studies, to be reported elsewhere, strongly demonstrate the power of evaluation apprehension in controlling experimental responding.

However, it is necessary that we go beyond such demonstration studies if these contaminating processes are to be better understood and thus more effectively controlled. A number of questions remain to be investigated. Do such personality variables as passivity, low self-esteem, and the need for social approval predict to the likelihood that evaluation apprehension will be aroused in the experimental situation? Does evaluation apprehension, once aroused, interact with experimenter bias (see Rosenthal, 1963) in a way that guides the subject in his hypothesizing about the kinds of responding that will win approval? Will exposure to psychological perspectives, as in the introductory courses from which so many subjects are drawn, tend to heighten the likelihood of experiencing evaluation apprehension in the experimental situation? Is there a minority of subjects who seek *negative* evaluation for masochistic purposes or as a way of asking for help, and will this affect their experimental responding? Can the presence of evaluation apprehension be uncovered by postexperimental inquiry? Comparable questions about the arousal of aggressive and other contaminating affective states could just as readily be formulated. Indeed it would seem desirable in further studies to attempt an operational separation of the two types of contamination that have been stressed in this paper.

In general the recently developed interest in investigating the experimenter-subject interaction as a source of bias in psychological research is a long needed innovation. The work of Orne (1962), Riecken (1962), Rosenthal (1963) and others has provided a most useful beginning. To the list of research contaminating processes that they have investigated, might well be added those that have been discussed here.

As regards the second major focus of this paper, do the present findings call the validity of dissonance theory into question? Recently there have been reported many challenging studies testing that theory's pertinence not only to attitude change but also to perceptual and motivational processes and even to learning phenomena.[8] Thus the present study, taken alone, cannot

---

[8] For example, and despite the fact that the author has found it possible to reinterpret one of the experiments reported by them, the work of Brehm and Cohen (1962) does seem to establish the relevance of the dissonance approach to the study of certain aspects of motivation and does so with considerable inventiveness and concern for methodological issues. Similarly the work of Lawrence and Festinger (1962) has opened a very interesting new line of inquiry on some problems in the psychology of learning.

be interpreted as challenging the general theory as such. However, it does seem to indicate that, at least in its account of the attitude-change consequences of counterattitudinal advocacy, dissonance theory has been overextended.

In the author's view the kind of counterattitudinal performance that best fits the dissonance paradigm is a simple overt act that directly violates one's private attitude (for example, eating or agreeing to eat a disliked food; expressing approval of a disliked proposal or candidate; merely *committing* oneself to develop counterattitudinal arguments; etc.). But when a person actually *does* elaborate a set of arguments opposite to his own attitude the dissonance he experiences is probably of much wider scope than dissonance analysis would have it; it encompasses considerably more than merely realizing that he has argued against his own position. The broader pattern of inconsistency that he encounters is that between the content and apparent plausibility, on the one hand, of the new arguments that he has developed and, on the other hand, his original affective judgment of the attitude object.

Thus the subject who opposes the Rose Bowl ban and then argues in favor of it may come up with some good arguments (for example, "If we ban going to the Rose Bowl we will improve our reputation as a serious University . . . we will draw better students," etc.). In so doing he may become convinced of the validity of those arguments. This will produce intraattitudinal inconsistency; that is, the newly established beliefs relating the Rose Bowl ban to positive ends and values will be inconsistent with the original negative affect toward the ban.

As was suggested earlier, the author's theoretical model (Rosenberg, 1956, 1960) takes this sort of inconsistency to be a basic condition for the occurrence of attitude change. It will be useful to show how this alternative model may be applied to interpreting the process of counterattitudinal advocacy. From this standpoint attitudes normally are stable, affective-cognitive structures and feature considerable internal consistency. It is assumed that the production of *inconsistency* through change in either the affective or cognitive component (the latter being more usual and likely) will, if it transcends the individual's tolerance limits, motivate further symbolic activity. This may lead either to the restoration of the original attitude or, if this line of defense is not available, to its reorganization in the opposite direction.

For the sequence that begins with cognitive alterations what is required is that the new cognitions be sufficiently internalized and difficult to reverse; then the most likely outcome will be for the affective disposition toward the attitude object to move in the direction consistent with the newly established cognitions. Thus attitude change in its conventional sense will have occurred.

In this context a basic question is: what will render the new, inconsistency-generating cognitions sufficiently internalized and difficult to reverse? Many variables could have this influence; but in the present study the necessary suggestion would be that the most important is the amount of reward expected and received for *developing* such cognitions. Putting this another way it may be hypothesized that the demonstrated influence of the magnitude of payment upon ultimate attitude change is mediated through its effects upon the cognitive processes that are activated during the essay-writing task.

Broadly speaking, two separate kinds of mediation are easily conceivable: the *expectation* of payment for counterattitudinal advocacy may operate as an incentive and thus affect the quality of the arguments advanced in support of the new cognitions; the *receipt* of payment may operate as a reinforcement that further fosters the internalization of the counterattitudinal cognitions; and of course the scope of these two processes would be expected to vary as a function of the actual amount of payment.

A subsidiary analysis of the essays themselves tends to support and clarify this view. One unequivocal finding is that the $.50 and $1 groups differ in the actual number of words per essay, the latter group writing the longer ones ($p < .05$).[9] However, the $1 and $5 groups do not show any such difference. Considering that the $.50 and $1 groups do not differ on the Rose Bowl issue while the $1 and $5 groups do, sheer verbal productivity does not seem to mediate the main effect. Further-

---

[9] All probability estimates reported in this discussion are based on a one-tailed interpretation of the Mann-Whitney statistic; in each case it was possible to make a unidirectional prediction about the attitude-change effects of the mediational variable under study.

more, separate analyses within each of the three experimental groups reveal absolutely no relationship between essay length and the postessay attitude toward the Rose Bowl ban.

But do the essays vary in quality, in the actual *persuasiveness* with which they are written; and if so does this relate to the postessay attitude score? Two judges, working without knowledge of the different reward conditions and using a 5-point scale, rated all the essays for their basic persuasiveness. As part of their instructions they were asked to ignore the length of essays "because a long one may often be less persuasive than a short one." The interjudge reliability of these ratings proved quite adequate: for 80% of the essays the two ratings were either identical or within 1 point of each other.

Six of the 20 subjects in the combined $.50 and $1 group had persuasiveness scores that were lower (1 and 1.5, based on the pooled ratings of the two judges) than any that occurred in the $5 group. Four of these 6 subjects also had extreme negative attitudes. A comparable finding is obtained when we split the $.50–$1 group into approximately equal low persuasiveness and high persuasiveness halves. Those who wrote comparatively unpersuasive essays show significantly more attitudinal negativism toward the Rose Bowl ban than those who wrote comparatively persuasive essays ($p < .03$). When the same sort of analysis is separately performed with the $.50 and $1 groups, respectively, similar findings are obtained with borderline significance ($p < .10$ in both instances). On the other hand within the high-reward group a division of the subjects into those who got the five lowest (though not as low as the comparable subjects in the low-reward group) and the five highest persuasiveness ratings does not yield any corresponding difference in attitudes toward the Rose Bowl ban.

An exactly similar finding is obtained when we use as the estimate of persuasiveness not the judges' ratings but the subjects' own postexperimental judgments of "how strong" their essays actually were. In the combined low-reward group those below the median in their self-ratings are less favorable to the Rose Bowl ban than those above the median ($p < .05$). Again no such effect is discovered in the high-reward group.

From these findings it may be concluded that one mediating source of the overall difference between the low- and high-reward groups is that some of the subjects in the former group were insufficiently motivated by the small reward that had been promised them: in consequence they wrote insufficiently developed essays, essays that were essentially unpersuasive to themselves. Thus it would seem appropriate to conclude that the overall positive relationship between reward and attitude change reflects the operation of an incentive or effort variable.

However, our analysis need not stop at this point. While some low-reward subjects wrote essays that are rated as extremely low on persuasiveness others did not. Thus it is possible to match the low- and high-reward groups on this factor and by so doing we can test for the presence of some other process that may also play a role in mediating the overall relationship between reward and attitude change. This was done by simply excluding from the analysis those low-reward subjects who got extremely low ratings (1 and 1.5) on the 5-point persuasiveness scale. With persuasiveness thus equalized (actually the mean persuasiveness score is then slightly *higher* for the remaining low-reward subjects than for the high-reward subjects) the high-reward group *still* shows significantly greater acceptance of the Rose Bowl ban ($p < .05$) and also of the proposal that athletic scholarships be abandoned ($p < .05$). These last findings do thus seem to confirm the expectation that, in addition to the incentive effect of variations in promised reward, there is yet another factor that contributes to the positive relationship between reward and attitude change. It would seem reasonable to interpret this other factor as based not upon the *promise* of reward but rather upon its *receipt;* thus our original conjecture that a reinforcement dynamic may be operative seems, on these grounds, to be rendered more plausible.

The use here of the term reinforcement should not, of course, be taken as referring solely to the kinds of relationships emphasized in conventional models of instrumental learning. In the present study the $5 payment, once received, could have increased the habit strength of the improvised counterattitudinal cognitions by directly increasing their attractiveness and credibility. Similarly, working for an expected large reward could have made the essay-writing a more ego-involving task and thus could have sensitized the subject to pay closer attention to the persuasive worth of his own arguments or to find greater merit in them. Furthermore, the amount of payment may also have affected the very clarity with which the new counterattitudinal arguments were remembered after the essay writing session.

In this discussion we have attempted to state, and also to present some additional data in support of, a consistency theory view of how counterattitudinal advocacy produces attitude change. That view can be summarized in the following set of propositions: the counterattitudinal improvisation establishes new cognitions that are inconsistent with the original attitudinal affect; the extent to which the affective judgment of the object will move toward the content of these new cognitions will depend upon the degree of affective-cognitive inconsistency they generate; this in turn will depend upon the strength and stability of the new cognitions; the strength and stability of the new cognitions are influenced, among other things, by the degree of reward received for their improvisation—and this is probably due both to the promised reward operating as an incentive and the received reward as a reinforcement; in consequence when counter-attitudinal advocacy is investigated in a way that circumvents certain biasing factors it will be found, as in the present study, that it produces attitude change in proportion to the magnitude of the reward for such advocacy.

Turning again to dissonance theory and shifting from its approach to one type of attitude change to its approach toward attitude change *generally,* the author would venture the judgment that dissonance research in this area has been complicated by certain difficult methodological and interpretive issues. Thus, as Chapanis and Chapanis (1964) have noted, it is common to many of these studies that they do not investigate the subject's personal reactions to the dissonance-arousing situation, that the magnitudes of attitude change are often quite small and that often a rather large number of subjects is, for one or another theory-based reason, eliminated from analysis. To this must be added the present demonstration that, in experiments on counterattitudinal advocacy, certain data-biasing processes may be invoked to account for reported findings. Indeed, since dissonance studies on other types of attitude change also place some, but not other, subjects in highly puzzling and unexpected situations it should be recognized that in these studies as well biased contamination may often affect the results obtained. In the light of all these points it would seem desirable to undertake an empirical reexamination of some of the major studies that have been offered as confirming the dissonance analysis of attitude change. In the opinion of the present author the consequence of such reexamination would not be the disconfirmation of the dissonance view of attitude processes but the discovery that its generality is of somewhat smaller scope than its advocates have estimated and that certain kinds of attitude change are better predicted and accounted for by other theories.

8

Counter-Norm Attitudes Induced by Consonant versus Dissonant Conditions of Role-Playing[1]

ALAN C. ELMS AND IRVING L. JANIS

While the Janis and Gilmore experiment was being conducted with Yale undergraduates, a similar study was in progress using volunteers at a small community college in a New Haven suburb. Presumably these students would not be so weary and wary of psychological research as those at Yale, Stanford, or Ohio State. In addition, a single unfamiliar researcher could himself play two rather more sharply differentiated roles before alternate groups of volunteers than would have been possible on his own campus.

Since experimenters' expectations do sometimes unconsciously influence results, the two researchers actually collecting data for these simultaneous experiments (Gilmore and Elms) purposely remained uninformed of each other's progress until the main statistical analyses for both studies were complete. This procedure, rather than later replication of a study whose results are already known, might well be used more extensively in research where experimenter bias is a potential problem.

This selection is reprinted with abridgments from the Journal of Experimental Research in Personality, *1965, 1, 50–60, with permission of Academic Press Inc. and the senior author.*

Incentive theory predicts that the amount of attitude change induced by role-playing will *increase* if a large monetary reward

[1] This experiment was conducted under the auspices of the Yale Studies in Attitude and Communication, which is directed by I. L. Janis and supported by a grant from the Rockefeller Foundation. The authors wish to express their thanks to Dean Robert Evans of Quinnipiac College for his helpful cooperation which enabled us to conduct the experiment with students at that college.

generates positive feelings of satisfaction, but will *decrease* if the same large reward generates negative affects, which tend to interfere with the type of open-minded set needed to be influenced by one's own improvised arguments as they are being scanned during the role-playing performance. Janis and Gilmore point out that an interaction effect might therefore be expected on the basis of incentive theory: *With positive sponsorship, a large monetary reward will have a predominantly positive incentive effect and thus make for an increase in the amount of attitude change; whereas with negative sponsorship, a large reward will tend to induce guilt, suspicion, or other negative affects that would give rise to interfering responses during the role-playing performance and therefore lead to less attitude change.* They point out that their finding that the $1 versus $20 payment had no effect does not necessarily tend to disconfirm this hypothesis because the ambivalent reactions evoked by the overpayment in the high-reward condition could obscure any such interaction effect. Moreover, in the unfavorable condition used in their experiment, the purpose of the role-playing task, despite the commercial motives of the sponsors, might have been regarded as socially accepted, since it involved helping to develop a legitimate advertising campaign. On the basis of these considerations, Janis and Gilmore point out that, in order to test the interaction hypothesis, the effects of a small reward should be compared with the effects of a more *plausible* large reward, and, in addition, a favorable sponsorship condition for the role-playing task should be compared with a more objectionable condition in which a distrusted sponsor asks *S*s to violate important social norms by deceiving their peers (as in the Festinger and Carlsmith experiment) or by helping a despised out-group to spread its propaganda.

With these considerations in mind, we designed the present experiment in a way that would enable us to investigate the same variables as in the Janis and Gilmore experiment, but with a role-playing task that requires *S*s to advocate a counter-norm attitude under conditions that are appropriate for testing the above-stated interaction hypothesis derived from incentive theory. Accordingly, we selected as the unfavorable (high-dissonant) condition, a role-playing situation that was defined as *helping the Soviet Union to prepare for a propaganda campaign to be directed to American students,* in contrast to the more favorable (low-dissonant) condition of *helping the United States govern-ment to prepare for a survey in order to take account of current attitudes among American students*. In both favorable and un-favorable sponsorship conditions, we used a plausible large monetary reward in contrast to a small one and, as in the Janis and Gilmore experiment, we also compared the effects of overt role-playing with a control condition in which the same information was given. In the latter condition, Ss agreed to perform the role-playing task and were paid for it, but the attitude effects were assessed before any overt role-playing took place. Thus, the present experiment involved a three-dimensional factorial design to investigate the amount of attitude change as a function of (1) overt vs. non-overt role-playing; (2) favorable vs. unfavorable sponsorship of the role-playing task; and (3) large vs. small monetary reward for the role-playing performance.

METHOD

The experiment was conducted in a New England Teacher's College with both male and female undergraduates, all of whom volunteered for the experiment following class announcements which promised payment to students who volunteered to par-ticipate in a new research project requiring less than 1 hour of time. The Ss were assigned, according to chance, to one of the eight experimental conditions within the three-dimensional fac-torial design. (The number of cases in each subgroup is shown in Table 1.)

All Ss were given an initial pretreatment questionnaire of ten items which asked them to express their personal attitude toward a new proposal that would involve sending American students to the Soviet Union to take their entire 4 years of college educa-tion in a Soviet university. They were assured that their answers would be kept anonymous.

After the initial questionnaire, all Ss were given the same instructions concerning the role-playing task, which was intro-duced in all conditions by the following standard background information:

Negotiations have been under way for some time between the Soviet Union and our Government, involving a joint program to send qualified U.S. students to study in the Soviet Union for 4 years. These American students would go through a complete 4-year course in a Russian university, where they would study the Soviet system of government and the history of Communism. Our Government is somewhat skeptical about the value of this training and will not agree to the program unless it can be shown that a significant number of eligible U.S. students favor the plan. The Soviet Government wishes to go ahead with the plan for obvious reasons. Although our State Department believes the program might have some serious disadvantages, in addition to any advantages, it is withholding final judgment until an accurate evaluation of student sentiment can be made.

In the *unfavorable sponsorship* condition, Ss were informed by the interviewer (*E*) that he was a representative of a private attitude-research firm which had contracted to carry out this study for the Soviet Embassy (after the firm had checked with the U.S. State Department and obtained permission to do so). The *E* asserted that the Soviet government had hired his firm to collect the materials needed to produce a pamphlet which representatives of the Soviet Union would distribute to all U.S. college campuses, presenting arguments in favor of the proposed program that would be appealing and convincing to American students. The Ss were then instructed to outline the most convincing arguments they could think of to use in the Soviet propaganda pamphlet aimed at students like themselves.

The Ss in the *favorable-sponsorship* condition, after being given exactly the same background information (quoted above), were told that the interviewer's firm had a contract with the U.S. State Department to help find out the attitudes of American students toward the program. The *E* said that his firm was getting ready to conduct a large-scale survey of U.S. students, whose opinions would be assessed after asking them to examine a pamphlet containing arguments on *both sides* of the question, which would make them fully aware of the issues involved. The Ss were then told that *E* had already gathered sufficient arguments *against* the program, and therefore he was now asking a few students to outline some arguments in *favor* of the program, to be inserted in the pamphlet.

Thus, the information presented in the unfavorable and favorable sponsorship conditions was identical, except for assertions about (a) the employer's being the Soviet Union vs. the U.S. State Department, and (b) the purpose of S's role-playing performances being to help the Soviet Union conduct a propaganda campaign vs. helping the U.S. State Department obtain information about the attitudes of American students.

Anonymity was again assured for both conditions and, in order to make the financial reward plausible, all Ss were told: "Please consider the arguments carefully and express them as clearly as possible, since our survey groups are small and the arguments you write down will almost certainly be included in the pamphlet." Within both sponsorship conditions, half the Ss were told that every participant would be paid a large amount of money ($10.00), which our pretesting results indicated would be regarded as a plausible large reward. The other half were offered a small reward ($0.50).

Before beginning the task, all Ss were paid the large or small reward in cash, *in advance*, and signed a receipt at E's request, after which they were assigned on a stratified random basis to the overt role-playing condition or the control condition. Those in the former condition were asked to write down their arguments and, after 2 minutes, E mentioned four general questions to consider, in order to stimulate their thinking about cogent arguments (e.g., "How would this program affect relations between the U.S. and the U.S.S.R., particularly with regard to world peace?"). After Ss had written for 5 minutes more, their outlines were collected and they were given the final (post-treatment) questionnaire. In the control (nonovert role-playing) condition, the same four "stimulating questions" were asked immediately after S agreed to perform the role-playing task. Then, instead of allowing the control S to write down his arguments, he was told that before beginning to think of arguments, there was one other thing to be done—to fill out another brief questionnaire.

The Ss in both the overt and nonovert role-playing conditions were given exactly the same rationale for the post-treatment questionnaire: Whereas the previous questionnaire had dealt with student opinion about study in Russia in general, the second questionnaire was to be used as part of an initial survey of student opinion concerning the specific "students-to-Russia" program, about which they had just been informed. The final questionnaire contained the same questions as the first one, except that the opening item made it clear that the students were to evaluate the new Soviet-sponsored proposal.[2] The other nine questions, which were worded in exactly the same way on both questionnaires, asked each S to indicate his personal desire to participate in the program, his expectations concerning its potentially favorable or unfavorable consequences, his judgments of its importance, and his anticipations of how it would be regarded by most other American students and by his parents.

After completing the final questionnaire, each of the overt role-players was asked to rate the quality of the arguments he had written in his essay. Then, after all the data were collected from each S, E carefully went through a dehoaxing procedure, correcting the misinformation given earlier and explaining that the procedure was part of a psychological study completely unconnected with the Soviet Embassy or the State Department. The Ss who had been given $10.00 returned the money and were paid the same standard amount as the controls ($1.50) for their participation.

Just before being dehoaxed, every S was asked several open-ended questions to find out whether he had accepted the various explanations E had given concerning the experimental procedures. The Ss' answers (as well as their spontaneous comments following the "dehoaxing" information, at the very end of the session) indicated that the information E had presented was generally regarded as genuine and valid. The comments by Ss in the favorable sponsorship condition indicated that they fully accepted E's statement that the study was being done as part of an educational survey for the U.S. State Depart-

---

[2] On the pretreatment questionnaire, the opening item was worded as follows: "Certain educators have proposed a program to send qualified American students to study in Russian Universities for a period of 4 years, beginning as freshmen and continuing through their complete undergraduate training there. If this program were permitted by the U.S. Government, would you favor or oppose the proposal?" On the final questionnaire, the opening item was modified in the following way, so as to provide the appropriate context for the post-treatment questions: "United States and Soviet governmental authorities are negotiating on a program to send qualified American students to Russian universities to study the Soviet system of government and the history of Communism for a period of 4 years. Would you favor or oppose this program?"

ment. Similarly, none of the Ss given the information about the unfavorable sponsorship expressed any disbelief about the alleged fact that the job was being done for the Soviet Union. Some of their answers, in fact, indicated that they perceived the purpose as being even more malignant than E had asserted. One S, for example, said he believed the real purpose was to try to pick up new recruits for the Communist Party and to help the Soviet Union in ways that would be just within the law.

The Ss in the unfavorable sponsorship condition, all of whom eventually complied, showed considerable hesitation, tension, and other manifestations of dissonance or conflict about writing an essay to help the Soviet Embassy conduct a propaganda campaign. Signs of disturbance were noted in their overt behavior at the time the purpose of the study was being described as well as in their written answers to the open-ended questions asked at the end of the session. For example, when we made completely blind ratings of the attitudes expressed in their responses to questions about how they thought their essays would be used, we found that none of the 36 Ss in the unfavorable sponsorship condition expressed any personal approval whatsoever; seven of them took pains to make it clear that they felt strong opposition or resentment, as compared with only one S in the favorable sponsorship condition. Moreover, at the beginning of the session, a number of additional Ss in the unfavorable sponsorship–low-payment group showed open reluctance to participate in the study. Several asked if they should take part even if they did not approve of the program or raised other questions that delayed their decision about whether or not to accept the job.

At the end of the session, when E told the truth about the purpose of the study, three Ss in the unfavorable sponsorship condition who had been paid $10.00 were disinclined to return any of the money, arguing that they had agreed to do the job because of the high pay. No such difficulties were encountered among the Ss who had been given the large payment in the favorable sponsorship condition. Another distinctive reaction, which was observed in most Ss in the unfavorable sponsorship condition, was the marked relief displayed when they were given the dehoaxing information.

Although the behavioral signs and the written answers to the post-treatment questions indicate that the high-dissonance condition succeeded in generating a relatively high degree of disturbance and conflict about engaging in the role-playing task, the amount of dissonance was nevertheless not so great as to interfere with the research by leading to a high incidence of outright refusals to participate in the study. Only one man (in the unfavorable sponsorship–low payment condition) refused to write the essay, and hence the differential loss of Ss was negligible among the various treatments to be considered.[3]

RESULTS AND DISCUSSION

The appropriateness of regarding the role-played position as a counter-norm attitude is indicated by results from the pretreatment questionnaire, which revealed that the Ss generally shared the widespread negative attitude of U.S. citizens toward Soviet institutions. The majority of students expressed strong opposition to the proposed educational policy of having American students receive their entire college education in the Soviet Union and asserted that their peers and their parents would also be opposed. There were no significant differences among any of the subgroups on the pretreatment attitude measures ($p > .20$, two-tailed, for every pair of means).

The attitude changes induced by the various conditions of role-playing were assessed by scoring the changes on each of the ten items in the attitude scale in terms of 0, $+ 1$ or -1, depending on whether the responses remained unchanged or shifted in the direction of favoring or opposing the Soviet-sponsored proposal. A net attitude-change score was computed for each S, and represented the total number of questions on which he changed positively from the "before" to the "after" questionnaire, minus the total number of those on which he changed negatively. (This measure was selected in advance because in our prior research on attitude change we have noted that a total score

[3] Two other Ss who wrote the essay were eliminated from the tabulations of the results because they expressed some vague suspicions that the large (10.00) payment might entail something more than E had asserted. One of the Ss was in the favorable sponsorship condition and the other in the unfavorable sponsorship condition of the overt role-playing treatment.

based on the presence or absence of change on each item generally entails less error variance than a score that summates the *amount* of change shown on every item.) The *mean* net attitude-change score for each condition is shown in Table 1.

It will be noted that the largest amount of attitude change occurred in the *overt* role-playing group that was exposed to the *least* dissonant condition, i.e., favorable sponsorship with large monetary reward. The mean net change of +2.4 shown by this group was found to differ significantly at beyond the 5% confidence level from each of the other groups of overt role-players (when *t* tests were computed in two different ways, one basing the standard error of the mean differences solely on the two distributions being compared and the other using an over-all error estimate obtained from an over-all $2 \times 2 \times 2$ analysis of variance). These findings indicate that overt role-playing is most effective when the inducements for performing the task are consonant with the Ss' personal values. The outcome clearly contradicts the dissonance-theory prediction and supports the incentive-theory prediction.

Further support for the same conclusion was obtained from the over-all analysis of variance of attitude change scores, which showed a significant triple interaction effect ($F = 7.88$, $df = 1/82$, $p < .01$ for favorable vs. unfavorable sponsorship $\times$ low vs. high payment $\times$ overt vs. nonovert role-playing). A separate analysis of variance for the four groups of overt role-players showed a significant main effect for the sponsorship variable ($F = 5.00$, $df = 1/66$, $p < .05$) and a near-significant interaction

TABLE 1

Mean Net Attitude-Change Scores[a]

Sponsorship of role-playing task		Control groups: No overt role-playing			Experimental groups: Overt role-playing		
		Small payment, $0.50	Large payment, $10.00	Total	Small payment, $0.50	Large payment, $10.00	Total
Favorable: U.S. Gov't.	N	5	5	10	18	16	34
	M	+0.2	+0.8	+0.5	+0.9	+2.4	+1.7
Unfavorable: Soviet Union	N	5	5	10	17	19	36
	M	−2.0	+1.6	−0.2	+0.6	−0.1	+0.3

[a] Positive scores indicate change in counter-norm direction.

of the sponsorship variable with the financial reward variable ($F = 3.66$, $df = 1/66$, $p < .07$).

In order to obtain some additional information about the effects of different amounts of monetary payment, we added two more groups of overt role-players to the experiment, one receiving favorable sponsorship ($N = 18$) and the other unfavorable sponsorship ($N = 17$), both of which were paid $1.50 in advance. The mean net attitude-change scores for these two additional groups were approximately zero (-0.1 and $+0.2$, respectively) and differed hardly at all from the near-zero means obtained from the corresponding two groups that had been paid $0.50. The findings indicate that a small reward of either $0.50 or $1.50 had essentially the same effect (and yielded essentially the same differences in attitude-change scores from a large reward of $10.00). This conclusion is supported by the data from a 2×3 analysis of variance for overt role-players, in which one variable was favorable vs. unfavorable sponsorship and the other was the three different amounts of financial reward. The results of this analysis of variance show a near-significant main effect for the sponsorship variable ($F = 2.60$, $df = 1/99$, $p = .11$) and a significant interaction of sponsorship with amount of financial reward ($F = 3.22$, $df = 2/99$, $p < .05$). It will be noted that this outcome is essentially the same as that obtained from the 2×2 analysis of variance (which gave corresponding p values of $<.05$ and $<.07$).

The above findings indicate that when the role-playing performance was carried out under *favorable* sponsorship conditions, the *large* financial reward produced *more* attitude change than the smaller financial rewards; but when the same type of performance was carried out under unfavorable sponsorship conditions, the large reward did not have a facilitating effect. This differential outcome, which is in line with predictions from "incentive" theory, is limited to the overt role-players. The four means for the control Ss who did not engage in role-playing (shown on the left-hand side of Table 1) do not duplicate the pattern found in the four experimental groups of overt role-players (shown on the right-hand side of Table 1). In contrast to the significant second-order difference noted among the overt role-playing groups, the corresponding second-order difference among the control groups is in the opposite direction, but it is nonsignificant ($F = 2.12$, $df = 1/16$, $p > .15$) and is attributable largely to the very low attitude change scores in the group of controls given the most dissonant treatment (unfavorable sponsorship with small reward, which had a mean net change of -2.0).

Interviews conducted at the end of the session indicated that, after having committed themselves, Ss in all four of the control conditions had silently started to think about supporting arguments, in anticipation of having to execute the role-playing task. Hence the controls apparently had engaged in *implicit* role-playing. But the attitude-change data provide no evidence at all that the control condition of nonovert role-playing produced any attitude changes, since none of the four control means in Table 1 differs significantly from zero. This finding cannot be taken at face value, however, because we did not have an additional "uncommitted" control group (given all the relevant background information but without any role-playing instructions at all) to compare with the nonovert role-playing condition. We cannot be sure that the latter condition was totally ineffective because, for example, the background information given about the Soviet-sponsored proposal might have had the effect of shifting attitudes in the negative direction, which would be manifested by a significant change in the negative direction by an "uncommitted" control group; the implicit role-playing that occurred among the Ss in our control groups, therefore, might have prevented them from changing in the anti-Soviet direction, resulting in manifestly zero change. What can be said with certainty, however, is that the nonovert role-playing condition was *relatively ineffective* as compared with overt role-playing carried out under favorable incentive conditions.

The large mean attitude-change score noted in the group of overt role-players given the favorable sponsorship information and the large monetary reward indicates that attitude change can be induced by role-playing even for a counter-norm type of attitude. Quite aside from the implications this finding has for opposing theories of attitude change, it helps to substantiate an empirical generalization inferred from prior role-playing experiments dealing with more innocuous types of opinion changes. The generalization in question is that the technique of improvised role-playing can exert a powerful influence to modify existing attitudes, including those anchored in social norms, which ordinarily are highly resistant to the usual forms of persuasive pressures.

Our finding that the greatest gain in attitude change was produced by overt role-playing under conditions of favorable sponsorship and large reward is similar to the outcome of the earlier experiment by Janis and Gilmore. In that experiment, too, the greatest amount of attitude change occurred in the group of overt role-players given favorable (public welfare) sponsorship and a large ($20) reward. The analysis of variance, however, showed that the only significant interaction effect arose from the sponsorship and the overt vs. nonovert role-playing variables, indicating that more attitude change occurred when overt role-playing was carried out under favorable sponsorship than under unfavorable conditions; the amount of attitude change was not significantly affected by the amount of financial reward. The incentive theory analysis was further borne out by the finding that, in the favorable sponsorship condition, the overt role-players improvised arguments of better quality than in the unfavorable sponsorship condition, as judged by two psychologists who made blind, independent ratings of all statements in the written essays.

The attitude change results of the present experiment are similar in that we again find that positive incentive conditions make for more attitude change. The sponsorship variable alone was found to have a positive effect on the amount of attitude change among the overt role-playing groups, but this effect was subordinate to the interaction of favorable sponsorship with the large monetary reward. This outcome, although somewhat different from that of the earlier experiment, bears out the prediction made by Janis and Gilmore for counter-norm role-playing, i.e., that a large monetary reward will have a positive effect on attitude change only when the role-playing task is sponsored by an acceptable group and is oriented toward a goal perceived by S as being consonant with his own; but the same large reward will tend to create suspicion, guilt, and other interfering responses that make for less attitude change when the role-playing task is sponsored by a distrusted sponsor and is perceived as having a purpose antithetical to one's own values. Thus, the findings from both experiments contradict the predictions from dissonance theory and support predictions from incentive theory concerning the conditions under which role-playing will be more effective in modifying attitudes.

There is one respect, however, in which the present experiment fails to parallel the earlier experiment: judgments of the quality of the essays written by the overt role-players did not yield the expected significant differences. Blind ratings of the essays by two independent judges revealed that every one of the overt role-players conformed with the demands of the task to write out arguments that were strongly in favor of the alleged proposal by the Soviet Union. Under favorable sponsorship conditions, the average number of "good quality" arguments was 4.2 in the group paid $10.00 as against 3.2 in the group paid $0.50; under unfavorable sponsorship conditions, the corresponding difference was approximately zero, both groups showing an average of about 3.9 "good quality" arguments. Although this second-order difference is in the expected direction and roughly parallels the attitude-change findings, an analysis of variance indicated that the interaction effect was not strong enough to be statistically significant at the 10% confidence level. The self-ratings of the arguments by the four groups of overt role-players showed uniformly high scores in all four groups, with no significant increases attributable to the variations in incentive conditions. The only significant difference found in the essays written by the four experimental groups is in the mean total number of words produced. On this variable, a significant main effect was found for the financial reward variable ($p < .01$), indicating that in both sponsorship conditions the large financial reward elicited more verbose essays than the small reward.

According to "incentive theory," the attitude changes produced by role-playing are mediated by intensive "biased scanning" of positive incentives, which involves two types of verbal responses: (1) fulfilling the demands of the role-playing task by recalling and inventing arguments that are capable of functioning as positive incentives for accepting a new attitude position, and (2) appraising the recalled and improvised arguments with a psychological set that fosters *open-minded cognitive exploration of their potential incentive value,* rather than a negativistic set of the type engendered by the arousal of feelings of hostility, resentment, or suspicion. Thus, for example, it would be expected that many intelligent American soldiers who were captured by the

Chinese Communists during the Korean War could comply with the role-playing demands of their despised "brain-washing" captors and nevertheless remain uninfluenced: While verbalizing "good" pro-Communist arguments, the prisoners could privately label all the improvised arguments with negative epithets or could think about counterarguments that would refute the statements they were overtly verbalizing (see Lifton, 1961; Schein, 1956).

In experimental research on role-playing effects, the first of the two types of response essential for effective biased scanning can be readily assessed by examining the manifest content of the role-playing performance to see if plausible-sounding arguments were improvised, but the second type is difficult to assess because it involves private verbalizations that occur silently, along with the overt statements that are being made. Judgments of the quality of written essays, as in the present experiment, are at best an indirect measure of the second type of response, based on the assumption that a hostile or closed-minded role-player will tend to be more perfunctory in his role-playing performance and hence produce arguments of poorer quality. On this indirect measure, our ratings of the essays fail to show that the incentive variables had a significant effect on the quality of the role-playing performance. But it is quite possible, of course, that this indirect measure is too crude to detect differences in psychological sets, and that research on this problem requires much more subtle measures, such as those provided by a content analysis of detailed interviews in which each S is asked to report on his covert subjective thoughts during the role-playing performance itself.

In summary, the predictions from "incentive" theory are borne out by the main results from this experiment, which show that a gain in attitude change was produced by overt role-playing under favorable inducement conditions. Our supplementary data on the quality of the essays, however, do not provide evidence that the gain was mediated by a corresponding increase in biased scanning while Ss were improvising arguments in favor of the assigned position. Obviously, the question of how the positive inducements lead to increased attitude change remains an open question to be settled by subsequent research.

9

Comment on "Counter-Norm Attitudes Induced by Consonant versus Dissonant Conditions of Role-Playing"

JACK W. BREHM

The initial response of dissonance theorists to the three pre-ceding studies was prompt and, naturally, critical.

This selection is reprinted from the Journal of Experimental Research in Personality, *1965, 1, 61–64, with permission of Academic Press Inc. and the author.*

The two apparent conclusions of Elms and Janis are (1) to accept incentive theory as an explanation of at least the major effects of role-playing on attitudes, and (2) to reject dissonance theory as an explanation of *any* of the effects of role-playing on attitudes. It may therefore be useful to remind the reader that dissonance theory takes a relatively limited position; under certain cond.tions, positive incentives reduce dissonance and the consequent pressure to change an attitude. The theory does *not* say that positive incentives have no other effects, and therefore incentive theory could be "true" at the same time that dissonance theory is "true." Leventhal (1964), for example, has proposed that incentives which have a value appropriate to an instrumental task result in no change in attitude toward the task, while those that are inappropriately low result in dissonance and positive attitude change, and those that are inappropriately high result in direct positive attitude change (following Peak, 1955).

In their discussion of previous relevant research, Elms and Janis dismiss an experiment by Cohen (Brehm and Cohen, 1962, pp. 73–78) on the basis of a report by Rosenberg which is in press. However, an ONR Technical Report with the same title and presumably reporting the same study provides less than convincing evidence that Cohen's study is weak in the ways specified. What primarily is missing is the establishment by Rosenberg that his experimental conditions would in fact produce the effects obtained by Cohen. For example, Rosenberg reports Ss in all his conditions indicated they were relatively free to refuse to write the discrepant essay. On the other hand, Cohen reports (Brehm and Cohen, 1962, p. 204) a fairly strong inverse relationship between amount of incentive and reported freedom to choose. Since Brehm and Cohen have taken the position that perceived choice may be a necessary condition for the arousal of dissonance, and that the magnitude of dissonance is therefore a function of the magnitude of perceived choice, it may not be so strange that Rosenberg failed to obtain attitudinal effects similar to those of Cohen. While Rosenberg's paper does point out a possible alternative interpretation of Cohen's experiment, it fails to provide convincing evidence that the alternative is the best explanation. The experiment by Cohen should not be so easily dismissed; it provides support for the assertion that dissonance and consequent attitude change are inversely proportional to the incentive used to obtain role-playing compliance.

A similar point can be made in regard to the criticism Elms and Janis make of the experiment by Festinger and Carlsmith (1959). After suggesting that $20 may have created suspicion, they cite as evidence a study by Janis and Gilmore (1965). In that study, Ss who were offered $20 "expressed a great deal of puzzlement. . . ." There is no doubt that Ss can be offered $20 in such a way as to be puzzling, but neither is there doubt that the same reward can be made to seem reasonable. An incentive which arouses suspicion entails processes other than consonant cognition, and would provide a poor way to contrive a "low dissonance" condition. Since Festinger and Carlsmith were trying to establish a low dissonance condition by offering $20, we may assume that they tried to make the amount seem reasonable. Specifically, they informed all experimental Ss that the money was not only for performing the immediate task but also to be on call in case their services should be needed again. The effect of "being on call" would be to make the $20 seem relatively reasonable and the $1 rather little. Personal communications from both Festinger and Carlsmith have indicated that there was little or no suspiciousness on the part of Ss about the

$20. While the possibility that suspicion was aroused cannot be completely ruled out, there is good reason to believe that this factor does not account for the results.

Disproving a dissonance hypothesis should be no more difficult, nor easy, than disproving other reasonable hypotheses about the same class of events. In the case of "forced compliance" one must be able to show that there are cognitions which lead the person not to comply, that there are cognitions which lead the person to comply, and (to insure relatively high dissonance) that the weighted cognitions leading to compliance are barely sufficient to obtain it. Furthermore, research (Brehm and Cohen, 1962; Festinger, 1964) has shown that dissonance effects may be clear only when the individual is committed to an alternative, an outcome, etc., so the disproof of dissonance must also rest upon a clear demonstration of commitment. If it can be shown that dissonance effects do not occur under these stipulated conditions, and if confounding effects can be ruled out, then the dissonance hypothesis tested would certainly tend to be disconfirmed.

What truth is there, then, in the assertion by Elms and Janis that "The outcome clearly contradicts the dissonance-theory prediction . . . ?" Aside from the possibility that the assertion is true, three answers might be given: (1) dissonance was not aroused by the experimental conditions; (2) dissonance was aroused but did not affect the attitude measured; and (3) dissonance was aroused and did in fact affect the attitude in a way consistent with the theory.

It is likely that dissonance was aroused, as Elms and Janis endeavored to show, because it seems that Ss in the unfavorable sponsorship condition were resistant to writing the essay and were quite uncomfortable about doing so. But a question may certainly be raised whether or not the aroused dissonance could be expected to result in positive change of the attitude measured. It will be recalled that the way in which dissonance is reduced is through change (or addition) of relevant cognitions, and those cognitions which are least resistant to change would be those most likely to exhibit change. Elms and Janis take pains to point out that the position of the essay is quite distasteful to the Ss and is clearly at variance with the popular position on the issue. Furthermore, the unfavorable sponsorship manipulation makes it even more difficult for Ss to favor the position of the essay since it highlights the negative aspects of the sponsor, e.g., propagandizing, dishonesty, ulterior motives, etc. Under these conditions, then, S's attitude would be highly resistant to change toward the position of the essay. Hence, if he did experience dissonance from agreeing to write the discrepant essay, he would have difficulty reducing the dissonance by becoming more favorable toward the discrepant stand. He would then be expected to attempt dissonance reduction in other ways.

Several ways of reducing dissonance can be distinguished in a relatively complex situation such as that used by Elms and Janis, and it is plausible that Ss used one or more of them. For example, a person might have subjectively magnified the pressure from E to comply, or, the approval of the project by our own government, or the belief that other students would not be taken in by one's own arguments. Similarly, an S might simply have admitted that he was wrong to write the essay, or he also might have attempted to belittle the importance of his role in the study, or the likely success of the study. The anecdotal evidence cited by Elms and Janis indicates not only tension but also attempts at dissociation and avoidance of responsibility for the decision; such attempts, if successful, would help to reduce dissonance. It is also interesting to note that Ss showed "marked relief" when they were "dehoaxed." This indicates not only that they experienced dissonance, but also that they had failed to reduce their dissonance successfully. In summary, the second answer concerning the truth of the Elms and Janis assertion that the data contradict the dissonance theory prediction seems at least partly true: since Ss found it difficult to become more positive toward the position of the essay, they attempted to reduce dissonance in other ways and were not altogether successful in their attempts at dissonance reduction.

When a person holds two cognitions or sets of cognitions which are dissonant with each other, and when each set is highly resistant to change, then dissonance can be reduced by adding cognitions consonant with one of the two sets (see Brehm and Cohen, 1962, pp. 55–59). In effect, this means that in the forced verbal compliance setting the individual bolsters his original position, or else he bolsters the act of writing the discrepant essay (or making a discrepant speech). As we have seen, the procedure in the Elms and Janis experiment made it difficult for Ss in the unfavorable sponsorship condition to change positively toward the position of the essay even though they experienced dissonance upon agreeing to write the essay. Thus, it would not be surprising to find these Ss attempting to bolster their original position, that is, changing negatively rather than positively in respect to the position of the essay. This effect would, of course, be greater where commitment to writing the essay was relatively low (control condition), and it would be greater in a high dissonance (low payment) than in a low dissonance (high payment) condition. In Table 1 of the Elms and Janis article there is a negative change in the appropriate condition: unfavorable sponsorship, low payment, no overt role-playing. Although, as Elms and Janis noted, one cannot be sure that this is true negative change, it is nevertheless clear that the low payment condition change (-2.0) is reliably different from the corresponding high payment change $(+1.6)$ with $p = .05$, an effect which Elms and Janis were unable to account for.

The effect of actually writing the essay is, of course, to increase commitment toward the position of the essay and thereby to make it more likely that an S would attempt to reduce dissonance by changing his attitude positively rather than negatively. The same Table 1 reveals the expected effect. For Ss who wrote the essay in the unfavorable sponsorship condition, there was a tendency for those who received low payment to change more positively than those who received high payment. While this tendency was not reliable in itself, it appears reliably different from the corresponding difference in the condition where Ss did not write the essay—again, an effect for which Elms and Janis give no explanation. In summary, the data in the unfavorable sponsorship condition are consistent with the view that writing a discrepant essay is dissonance-arousing, and the tendency to reduce dissonance by changing one's attitude negatively rather than positively (toward the essay position) is an inverse function of the strength of one's commitment to the essay position. It is reasonable to say, then, that Elms and Janis were incorrect in asserting that the outcome clearly contradicts the dissonance theory prediction. It seems more likely that dissonance was aroused and did in fact affect attitudes in a way consistent with the theory.

The problem here is not so much in how one reads the data,

because the present analysis is post hoc and is admittedly in defense of dissonance theory; rather, the primary problem is in providing an adequate test of the dissonance hypothesis of central interest. In attempting to obtain positive evidence for a hypothesis, an investigator must immerse himself in the relevant theory and must be sure that the methods provide an adequate test. But to *disprove* a hypothesis is even more demanding of an investigator in terms of familiarity with the theory and providing adequate methods. He must be able to make a case, quite independently of the expected outcome of "no effect," that his use of the theory is accurate, his manipulation effective, his measures sensitive, and confounding factors are absent. In the experiment under discussion, the dissonance manipulation of unfavorable sponsorship also made the dependent attitude relatively resistant to positive change. Thus, the conditions for an adequate test of the dissonance hypothesis were not provided. The fact that dissonance effects apparently did occur is then due more to accident than to the experiment's having provided a good test.

Perhaps in practice the person best equipped to disprove a dissonance hypothesis is one who has been successful in supporting it. When such a person designs a test, he is more likely to do so in a sensitive and adequate way and is thus in a position to produce and to recognize disconfirming evidence when it appears. An example is Walster's experiment (in Festinger, 1964, pp. 112–127) in which she found that post-decisional re-evaluation of choice alternatives disappeared rather soon after the choice.

The application of dissonance theory to role-playing must take into account not only the decision to play the counter-norm role but also the effect of inventing, and perhaps publicly stating, the arguments themselves. If the decision to comply arouses relatively low dissonance because the force to comply is great, the behavior of inventing or stating arguments, or both, may in itself arouse further and significant amounts of dissonance and consequent attitude change. However, where a considerable amount of dissonance is aroused by the decision to comply, the invention or statement of arguments could on the one hand contribute to the dissonance, but may, on the other, simply help to reduce dissonance by facilitating attitude change. The relevant data are ambiguous (Brehm and Cohen, 1962, pp. 248–258).

This attempt by Elms and Janis to disprove a dissonance hypothesis, though inadequate in itself, still serves to point up the methodological problems which must be solved if this type of disproof is to be produced. More valuable, however, is their test of the application of incentive theory. For it is apparent that the relatively obvious implications of dissonance theory for the understanding of role-playing effects on attitudes have been tested and supported, and if there is to be a confrontation of dissonance and incentive theories, incentive theory must be made more explicit and tenable through this type of empirical demonstration.

10

Studies in Forced Compliance: I. The Effect of Pressure for Compliance on Attitude Change Produced by Face-to-Face Role Playing and Anonymous Essay Writing

J. Merrill Carlsmith, Barry E. Collins, and Robert L. Helmreich

An experiment is best criticized with another experiment. Previous studies indicated that in at least some circumstances, higher rewards for role playing failed to produce the lower opinion change predicted by dissonance theory. But did these results really invalidate the usefulness of dissonance theory in accounting for role-play effects, or did they point to complications unanticipated by any *researchers? The authors of this paper favored the latter view. As Barry Collins later said, "It was our notion that there were some circumstances where dissonance theory was correct and other circumstances where it was irrelevant" (Collins, 1967). They set out to find which situations were which, experimentally.*

This selection is reprinted with abridgments from the Journal of Personality and Social Psychology, *1966, 4, 1–13, with permission of the senior author and the American Psychological Association.*

Since most of the criticisms which are applied to one individual study do not apply to the others, the meaning of all studies, in concert, is not clear. At the very least, these data suggest that the original formulation of the attitude-change process by Festinger and Carlsmith was incomplete. At the most, they suggest that the dissonance results were due to trivial artifacts. Because of the many differences in procedure among these various studies, it would be worthwhile to study differences in procedure which might have produced different results.

There are, of course, many differences, but let us turn our attention to just one. Contrast the Festinger and Carlsmith experiment with, say, that of Elms and Janis. In the study by Festinger and Carlsmith, the subject is asked to make a public statement (at least in front of one other person) which conflicts with his private belief. Furthermore, the person to whom he is making this statement is *unaware* that this is in fact in conflict with the private belief. Such a situation is certainly one in which dissonance would be aroused.

Consider on the other hand the position of the subject in the Elms and Janis experiment. He is being asked to write an essay in favor of a position which he does not agree with. He is assured that his essay will be kept anonymous—no one will ever know that he wrote it except the experimenter. And the experimenter —the only person to read the essay—knows full well that the essay does *not* express the subject's private opinion. The experimenter, in essence, is asking him whether he has the intellectual ability to see some arguments on the opposite side of the issue from that which he holds. It can be argued that writing such an essay will create no dissonance. Stated in an extreme form, the question is whether the cognition "I am, for good *reasons,* listing some arguments in favor of the position 'not-X' " is dissonant with the cognition "I believe 'X.' " It is plausible that, especially among college students, the cognition that one is listing such arguments is not at all dissonant with the cognition that one believes the opposite. Rather, the ability intellectually to adopt such a position is the hallmark of the open-minded and intellectual.

The argument in the paragraph above is not altogether different from the emphasis which Brehm and Cohen (1962) have placed on the role of commitment in the arousal of dissonance. A person who is merely writing arguments in favor of a position, but who has not committed himself to that position, would not experience dissonance *about the fact that he was writing arguments.* This is not to say that there may not be dissonance of some other kind, or that there may not be other nondissonance processes operating to produce attitude change as a result of writing these arguments. For example, insofar as the arguments he produces are good ones, there is dissonance aroused between the cognition—"This good argument in favor of not X exists" and the cognition "I believe X." This dissonance-theory process sounds quite similar to the incentive-theory process which Janis and Gilmore posit to explain attitude change produced by role playing. The point to be made here is that writing an anonymous essay may not produce dissonance *of the particular kind* studied by Festinger and Carlsmith, and that the predictions from dissonance theory about incentive effects may not be relevant in such situations.

In order to test this post hoc explanation, we attempted to design an experiment which would demonstrate that the results reported by Festinger and Carlsmith could be repeated under appropriate conditions, whereas the opposite kind of results might be expected under different conditions.

One further difference between experiments which have obtained results consistent with the dissonance-theory predictions and those experiments which have not has been the theoretical predilection of the experimenters. With the exception of the work of Nuttin, the results in line with dissonance-theory predictions have been obtained by experimenters who were to some extent identified with dissonance theory and who might be expected to "hope for" results consistent with dissonance theory. The converse has been true of experimenters who have obtained results inconsistent with dissonance theory. In light of the increasing interest in subtle effects of so-called "experimenter bias" (Rosenthal, 1963) we carried out the present experiment using two experimenters of different theoretical backgrounds. One of the experimenters (JMC) was presumably identified with a dissonance-theory approach; the other (BEC) was somewhat identified with a more behavioristic or reinforcement theory approach.

The basic design of the experiment to be reported here is a $2 \times 2 \times 4$ factorial. Subjects were asked to adopt a counterattitudinal position in two very different ways. Half of the subjects were asked to lie to a confederate in a face-to-face confrontation. They were asked to tell a confederate that a decidedly dull task was, in fact, interesting—a manipulation essentially identical to that of Festinger and Carlsmith. The other half of the subjects were asked to write an anonymous essay in favor of the same position—an essay which would ostensibly be used to help the experimenter prepare another description which would then be presented to future subjects. Half of the subjects were run by each experimenter. Finally, experimental subjects were paid one of three different amounts of money for performing the task, while a control group was paid no additional money and performed no counterattitudinal responses.

METHOD

Subjects

An advertisement was placed in the local paper offering to pay high school age students (14–18) $2.50 for 2 hours of participation in a psychological experiment. When males called the listed number, they were given appointments for the experiment. Females were put on a "waiting list."

Two hundred and two male subjects participated in the experiment. A total of 11 subjects were eliminated from the reported results. Four subjects (2 pairs of brothers) were discarded because, in the judgment of the experimenter administering the posttest, they did not comprehend the meaning of the 11-point rating scale. Typically they expressed strong approval or disapproval and then chose a number on the opposite end of the scale. The posttester did not know which condition the subject was in, and, therefore, could not bias the results by selective elimination. Four more subjects (2 $.50 role play, 1 $1.50 role play, and 1 $.50 essay) were discarded because they did not follow through on the assigned role play or essay. Typically they admitted the task was dull and stated that they had been asked to say it was interesting. Only 1 subject showed any detectable sign of suspicion, and he was eliminated before he took the posttest. One subject accidentally saw the confederate in conversation with one of the experimenters. Finally, 1 subject, when he heard from the confederate that her friend "told her it was kind of dull," called in the experimenter and suggested that the accomplice be assigned to a control group since she knew the task was dull.

The subjects were extremely heterogeneous. They ranged from those who could barely master the complexities of an 11-point scale or could produce only 20 or 25 words of essay in 10 minutes to numerous prep-school students and children from professional families. The sample included a substantial number of Negroes.

Setting and Personnel

The study was conducted in six rooms of the Yale Psycho-Educational Clinic over a 3-week period. The five personnel conducting the experiment were the two principal investigators (BEC and JMC, who alternated as "project director" and "posttester"), a graduate assistant who served as experimenter (RLH), a receptionist, and a female high school age accomplice.

Overview of Design

The basic procedure was similar to that used by Festinger and Carlsmith (1959). Experimental subjects were asked either to write an essay or to tell a second, presumably naïve, subject that the experimental task was fun, interesting, exciting, and enjoyable. The subjects knew from their own experience with the task that it was dull and uninteresting. Subjects were paid an *additional* $5, $1.50, or $.50 to role play or write the essay. Control subjects were paid no additional money and were not asked to role play or write an essay. One-half of the subjects were run with BEC as project director and JMC as posttester, and the other half were run with the roles reversed. Attitudes toward the experimental task were then measured in a posttest-only design. The accomplice rated the several dimensions of the role-play performance, and the transcripts of the role plays and the essays were rated on a number of variables by three judges.

Procedure

All subjects. On arriving at the building, each subject was greeted by the receptionist who verified his age and high school status and conducted him to an experimental room furnished with desk, chairs, and writing materials. After the subject had waited alone for several minutes, the experimenter entered the room, introduced himself as Mr. Helmreich, and announced that he was ready to start the experiment. The experimenter then explained that the experiment itself would only take a little over an hour and that since subjects were being paid for 2 hours' participation, arrangements had been made for every subject to take part in a record survey being conducted in the building by a "man from some consumer research outfit in New York." At this point, the subject was presented with the experimental task—20 5-page booklets of random numbers. Each booklet had a cover sheet which instructed the subject to strike out each occurrence of two of the digits (e.g., 2s and 6s) contained in the booklet. The subject was told that he should work at a comfortable rate, correct mistakes, and continue working until stopped by the experimenter. The experimenter then explained that he would describe the purpose of the study when he stopped the subject on completion of the task. The subject was then left alone to work for an hour. The supply of booklets left with the subject was many times the number which could be completed in an hour. The task itself was designed to be so dull and repetitious that the subject would leave with a generally negative feeling.

At the end of an hour, the experimenter reentered the room and told the subject that he could stop as the experiment was completed. The experimenter then seated himself next to the subject and said he would explain the purpose of the study. The experimenter described the project as a large-scale study designed to investigate how a person's prior expectation of the nature of a task might affect the amount and accuracy of work performed. The subject was told that the project was investigating the best ways to describe routine tasks so that people would be motivated to work hard and accurately. Each subject was told that he was in a control condition and, therefore, had been given no expectation about how pleasant the task would be. He was told that his group would serve as the standard comparison for other groups which were given positive expectations.

At this point the explanations began to differ according to the experimental condition to which the subject was assigned. Four different procedures were used: role-play control, role-play experimental, essay control, and essay experimental.

Role-play control subjects. Subjects in this condition were told that subjects in the other condition were introduced by the experimenter to a high school boy named Anderson who, presumably, had just finished the experimental task. In fact, continued the experimenter, the boy was paid by the experimenter to say the task was fun, interesting, exciting, and enjoyable. The experimenter remarked that after the paid assistant had been with a subject in the other condition 2 minutes, telling the subject how the experiment was fun, interesting, etc., the experimenter would return to the room, excuse the assistant, and start the subject on the same random-number task. The experimenter pointed out that a high school age assistant was necessary in order to make the description of the task plausible.

At this point, the experimenter asked if the subject had any questions concerning the purpose of the study. After dealing with any questions, the experimenter stated that the project director (BEC or JMC) would like to thank him. The experimenter then left the room and returned with the project director, who then gave the termination speech.

Role-play experimental subjects. In this condition, as the experimenter was finishing the same description given to role-play control subjects and asking for questions, the project director knocked on the door, entered the room, excused himself, and asked the experimenter if he knew where Anderson was. After the experimenter replied that he had not seen him, the director remarked that a subject was waiting in a condition where he was supposed to be told that the task was fun and interesting. He then asked the experimenter if he knew how to get in touch with Anderson and received a negative reply. After a pause, the director asked the experimenter if the subject with him was finished. The experimenter replied that the subject had completed the task and that he was explaining the purpose of the study. The director then remarked that perhaps the subject could help them; that, as the experimenter had no doubt explained, Anderson had been hired to tell some of the waiting subjects that the task was fun, interesting, exciting, and enjoyable. The subject was told that he could help the director out of a jam by describing the task in those terms to a girl who was waiting to start the experiment. The director said that since he was in a bind, he could pay $.50 ($1.50, $5) for doing this job. After the subject agreed (every subject agreed to undertake the task), the experimenter was sent to obtain the proper amount of money and a receipt form. While the experimenter was gone, the director rehearsed the points (fun, interesting, exciting, enjoyable) that the subject was to make to the waiting confederate. After the experimenter returned, the subject took his money, signed a receipt, and was conducted by the director to another room where the female confederate was waiting, ostensibly to start the experiment.

The director told the confederate that the subject had just finished the experiment and that he would tell her something about it. He then left, saying he would be back in a couple of minutes. The girl said little until the subject made some positive remarks about the task, then remarked that a friend of hers had taken the test and had not said much about it except that it was rather dull. Most subjects attempted to counter this evaluation, and the accomplice listened quietly accepting everything the subject said about the task. The interaction between the subject and the accomplice was recorded on a concealed tape recorder.

After 2 minutes, the director returned to the room, told the accomplice that the experimenter would be in to get her started on the experiment, and led the subject from the room. The director then gave the termination speech common to all subjects.

Essay control subjects. Procedures in this condition were the same as in the role-play control condition except that subjects were told that subjects in the other condition read a short essay describing the task positively. The experimenter stated that after reading the essay, subjects in this other group were given the same random-number task. After answering any questions concerning the purpose of the study, the experimenter brought in and introduced the project director who gave the termination speech.

Essay experimental subjects. In this condition, subjects were treated in the same manner as essay controls until the project director was introduced. At this point the director seated himself beside the subject, stated that he had a problem and that the subject might be able to help. He remarked that, as the experimenter described, some subjects in other conditions read an essay describing the task as fun, interesting, exciting, and enjoyable. But he further commented that the experimenters were unhappy with this essay. The director felt that the essays were unsatisfactory because they did not sound like they had been written by high school students and that they did not have the perspective of someone who had taken the experiment. The experimenters had decided to write a new description of the task and felt that the best way to proceed would be to ask a few of the subjects to write positive descriptions of the task. He emphasized that no other subjects would read these essays because he would merely use them as sources of phrases and ideas for an essay which he, the director, would write. He then added that since they were "in a bind" he could pay the subject $.50 ($1.50, $5) to write a 5- or 10-minute description of the task. After the subject agreed to do so (all subjects agreed to write the essay), the experimenter was sent to obtain the proper amount of money and a receipt form. While the experimenter was gone, the director rehearsed with the subject the points that he should make in the essay— that the task was fun, interesting, exciting, and enjoyable. After the experimenter returned, the subject took his money, signed a receipt, and followed the director to another office where he was given paper and pen and told to write for 5 or 10 minutes. He was to press a buzzer which would notify the director when he was finished. The subject was then left alone, and an electric timer was started in the adjoining office. The subject stopped the timer when he pressed the buzzer to signify that he had finished the essay. If the subject had not completed the essay by the end of 15 minutes, the director appeared in the room and told him that he had been working about 15 minutes and should finish up in the next couple of minutes. If still working, subjects were told to stop at the end of 17 minutes (1,000 seconds). After collecting the essay, the director gave the termination speech.

Termination speech. (Identical for all subjects.) While walking away from the experimental room, the director remarked that, as the experimenter had mentioned, a man from Consumer Research Associates had asked if he could have the subjects rate some records since the experiment did not last the full 2 hours. He stated that he did not know much about what the survey was about, but he would show the subjects where to go. As in the Festinger and Carlsmith (1959) study, the experimenter then stated, "I certainly hope you enjoyed the experiment. Most of our subjects tell us they did." He then directed the subject to the posttest room, thanked him, and made a strong request for secrecy about the experiment. It was clear to the subject that the experiment was over at this point.

Posttest. The subject then arrived at a comfortably appointed office labeled Consumer Research Associates on the door. As the subject entered the office, he was greeted by the posttester (BEC or JMC) who introduced himself as Ted Johnson of Consumer Research Associates. Johnson then ushered the subject into the office and seated him before a desk. Next to the desk was a portable record player equipped with stereo earphones. The desk itself was littered with papers bearing Consumer Research Associates' letterhead and titled "Teen Age Market Survey—Connecticut." Johnson introduced the posttest by saying that his company was interested in the type of music teen-agers listened to and the types of music they liked for specific activities. He added that this was important because teen-agers bought 68% of the records sold in this country.

The subject was then asked to listen to a "practice" record for 30 seconds. Johnson then asked the subject to rate the practice record on several questions. He explained the use of an 11-point scale running from −5 to +5 using a graphic illustration of the scale. The subject rated the record as to how much he liked it generally, how much he would like to listen to it on a date, how much he would like to dance to it, and how much he would like to study by it—each rating on the 11-point scale. After the practice record, Johnson announced that they were ready to start the survey. As he started to hand the earphones to the subject he stated:

Oh. There is one thing I forgot. As you might imagine, the kind of mood you are in and the kind of experiences you have just had might influence the ratings you give in a situation like this. [The preceding spoken slowly to give the subject opportunity to agree.] If you had a splitting headache, you would not like much of anything we played through those earphones. [Subjects usually laughed— the volume was moderately high.] So I do want to ask you a question or two about that sort of thing. I don't know much about what they are doing up there, but would you say the test they had you working on was sort of pleasant or unpleasant? [slight pause] As a matter of fact, why don't we put it in terms of the same scale we used for the records? A minus 5 would be very unpleasant and a plus 5 would be very pleasant.

Since the subject had already used the rating scale for the practice record, the other five questions were covered quickly, and the subject immediately began to listen to the first "survey record." The word "test" was used in each question to make sure that the subjects were reacting to the experimental task only, and not the total experiment.

The six questions asked in the posttest were:

1. How pleasant did you find the test?
2. Was it an interesting test?
3. Did you learn anything from the test?
4. Would you recommend the test to a friend?
5. Would you describe the test as fun?
6. What is your general overall mood at the present time?

In each case a $+5$ represented a highly positive reaction and a -5 a strongly negative reaction. All subjects seemed convinced about the genuineness of the posttest; several hesitated to discuss the test because the project director had cautioned them to secrecy.

RESULTS

There are 15 subjects in each of the four control groups, and 11 subjects in all but one of the 12 experimental groups. There are only 10 subjects in the $.50, BEC, essay cell. The results can be discussed in three broad categories: the six questions in the posttest, measures evaluating the quality of the role-play performance and of the essays, and experimenter effects.

Posttest Variables

The mean response for each of the six questions in the posttest is shown in Table 1. Consider first the questions dealing with words the subject actually used while role playing or essay writing —"How interesting would you say the test was?" and "How much fun would you say the test was?" Table 1 shows that both essay and role-play control subjects found that the test, or random-number task, was uninteresting ($M = -1.2$) and not much fun ($M = -1.4$).

Our major hypotheses concerned the differential effects of pressure for compliance in the role-playing and essay-writing situations. Specifically, it was anticipated that subjects who en-

TABLE 1

Means for Posttest Variables Collapsed over Experimenters

	Control	$.50	$1.50	$5
Interesting				
RP	−1.43	1.23	−0.86	−1.18
E	−1.00	−0.86	1.32	2.41
Fun				
RP	−1.43	0.76	−0.81	−1.10
E	−1.28	−0.80	1.62	1.55
Fun plus interesting				
RP	−2.71	1.81	−1.62	−2.19
E	−2.14	−1.80	3.24	3.95
Pleasant				
RP	0.77	1.18	0.82	1.55
E	0.93	0.86	2.14	2.55
Learn anything				
RP	−0.37	−0.50	−2.00	−0.32
E	−2.27	−0.10	−0.41	−0.64
Recommend				
RP	2.53	2.50	1.59	2.27
E	2.33	2.38	2.50	3.56
Mood				
RP	1.83	2.18	2.27	3.41
E	2.83	2.19	3.32	3.36

Note.—Scores from single questions range from −5 (extremely negative toward the task) to +5 (extremely positive). Fun plus interesting can range from −10 to +10. RP = role play; E = essay.

gaged in a face-to-face confrontation (role play) would show a *negative* relationship between money offered for the role playing and attitude change. Thus subjects offered $.50 to role play should show maximal change, followed by subjects offered $1.50, and then those offered $5; the control subjects should, of course, be lowest.

Subjects who had written counterattitudinal essays, on the other hand, should show exactly the opposite trend. In this case, those subjects paid $5 should be most positive toward the task, followed in order by subjects paid $1.50, subjects paid $.50, and control subjects. In order words, the hypothesis anticipates a

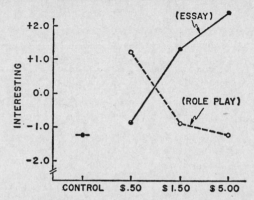

Fig. 1. Responses to posttest question on interesting. (The value drawn for the control group represents the average on all control groups.)

positive relationship between attitude change and money for subjects who wrote essays.

Figures 1 and 2 reveal two facts. First, it can be seen that subjects who adopted a counterattitudinal position, whether this was done by publicly announcing the position or by privately writing an essay adopting the position, changed their attitudes to bring them into line with the counterattitudinal position. That is, they felt that the experiment had been relatively more fun and interesting than did control subjects.

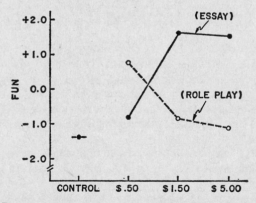

Fig. 2. Responses to posttest question on fun. (The value drawn for the control group represents the average of all control groups.)

Moreover, both hypotheses are strongly confirmed. The amount of money offered to adopt this counterattitudinal position had sharply different effects for role players and essay writers. When a subject is asked to publicly adopt a position which he does not privately believe in a face-to-face confrontation, he changes his attitude less if he is paid large amounts of money to adopt this position. Thus subjects paid $5 thought that the experiment was much less interesting and fun than did subjects paid $.50. An analysis of variance showed that the test for linear trend in the role-playing conditions was significant at the .05 level or better (see Table 2).

When a subject is asked to write a private essay which disagrees with his beliefs, however, the effect is exactly the opposite. The more the subject is paid to write this essay, the more his attitude changes in the direction of the position he is adopting. Thus, subjects paid $5 thought the experiment was more fun and interesting than did subjects paid $.50. Again an analysis of variance shows a significant linear trend in the hypothesized direction (see Table 2).

In general, essay subjects evidenced more attitude change. This finding should be interpreted with some caution, however. A glance at Figures 1 and 2 suggests that, if the study had used only $.50 incentives, it would have been the role-play subjects who evidenced the most attitude change.

As can be seen from the last line in Table 2, the two a priori hypotheses and the role play-essay main effect account for most of the between-cell variance for fun and interesting. The fact that these 3 degrees of freedom (out of a total of 15) account for so much of the variance indicates the unimportance of experimenter main effects and higher order interactions.

As Festinger and Carlsmith found, this effect seems to be quite specific to the particular words used in adopting the counterattitudinal position. When subjects were asked how pleasant the experiment had been, or how much they had learned from it, or whether they would recommend it to a friend, there were no effects in the role-playing conditions, and only one significant effect in the essay-writing condition (see Tables 1 and 2). Only the questions asking the subjects how interesting and how much fun the experiment had been seem to show the effects of role playing which are predicted.

TABLE 2

A Prior Hypotheses for Posttest Variables plus Main Effect for Role Play-Essay

	Interesting	Fun	Fun plus interesting	Pleasant	Learn anything	Recommend	General mood
Role play, rank-order linear trend	8.1*	5.4*	7.1*	<1	<1	<1	<1
Essay, rank-order linear trend	18.1***	13.6***	19.3***	8.5***	1.6	1.6	2.0
Role play versus essay (from Table 3)	5.0*	4.0*	5.7*	2.7	<1	1.0	2.9
Percentage of between-cell variance contributed by 3 hypotheses	73	73	74	63	23	23	20

Note.—Unweighted mean solution. Error term from Experimenter × Role Play-Essay × Money analysis (Table 3).
* $p < .05$.
** $p < .01$.
*** $p < .005$.

TABLE 3

Experimenter, Role Play-Essay, and Money Analyses (2 × 2 × 4 Analysis of Variance)

Source	df	Interesting	Fun	Fun plus interesting	Pleasant	Learn anything	Recommend	Mood
Role play versus essay	1	5.05*	3.98*	5.73*	2.69	<1	1.02	2.90
Money	3	3.05*	2.90*	3.42*	2.60	<1	<1	3.17*
Interaction	3	7.04**	4.74**	7.15**	1.28	1.60	<1	<1
MS_e		9.91	9.75a	31.64a	5.14	15.67	10.05	4.22
df error		175	167a	167a	175	175	175	175

Note.—Since none of the experimenter main effects and none of the experimenter interactions reached the .05 level (only 1 of 28 reached the .10 level), they have been omitted from the table. The unweighted mean solution was used.
a The fun measure was not included in the posttest until 8 subjects (all in different cells) had been run. Consequently the N for fun and for fun plus interesting is only 183.
* $p < .05$.
** $p < .01$.

Subjects were also asked to rate their general mood, and on this question an interesting trend appears. Although the effect of incentive is not significant for either essay-writing or role-playing subjects taken individually, the trend is identical in both cases, so that there is a significant main effect of money. As inspection of Table 1 shows, the more subjects were paid, the better the mood they were in at the end of the experiment, irrespective of whether they were paid to write essays or to engage in face-to-face role playing. Such an effect may seem hardly surprising for the subjects who wrote essays. Essay subjects said that they were in a better mood after they had been paid $5; they also said that the experiment had been more fun and more interesting.

However, subjects who had engaged in face-to-face role playing and were paid $5 said that they were in a better mood, but thought that the experiment had been *less* fun and *less* interesting than subjects paid $.50. Thus, the results for essay-writing subjects might be interpreted as a simple generalization: they had been paid more money, were consequently in a better mood, and consequently rated the experiment as more fun and more interesting. Such a possible effect is, of course, impossible for the role-playing subjects. The more they were paid, the better the mood they were in, but the less they thought the experiment was fun and interesting. Such a finding is especially interesting in view of the interpretation of the results of Festinger and Carlsmith offered by several writers (e.g., Elms & Janis, 1965) which focuses on the hypothesis that subjects paid $20 failed to show attitude change because they felt anxious or guilty. Insofar as this question about mood can tap some of these presumed feelings, we find that contrary to this hypothesis, the more subjects are paid for performing a task like this, the better they feel.

Role-Play and Essay Performance

Evidence on the subjects' actual performances was gathered when all three authors independently rated the essays and transcripts of the role plays. Transcriptions of role-play performance were rated on the following six scales:

1. Persuasiveness and emphasis before the accomplice remarks that she has heard the task is dull.

2. Persuasiveness and emphasis after remark.
3. Overall positiveness.
4. Overall persuasiveness and conviction.
5. Percent of time spent on assigned topic.
6. Dissociation of self from content of message.

Ratings by the accomplice are also available on role-play subjects for the first four scales and for:

5. Apparent conflict.
6. Signs of discomfort.

Essays were rated on the following four scales:

1. Emphasis used in making points.
2. The extent to which the subject went beyond the statements given and created reasons in support of his general theme.
3. Overall quality and persuasiveness.
4. Apparent effort (with an attempt to control for ability).

It was anticipated that, if any differences were found at all, high incentives should improve the quality of both role-play and essay performance. (Control groups were, of course, omitted from all analyses, and separate analyses were performed for essay and role-play measures.) The interjudge reliabilities were typically in the 70s and 80s, and the various performance measures were highly correlated among themselves. None of these ratings of role-play transcripts showed even a .10 trend in any analysis of variance. Similarly, evaluations of the content of the essays show no glimmer of a difference among treatment groups. Also, there is no evidence that any of the measures of role-play or essay performance were correlated with posttest attitudes. According to the ratings made by the accomplice, role-play subjects showed highest conflict when they were paid only $.50 (the $F = 5.58$, $p < .01$, for the 2×3 Experimenter $\times$ Money analysis of variance). But this is the only "quality of performance" accomplice rating which shows any sign of a money effect.

Experimenter Effects

The results from the two experimenters are remarkably similar. The Fs for experimenter main effects and experimenter interactions are, in general, smaller than might be expected by chance. There are two variables, however, which produced significant experimenter effects: the accomplice's ratings of conflict (necessarily for role-play subjects only since it is an accomplice rating) and the "number of words used once" measure. According to the accomplice's ratings of conflict, subjects run by BEC indicated more conflict than those run by JMC ($p < .05$). Since the role play occurred before the subject met the posttester, we can safely assume the effect was created in the experimental manipulations and not in the posttest. Posttest attitudes show no parallel trend.

Subjects were told to use four words: interesting, exciting, enjoyable, and fun. Each role play and essay was scored for the number of these words which were used at least once. Both role-play ($p < .05$) and essay ($p < .01$) subjects run by BEC used more words than subjects run by JMC in both conditions. This effect is easily understood in terms of the heavier emphasis placed on the four words by BEC. In contrast to JMC, he asked the subjects to repeat the words back to him after he had stated them to the subjects. For the *role-play subjects only*, subjects run by JMC tended to use more words in high-incentive conditions, while BEC's subjects show no such trend (interaction $p < .05$). The attitude data show no patterns similar to any of those revealed by the number of words measure.

DISCUSSION

As can be seen in Figures 1 and 2, the major hypotheses from the study have been dramatically confirmed. There is one set of circumstances where increasing pressure for compliance leads to smaller amounts of attitude change. A subject who was enticed to make a patently false statement before a peer who believed the subject was sincere showed less attitude change with increased pressure for compliance. Figures 1 and 2 clearly indicate that the comparison between the $.50 group and the $1.50 group is the more crucial for role-play subjects. The highly significant difference between these two relatively small rewards represents a very strong replication of the original Festinger and Carlsmith study. These results, taken in conjunction with those of Cohen (Brehm & Cohen, 1962), make it highly unlikely that the original

Festinger and Carlsmith result is an artifact of the unusual magnitude of the $20 reward.

It is equally clear, however, that there is another set of circumstances in which increasing pressure for compliance produces more attitude change. A subject who wrote an anonymous essay (to be read only by the experimenter) showed more attitude change with increasing pressure for compliance. This dramatic interaction is quite consistent with the theory outlined in the introduction.

The results for the experimenter manipulation are also encouraging. The two experimenters produced remarkably similar effects. It is clearly the case that the differing theoretical orientations of the experimenters—and their somewhat different expectations about the outcomes—had no effect whatsoever on attitude change.

What remains unspecified, however, is the crucial difference between the role-play and essay-writing conditions. The following list describes just a few of the many components in the complex manipulation used in this study: The essays were written while the role plays were oral; the role-play sessions lasted for a maximum of 2 minutes while the essay sessions lasted for a maximum of 17 minutes; as a result of the differing justifications used to entice compliance, role-play subjects performed under somewhat more "hectic" or "crisis" circumstances than essay subjects; finally, if looked at from the subjects' perspective, the social consequences or implications of the compliant act differed greatly between the two conditions. In the essay condition, the only reader of the essays would be the experiment, who understood why the essay had been written. In the role-play condition, however, the audience—the experimental accomplice—presumably believed that the subject was sincere when he said that the task was fun, interesting, exciting, and enjoyable. It seems quite clear that the latter condition is more dissonance producing.

What is unclear from dissonance theory, however, is why the essay condition should show an *increasing* amount of attitude change with increased incentive. If there is no dissonance at all produced in the essay condition, then the different incentives should have no effect on attitude change—there should, in fact, be no attitude change. If the amount of effort is greater for high-incentive subjects, then dissonance theory can predict a positive relationship between the amount of incentive and attitude change. *If* subjects in the high-incentive conditions exerted more effort, then this greater effort should lead to greater dissonance in the high-incentive conditions, and, consequently, greater attitude change. A long and careful examination of both essays and role-play performance, however, unearthed no evidence whatsoever that the high-incentive essays were in any way superior. The fact that the finished product in the high-incentive condition is not better, of course, does not imply that the students did not try harder. Subjects were given four words to repeat, and there was little else that they could do other than repeat the four words and include them in complete sentences. It is possible that an increased effort in the high-incentive condition would not be reflected in higher quality essays.

It is probably necessary to turn somewhere other than dissonance theory for an explanation of the positive relationship between pressure for compliance and attitude change. One very plausible explanation of our results for the essay-writing subjects is a simple generalization phenomenon. We know that the more subjects were paid the better the mood they were in. It would not be surprising if this good mood generalized to the task they had been doing, so that they would report that the task had been more fun and interesting. This explanation would assume that in the role-playing conditions, this tendency to generalize was overcome by the dissonance produced.

Alternatively, it is possible that the theoretical orientation proposed by Hovland (Hovland, Lumsdaine, & Sheffield, 1949) and Janis (Janis & Gilmore, 1965) is needed in order to explain the attitude change in the essay condition. But, as we understand them, these theories also must predict that the performance in the high-incentive condition will be superior in some way to the performance in low-pressure conditions. Nor do they make clear why the opposite effect should be found in the role-play conditions.

One final point should be made about the sensitivity of the incentive manipulation. A quick glance at Figures 1 and 2 indicates that the results would have appeared quite different had the $.50 group been omitted. There would have been no incentive effects for either essay or role-play subjects, and there would have remained only the main effect indicating that essay subjects showed more attitude change than role-play subjects.

Finally, it should be noted that our results for the role-playing subjects are consistent with several other experiments using different techniques for varying pressure for compliance. Studies on the use of strong or weak threats to induce counterattitudinal behavior (Aronson & Carlsmith, 1963; Freedman, 1965; Turner & Wright, 1965) have consistently shown more attitude change when weaker pressures are applied for compliance. Another kind of evidence comes from experiments by Freedman (1963) in which he shows more attitude change when little justification is provided for the counterattitudinal behavior than when high justification is provided.

11

Attitude Change after Rewarded Dissonant and Consonant "Forced Compliance": A Critical Replication of the Festinger and Carlsmith Experiment[1]

JOZEF M. NUTTIN, JR.

Cross-cultural replications are unfortunately still rather rare in social psychology. However, interest in the influence of role playing on attitudes appears to be international. Mario von Cranach (1965) has performed a set of role-play experiments in Germany which he sees as generally supportive of dissonance theory. At the Laboratorium voor Experimentele Sociale Psychologie, University of Louvain, Leuven-Nederlands, Belgium, Jozef Nuttin has conducted repeated replications and modifications of several of the studies reprinted earlier in this book. Not all of his experiments have yet been published (in his letter of reprint permission, Professor Nuttin enviably writes, "We lack publication pressure"), but those described in the present paper constitute one of the more engaging efforts to explore further the variables involved in the situation devised by Festinger and Carlsmith.

This selection is reprinted with abridgments from the International Journal of Psychology, *1966, 1, 39–57, with permission of the author, the International Union of Psychological Science, and DUNOD, Publisher, Paris.*

[1] The data of this article were first presented in the second part of a report discussed at the Second Conference of Experimental Social Psychologists in Europe, Frascati 1964. I wish to thank Professor L. Knops for his statistical advice and also the experimental staff, Dirk Eeckhout, Annie Janssen-Beckers, Magda Mertens, Erik Billiaert, Dirk Logghe, and Joan Rijsman.

In general, we would like to state that the Festinger and Carl-smith interpretation needs to be tested out by using a more adequate experimental design which enables us to identify the crucial factors which are responsible for the obtained results. It seems to us that the dissonance interpretation of the results is based on the pretended manipulation of an independent disso-nance variable for which there is no control whatsoever that it was manipulated. Moreover, even if the over-all dissonance was really different in the low and high reward condition, there is still no sufficient guarantee to handle the control condition as one which only differs *qua* manipulated dissonance.

Cognitive dissonance is, of course, an intervening variable whose antecedents are private cognitive elements. The independ-ent variable, manipulated in the dissonance creation phase, is constituted by a set of three experimentally induced cognitions whose dynamic interrelations would lead to different degrees of dissonance reduction: 1. "the tests are dull"; 2. "I told the waiting subject that the tests are enjoyable"; 3. "I received money for telling that the tests are enjoyable".

The interpretation is based on the assumption that the Ss do experience cognitive dissonance as a result of the presence of cognitive elements 1 and 2 and that the amount of over-all dissonance is inversely influenced by the size of the reward in cognitive element 3. The difficult point however is that the Es do create in the second phase of both experimental conditions, —and not in the control condition—a very long chain of cogni-tions, feelings, and overt behavior and that they define the inde-pendent variable as a system of three selected cognitions without providing the necessary proof that it is precisely this dynamic interrelation between the three cognitive elements selected which is responsible for the obtained effect. The control condition used is not one in which the crucial aspect of this cognitive system is systematically different, but is a situation in which only cognitive element 1 is given, whereas other—possibly relevant—features of the "dissonance creation phase" are absent. Furthermore, we would like to stress the point that the very term "forced compli-ance" used in the title of Festinger and Carlsmith's publication, is itself a most ambiguous interpretation, not of the results, but of the manipulated independent variable.

In the opinion of the authors, there is no forced compliance in the control condition and there is forced compliance in the two experimental conditions, the force being weaker in the one dollar than in the twenty dollar condition. The term "forced compliance" refers however simultaneously to two different variables.

(1) The force which is manipulated is the monetary reward. It is however not clear at all that the money offered has any coercive function in the situation created. Nevertheless, the reward continuum is described as starting from "just barely sufficient to induce the person to say . . ." and the 20 dollar reward is situated at the opposite end of the same continuum. (2) The force is defined as a pressure which induces the person to say "not X" (cognitive element 2) (Festinger and Carlsmith, 1959, p. 204), or, as described elsewhere (Festinger and Aronson, 1960, p. 225) "the subject makes a public statement which is dissonant with his beliefs in order to receive a small reward." This means that the authors presume that the subjects do experience the reward as "being paid for telling a lie."

This is an interpretative description of what could happen in the experimental situation. It is however equally possible that the dynamic structure of subject's cognitive world was quite different. Since the experimenter was in a situation of relative emergency, he asked a favor of his subjects and expressed his gratitude by paying a reward. The favor asked for was meaningful to the Ss, since E had already explained why a student role-plays for the experimental condition. So it might be that the specific dissonance created by the role-playing is completely irrelevant and that the observed difference between the one and twenty dollar condition is a function of the size of reward offered for extra help to an experimenter. In other words, there is no guarantee that the reward would not have had the same effect in a consonant compliance condition, i.e. cooperation by a role playing in which S tells that the boring tasks were boring.

Since it is very difficult to ask the Ss how they perceive the various features of the experimental situation without interfering with the cognitive process itself, the only solution, in our opinion, can be found in an experimental design which controls for the crucial factors. Therefore, it seemed to us that the most appropriate way of doing this would be in manipulating separately the cognitive nature of the compliance and the size of the reward.

In order to stay as close as possible to the terms used in the original experiment, we will distinguish between "consonant," "dissonant" and "no" compliance. The term compliance here only refers to the yielding of the S to the demand of the E to do him a favor by role-playing. "Dissonant compliance" means that the actual content of the role-playing implies the creation of cognitive element 2 which is supposed to be dissonant with element 1; whereas "consonant compliance" refers to a role-playing which is in all aspects identical to the former, except for the crucial dissonance creating quality of the conversation with the stooge. This means that the Ss accept to do the favor, and eventually are rewarded for it, but that the favor consists of telling the stooge that the tasks were dull and boring, which is consonant with cognitive element 1.

Independently of the consonant or dissonant nature of the compliance, we will also manipulate the reward factor. If it is true that the reward has an effect in the one dollar condition because of its interaction with the dissonant quality of the compliance, the same effect should not be observed in a consonant compliance condition and *a fortiori* be different from the one in a no compliance situation. Moreover, if the reward is to be seen on a continuum of force for the compliance, there should be even less force in a no reward dissonant compliance. Consequently the so-created dissonance should be greater and the attitude change different from the change observed in a consonant or no compliance condition without reward.

EXPERIMENTAL PROCEDURE

Subjects and Preliminary Instructions

The experimental subjects were 120 volunteering male second year students of the University's Dutch-speaking Department of Sciences, who follow the author's course on Experimental Psychology.[2] They were informed that the duration of the experiments would vary between 30 and 90 minutes, and that after the experiment was finished, they might be approached by a certain Mrs. J. (this was said in a humoristic way in order to

[2] It should be noted that the students do not expect to be paid for their participation in experiments.

assure a good imprinting of the name of Mrs. J.) who, from time to time, interviews students, military servicemen, children and aged subjects, who serve in the wide variety of experiments run at the Psychological Institute. There were no compelling reasons found to reject subjects from the final analysis. It will be noticed that several changes in the instructions were made in order to maximally avoid any suspicion on the part of the subjects.

Experimental Design

Our critical replication of the Festinger and Carlsmith experiment consists of 8 different conditions with 15 replications per cell. Basically, it is a 3×3 design in which unfortunately one cell could not be filled. We decided this beforehand on the only basis of time considerations. The eight conditions enable us to constitute two different 2×3 factorial designs. Design I having a first factor with two levels: dissonant and consonant compliance; and a second factor with three levels: zero, 20 and 500 BF (Belgian France) reward. Design II having a first reward factor with two levels: zero and 500 BF and a second factor with three levels: dissonant, consonant and no compliance (see Table 1, p. 145).

We briefly identify each of the 8 conditions, keeping the original codes from F 13 up to F 20 (F as in *F*estinger) which were preceded by codes R (R as in *R*osenberg) from R 1 up to R 12 for the twelve conditions of our critical replication of Rosenberg's experiment and which all belong to the same initial report of this research project (Nuttin, 1964).

It will be recalled that Festinger and Carlsmith had three conditions: a control condition, which in our design is a no compliance and no reward condition; a one dollar dissonant and a twenty dollar dissonant compliance condition.

These original Festinger and Carlsmith conditions are hopefully replicated by the following three conditions:

F 13: no compliance—no reward
in which the Ss were only submitted to the attitude creation and the attitude measurement phase and did not receive any monetary reward. This should be equivalent to the only control condition of the original experiment.

F 14: dissonant compliance—500 BF reward
in which the Ss passed through the dissonance creation phase, receiving our high monetary reward. This condition should be equivalent to the original 20 dollar condition. Although the bank countervalue of 500 BF is only 10 dollars, its psychological value for most Flemish students would be between 15 and 20 dollars.[3]

F 15: dissonant compliance—20 BF reward
this condition should be equivalent to Festinger and Carlsmith's most dissonance creating 1 dollar condition. Twenty BF is the smallest banknote in Belgium.

The following conditions were added to the replicated design:

F 16: dissonant compliance—no reward
the treatment is identical to F 14 and F 15 except for the reward. According to Festinger's conception of "forced" compliance, this condition should be even more dissonance creating than the F 15.

F 17: consonant compliance—500 BF reward
which is identical to F 14 except that S has to convince the stooge that the boring tests are boring. Here the crucial cognitive relation of the role-playing with the private opinion is assumed to be consonant.

F 18: consonant compliance—20 BF reward
which is identical to F 17, except for the size of the reward.

F 19: consonant compliance—no reward
which is identical to F 17 and F 18, except for the reward.

F 20: no compliance—500 BF reward
which is identical to the control condition of the original experiment, except that S received a 500 BF reward for having completed the two boring tasks.

Experimental Situation and Instructions

Although we do not think that cross-cultural replications should be literal translations of the original research, there were no compelling reasons found for having major changes in the experimental situation and instructions. Since the instructions of the original study were followed as closely as possible, special

[3] 500 BF = 20 hot meals in the University restaurant; 20 BF = 25 cigarettes + a glass of beer.

attention will be given in this section to some modifications which were introduced mainly in order to increase the validity of the experimental situation, to make the task situation even more dull and boring than it was in the original study and to avoid suspicions among the Ss.

The description of the instructions and experimental situation will be given for each of the four phases of the experiment: 1) the attitude creation phase; 2) the compliance phase which for the dissonant compliance conditions corresponds to the dissonance creation phase of the original experiment; 3) the attitude measurement phase and 4) the post-experimental treatment phase. It is clear that all Ss went through phases 1, 3 and 4, whereas only the Ss of the dissonant and consonant compliance conditions went through phase 2.

Phases 1 and 2 were conducted by three different male E's who were unknown to the Ss and who could be perceived as young research assistants preparing a thesis. Each E conducted five experiments of each condition, following a balanced time schedule. An analysis of variance failed to show any systematic experimenter-bias. The stooge of phase 2 was a candid looking female student, unknown to the Ss and of about the same age. She did not know to which reward condition S did belong. The Interviewer of phase 3 was a female research-assistant. Needless to say that the Interviewer was always kept in complete ignorance of which condition S was in. Phase 4 was always conducted by the author.

1. *Attitude creation phase*. After a few minutes waiting in a "waiting-room for Ss with code A," the S was welcomed by E. While they were walking together to the experimental room, E reassured S that the experiment would not exceed 90 minutes. Off-hand he hinted at the possibility of an interview with Mrs. J. who proved to be well-known to all Ss. (*cf*. preliminary instructions).

As soon as S entered the room, he was invited to sit down at the table and with no further introduction he was given a square board containing 7 × 7 metal winged nuts which were so mounted that they could be turned infinitely in the same direction. S was simply asked to turn each of the 49 nuts a quarter turn clockwise, then another quarter turn, and so on. He was told to use one hand, at his own choice, and to work at his own speed. We intentionally avoided identifying the task as a performance test. E was sitting slightly behind S in order to prevent any face-to-face contact, and in addition, S was not allowed to talk. After half an hour work, E replaced the board by a tray containing 12 small wooden cylinders. S was asked to empty the tray, to refill it with the spools, to empty it once more, and so on. S was left ignorant about the duration of the task and again was prevented from asking questions, was told to use one hand and to work at his own speed.

While S was working on the tasks, E took some notes in order to make it convincing that this was "the" experiment. In contrast with the original study, however, E was not equipped with a stop watch. This, we thought, might have invited S to perform a speed-test when we really wanted to make the whole task as empty and dull as possible.

After half an hour, the second task was completed, and E falsely explained the purpose of the experiment. S was told that he was in the control condition A, but that the Ss in the experimental condition B, while waiting before the experiment, were introduced to a hired accomplice student who role-played that the tasks were enjoyable, interesting and lots of fun. The main purpose of the experiment was indeed to see whether students perform differently on the tasks if they are told beforehand that the tasks are interesting and enjoyable than if they are not told anything. For the Ss of our consonant compliance conditions, the relevant parts of the instructions were replaced by boring, uninteresting and not enjoyable.

2. *Compliance phase.* From our experience during a long pretesting period, it appeared that the experimental situation in which the original compliance instructions were given could be improved. The compliance phase is indeed the most difficult and crucial one of the whole experiment. On the one side, one should avoid a self-selection of the Ss who become suspicious or refuse the role-playing. On the other side, one should not really force them to role-play, since this would damage the subtle dissonance manipulation itself. We hope to have succeeded in presenting the emergency situation for which the help of the subject was needed, in a more realistic way as follows.

When E was about to finish his explanation, he gave a secret light signal to another E who was waiting in the corridor and who came immediately to the door, knocked and waited. While S still had his back turned to the door, E opened and said, with a show of surprise in his voice, "Ah! Professor!", went out and closed the door, leaving S alone for 2 minutes. Upon re-entering, he said "I will try, Professor." In the rewarded compliance conditions, E held the monetary reward in his hand. E then appeared rather uncomfortable and explained that Professor N. (the author) had just come to tell him that the hired student had phoned saying that it was impossible to come and that Professor N. suggested that S might be willing to substitute for him, since the next subject was already waiting in the waiting room for experimental condition B. "Of course you do not have to, but you see, this is the kind of emergency situations which cause unnecessary loss of time for my thesis work."

All Ss of the compliance conditions agreed with this proposition and memorized the items to be said to the waiting student "who happened to be a girl." The items for the dissonant compliance were:

—I found the tests most enjoyable;—very interesting;—it really was worthwhile to cooperate in this experiment;—as far as I am concerned, N. can give me more of these tests;—psychology really is an interesting subject matter.

For the consonant compliance, Ss memorized the following points:

—I found the tests extremely boring;—not interesting at all; —such cooperation is just a loss of time;—N. will not see me again in this Institute;—I just do not understand what those psychologists are doing.

The Ss of the reward conditions were given the monetary reward after signing a hand-written receipt (for budgetary reasons). Just as in the original experiment, it was said that S might serve as a substitute accomplice in case of future emergencies.

E took S to the waiting room, introduced himself to the stooge, asked for her appointment card and said "just a minute, Miss M.," continuing to S: "I'll go and see if Mrs. J. wants to interview you." As soon as S had said some positive (or negative for the consonant compliance conditions) remarks about the tests, the stooge said that she was surprised because a friend of hers—she just had seen at the Alma (university restaurant)—had told her that she found the experiment boring and dull (or enjoyable and interesting for consonant compliance conditions). After this, the stooge listened quietly in a standardized way.

As soon as S changed the topic of conversation, she gave a secret light signal to E who entered and said to S: "Mrs. J. would indeed very much like to see you" and took him to the room of the Interviewer (Mrs. J.), situated on another floor at a distance of about 80 meters from the experimental and waiting rooms. Meanwhile, E thanked S and, just as in the original experiment, E said "I hope you did enjoy it. Most of our subjects tell us afterwards that they found it quite interesting. You get a chance to see how you react to the tasks and so forth."

It should be noted that the Ss of the no compliance conditions had the same preparatory treatment for the interview, immediately after E gave his false explanation of the experiment. Before entering the room of the Interviewer, they had however to wait about 4 minutes, in order to keep the time interval between the first and third phase more or less constant.

3. *Attitude measurement phase.* The interviewer introduced herself (*cf.* preliminary instructions). She urged S to answer frankly, assuring him that his answers would be handled with the utmost discretion. Then she asked in which kind of test or experiment S had served. She reacted in a neutral way to the answer of S, saying that, for her sake, this was to be considered as a cooperation in a test and not in an experiment. She then chose from a large variety of rating forms, a booklet "For Male Students who have served as S in A tests." These precautions were taken in order to avoid a rating of the whole experimental session, with the possible rewarded compliance included. Whenever a S spontaneously alluded to the cooperation with E, the Interviewer reacted as if she never had heard about this, and that this was certainly not to be taken into account for her interview.

After some introductory questions, the Interviewer verbally commented the ratings presented in a 20 page printed booklet. The S marked his answer on each page and could give comments if he wished. All verbal interactions were tape-recorded.

The main questions asked were the following.

—*Rating A:* "Did you find the tests enjoyable?" An 11-point scale from -5 to $+5$ was labeled at each point from "extremely disagreeable" (-5) over "neither enjoyable nor disagreeable" (0) to "extremely enjoyable" (+5).—*Rating B:* "Did you find the tests interesting?" An 11-point scale from "extremely boring" (−5) over "neither boring nor interesting" (0) to "extremely interesting" (+5).—*Rating C:* "Did you find the tests varied?" An 11-point scale from "extremely monotonous" (−5) over "neither monotonous nor varied" (0) to "extremely varied" (+5).—*Rating D:* "Would you be willing to participate in another similar experiment?" A 6-point scale going from "completely willing" (6) to "not willing at all" (1).—*Reward ratings:* Six ratings had to do with the attitude toward financial payment of Ss. "The payment of . . . BF for cooperation in a psychological experiment of maximally two hours is, in my opinion . . . 'too little' (0) over 'just sufficient' (5) to 'much too much' (10)." A different form was presented for payment of 5, 20, 50, 100 and 500 BF. A sixth question was completed: "According to me, it is appropriate to pay . . . BF to a student who volunteers for a two-hour experiment."

4. *Post-experimental treatment phase.* At the end of the attitude measurement phase, the Ss from all conditions were taken to my office, where I conducted a final (recorded) interview. I started by saying: "I guess you participated in the experiment with the two manipulation tasks. The two tests you took there have some importance to me and I want to ask you to think once more about these two tests, and to answer the following three questions." The S was given a second time the ratings A, B and C.

After this, S was asked to give his description of the experiment and to tell me what he thought it all was about. A very few Ss expressed their suspicions about the compliance being part of the experiment. It was however difficult to judge from their reactions if this suspicion was aroused by my first questions or really had happened at the very moment of the compliance. All symptoms of suspicion, as well in phase 2 as in this last phase, were carefully registered. An inspection of these data made it clear that the amount of suspicion was very small and that there were no differences between compliance conditions at all. With regard to the Interview of the attitude measurement phase, not one single subject had perceived this to be linked with the first two phases.

As soon as the S finished his version of the experiment, I told him the truth and explained the reason for the deception used. All rewarded Ss were informed that there were no funds available. After the money was returned, all Ss, those of the no reward conditions included, were given a very much appreciated non-monetary reward. Each student gave me in his turn a formal promise to talk to other people neither about the experiment nor about the non-monetary reward.

RESULTS

1. Rating A: "How Enjoyable the Tasks Were"

This rating can be considered as the closest approximation of the original assessment of the attitude toward the tasks. As a matter of fact, judging from the titles used in their publication, Festinger and Carlsmith do consider the reactions on their first question (interesting and enjoyable) mainly as a description of the hedonic and enjoyable aspects of the task performance.

It will be recalled that the answers given on this rating were the only significant results of the original experiment, *viz.* −.45 in control; +1.35 in one dollar and −.05 in 20 dollar condition.

In Table 1, the average ratings are given for the eight conditions of our replication. Looking only at the three cells which are

TABLE 1

Means for Rating A (from −5 to +5) for Each
of the 8 Experimental Conditions

	REWARD		
	o BF	20 BF	500 BF
Dissonant compliance	− .9 F 16	− .4 F 15	− .9 F 14
Consonant compliance	− .8 F 19	+ .4 F 18	− 1.8 F 17
No compliance	− .9 F 13		− 1.2 F 20

replications of the original study (F 13: original control; F 15 and F 14, original one and 20 dollar conditions), we find the observed means in the dissonance predicted direction: the mean for the large reward being the same as the control condition, whereas the mean for the small reward condition is slightly less negative. This result is obviously very weak and not significant at all. The observed differences are however in the same direction as in the original study. The dissonance direction of these results becomes even somewhat clearer if we dichotomize the self-ratings in those which were at the negative side of the continuum and those which were not. As a matter of fact, for both the control and the high reward condition (F 13 and F 14), 10 out of the 15 Ss rated on the negative side of the continuum, whereas this was the case for only 6 out of the 15 Ss from the small reward condition (F 15). So we could conclude that as far as the replicated conditions are concerned, we do have a weak confirmation of the original results.

What about the dissonance prediction, the smaller the reward, the greater the dissonance and hence the attitude change, for a zero value of the reward? The data of condition F 16 (dissonant compliance—no reward) are not in line with this specific prediction. The average rating is identical to the ones of the 500 BF reward dissonant compliance and of the no compliance with no reward conditions (F 16 = F 14 = F 13). Condition F 16 gives us 9 ratings at the negative side of the continuum.

A further inspection of our consonant compliance conditions reveals a most interesting pattern. As a matter of fact, we do find the most positive and most negative average rating in the whole design precisely in the low and high reward consonant compliance conditions: the only mean rating, in the whole design, which is at the positive side of the continuum, is found in F 18, where a small reward was given for telling that the boring tasks were boring. A 500 BF reward given for the same consonant role-playing results in the most negative reaction toward the same tasks. As a matter of fact, in the 500 BF consonant condition, there was not a single subject rating at the positive side of the continuum, whereas 8 out of the 15 Ss of the 20 BF consonant condition reacted positively towards the dull tasks after having been paid a small reward for the same consonant role-playing.

It is clear that these results, obtained in our consonant compliance conditions do follow exactly the same pattern as the

results obtained in the original Festinger and Carlsmith dissonant
compliance conditions. (See Fig. 1, where the gap between the

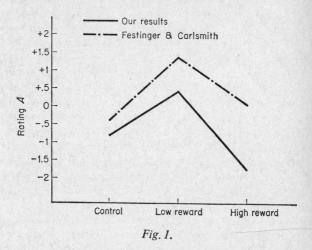

Fig. 1.

original results and our consonant compliance might be due, *e.g.*,
to the fact that our experimental tasks were even more boring
and dull than those of the original experiment).

Considering the eight cells of Table 1, the global pattern could
be structured as follows: the small 20 BF reward, whether for
consonant or dissonant compliance, results in the most positive
attitude toward the tasks, the high 500 BF reward results in the
most negative attitude even if the reward is just given for the
performance of the tasks (F 20) and the attitude toward the
tasks is not affected by the compliance if there is no reward
given. This weak trend is graphically presented in Fig. 2.

The trend is weak indeed. An analysis of variance for each of
the two 2×3 designs (I and II) fails to result in a significant F
($F = 1.84$ for Design I, reward factor with 3 levels; $F = .54$ for
Design II, compliance factor with 3 levels). A non-parametric
one-way analysis of variance leads to the same lack of over-all
significance.

2. Rating B: "How Interesting the Tasks Were"

The mean scores for Rating B are presented in Table 2.
This time, the small reward for dissonant compliance results

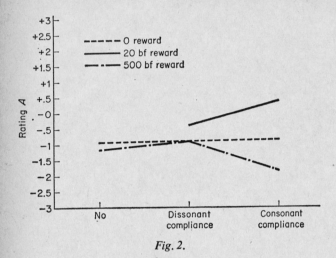

Fig. 2.

in an observed mean which is even more negative than either the control or the high reward condition. Once more however, the small reward for consonant compliance leads to the most positive reaction, whereas the large reward for consonant compliance

TABLE 2

*Means for Rating B (from −5 to +5) for Each
of the 8 Experimental Conditions*

	REWARD		
	0 BF	20 BF	500 BF
Dissonant compliance	— 1.1	— 1.7	— .7
	F 16	F 15	F 14
Consonant compliance	— 1.9	— .6	— 2.8
	F 19	F 18	F 17
No compliance	— 1.5		— 1.7
	F 13		F 20

results in the most negative mean attitude. Taking into account the rather low correlation ($r = .66$) between the "enjoyable" and "interesting" ratings, this similarity between the two patterns is rather striking.

An analysis of variance for the 2×3 factorial Design I with 3 reward levels, gives an F of 2.46 which is significant at the .05 level. As is shown in Table 3, a further elaboration of the same

TABLE 3

Analysis of Variance for Data from Table 2 for the 2×3 Factorial Design with 3 Reward Levels

Source	SS	df	MS	F	Fc
Reward factor	4.9	2	2.45	.56	3.12
Compliance factor ..	7.92	1	7.92	1.82	3.98
Interaction	40.76	2	20.38	4.67*	3.12
Within	366.01	84	4.36		
Total	419.59	89			

* $p = .05$

experimental design fails to show a main effect, either from the reward or from the compliance factor. There is however a significant interaction between the two factors.

A further breakdown of each of the factors gives us the following. The overall F between the three reward conditions for dissonant compliance is not significant ($F = 1.04$). The over-all F between the three reward conditions for consonant compliance is very significant ($F = 10.83$; $p = .01$). The Duncan Multiple Range Test shows that only the difference between F 17 and F 18 (500 and 20 BF reward) is significant ($p = .01$). The F between the two compliance conditions (dissonant and consonant) for both the zero and 20 BF reward is not significant ($F = .77$ and 2.37). The F between the two compliance conditions for the 500 BF reward (F 14 and F 17) is very significant ($F = 9.66$; $p = .01$). A non-parametric analysis of the variance of the ranks for the same six conditions leads basically to the same results (Kruskal-Wallis' $H = 11.45$; significant at the .05 level). The only differences between specific groups which have a significant U are: between F 17 and F 14 (consonant and dissonant compliance with high reward), $U = 47.5$ and between F 17 and F 18 (low and high reward with consonant compliance), U also of 47.5, both being very significant at the .01 level.

From the above results it is clear that the high reward has an effect, depending on the dissonant or consonant nature of the compliance. The results however do not support the dissonance prediction as formulated in the original experiment. The data can be read as follows: a reward of 500 BF, received for telling that the boring tests are boring, results in an attitude response (on the rating B) which is "more boring" than if only 20 BF is received for the same consonant compliance; a reward of 500 BF received for telling that the boring tests are interesting, does result in a less unfavorable attitude toward the boring tests, but this attitude is not significantly different from the one observed in Ss who received only 20 BF or no reward for having played the same dissonance creating role.

How ever tempting the interpretation of the results of this first experimental design might be, one is again frustrated when considering the second 2×3 design which offers a zero and 500 BF reward at each of the three levels of the compliance factor: dissonant, consonant, and no compliance. Here the over-all F ($F = 1.84$) does not meet the criterion for significance, leaving us with the final conclusion that we had better not reject the null-hypothesis stating that attitude responses (on rating B) coming from high or no reward, either for dissonant, consonant or no compliance are all drawn from the same attitude population.

3. Rating C: "How Monotonous the Tasks Were"

Table 4 shows that all Ss agreed that the tasks were quite monotonous. A mere glance at the various means offers ample evidence that there are no systematic differences due to the induced factors (over-all $F = .84$). One could point to the fact that both the consonant and dissonant low reward (20 BF) conditions have the least unfavorable means just as they also had the most favorable answers on rating A.

4. Other Replicated Ratings

Besides the main question "Were the tasks interesting and enjoyable?", Festinger and Carlsmith asked three more questions:

TABLE 4

*Mean Scores for Rating C (from −5 to +5) for Each
of the 8 Experimental Conditions*

| | REWARD | | |
	0 BF	20 BF	500 BF
Dissonant compliance	− 3 F 16	− 2.3 F 15	− 2.7 F 14
Consonant compliance	− 2.7 F 19	− 2.6 F 18	− 3.4 F 17
No compliance	− 3.3 F 13		− 3.5 F 20

"Would you have any desire to participate in another similar experiment?" "From what you know about the experiment and the tasks involved in it, would you say the experiment was measuring anything important?" and "Did the experiment give you an opportunity to learn about your own ability to perform these tasks?"

These three questions were also rated during the attitude measurement phase of our replication. For the first of these questions, desire to participate in another similar experiment (our rating D) Festinger and Carlsmith did get "almost" significant results (.08 and .15 level). The mean ratings obtained for our conditions on a scale from 1 to 6 are all very similar, varying between 4.4 and 5.3 for the eight conditions. It is clear that none of the experimental manipulations is reflected in these results. The only point worth noting is that the answers on this rating are very significantly less favorable than the answers given on the same rating by similar Ss who participated in a similar experiment, also with high rewards but without the dull task. Even the mean answers of our high reward conditions are less favorable than the mean answers of the no reward condition of the experiment referred to. This might be an indirect illustration of the validity of the experimental situation: the tasks were boring indeed.

Our answers for the last two ratings, for which Festinger and Carlsmith did not really expect dissonance results, and did not get either, are also lacking any significant difference or trend.

DISCUSSION OF RESULTS

The essence of the so provocative Festinger and Carlsmith experiment can be summarized as follows: if you want to change an individual with attitude A in the direction of not A, pay him the smallest sum necessary to compel him to public behavior in a direction contrary to his attitude. The higher the reward, *i.e.* pressure, the smaller the effect will be.

It seems to us that the results of our critical replication do put a serious question mark behind the specific formulation of the dissonance theory interpretation of the original data. Festinger and Carlsmith's interpretation was indeed completely based on the dissonance created by the public statement in role-playing. We have shown that one gets exactly the same inverse effect of size of reward if the public statement is consonant with the private attitude. Considering ratings A and B together, which replicate very closely the original question "How enjoyable and interesting were the tasks?" we observe in the consonant compliance with low reward condition, fourteen positive reactions toward the dull tasks (8 for A and 6 for B), whereas there is not a single positive reaction (out of 30) in the consonant compliance with high reward condition, the latter being not signficantly different from the replicated original control condition, in which we find only four ratings on the positive side of the continua (2 for A and 2 for B).

These results are furthermore corroborated by the answers given on rating C which was not used in the original study. In Fig. 3, the global pattern is given for the summated mean ratings of A + B + C.

It is not easy to interpret the global results of our replication. Our personal effort would lead us in the following direction. First, it seems reasonable to accept that the role-playing, either dissonant or consonant, does not have any systematic effect on the private attitude toward the dull tasks if there is no reward

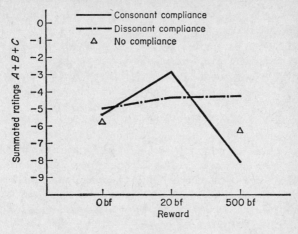

Fig. 3.

offered. From this result, it becomes difficult to accept Festinger and Carlsmith's interpretative definition of the reward as having a coercive function with regard to the "forced compliance."

When looking now to our reward conditions, we would like to consider a distinction between a realistic and plainly acceptable 20 BF reward and a disturbing or much less justified 500 BF reward. The 20 BF reward was not expected by the Ss, but it was very welcome and useful to students who after all did an extra favor to the E. It was an agreeable surprise at the end of a dull experiment and one of its generalized effects might have been to temper somewhat the negative attitude toward the dull tasks, especially in the consonant low reward condition (but also in the dissonant condition, *cf.* rating A) where the total effort asked from the S presumably was less than in the dissonant compliance. (For further evidence on this point, *cf. infra.*)

The 500 BF reward however, might very well have been a rather disturbing surprise. As a matter of fact, we do not know what we are doing when we force a poor student to accept such a high reward. Maybe we are not any more manipulating reward, but mere embarrassment. The student could of course refuse the reward, but the E wanted him to accept the money and the receipt was written and signed in a hurry since the next S was already waiting. Maybe the acceptance of the high reward was much more "forced acceptance or compliance" than the role-playing itself. We would like to stress the point that it became very clear from the reactions of the high reward Ss during the post-experimental interview that they all did believe that the 500 BF were theirs and that nobody ever would take it back. It certainly was, on deontological grounds, most appropriate to give them instead a much appreciated non monetary reward.

Let us suppose now that the reward was disturbing because unjustified. What can a subject do in order to make such a reward more justified? He can do many things, which are unpredicted by the experimenters, even *e.g.* change his attitude toward the USA just by guessing that the research money used could not have been given by a Belgian research foundation.[4] He could also try to justify keeping the reward just by trying to deserve it more. One way to reach this goal could be by accentuating the negative aspects of the experimental tasks: "After all it was a hell of a boring job I did for those psychologists." We realize that this does not fit into the E's definition of the experimental manipulation: E gave the high reward for the compliance and even for staying on call and not for the task. But the experimenter cannot prevent the subject from having his own definition, his own perception of the experimental situation, which ideally should coincide with the *a priori* imposed structure of the research people, but which does not necessarily coincide. So the final result would be that there is no pure reward effect in the 500 BF conditions and that the mean attitude rating, as well in the original study as in our replication, becomes lower in the high reward than in the low reward conditions for the above reasons.

But, what about the observed differences in the three high reward conditions as a function of compliance? We do have some reasons to conjecture that the need for justification of the high reward might not have been the same in the three different compliance conditions.

The reader will recall that each S was asked, during the attitude measurement phase, how much a volunteering student should get paid and what his opinion was about a reward of 5-20-50-100 and 500 BF. An analysis of the ratings for the payment of 500 BF shows the following trends: there is only one cell in the whole design in which 14 out of the 15 Ss did rate at the very extreme "much too much" side of the continuum. The average rating for

⁴ This research project was not supported by any grant.

the consonant high reward is indeed 9.9 (one S scoring 8) on a scale from 0 to 10. The no compliance with high reward condition has ten maximal ratings, four 9 and one 7 whereas the dissonant with high reward compliance does have the lowest mean of the whole design, with one 5 (just sufficient), two 6, one 8 and two 9. The same trend is also clearly reflected in the answers given on the question "How much should a student be paid for a two hour cooperation?" In the no reward and the low reward cells the average is about 20 F, the dissonant compliance conditions both being some 5 F higher than each of the consonant compliance conditions, which points in the direction of higher perceived effort in dissonant role-playing. In the high reward conditions however, the Ss of the consonant compliance do ask exactly the same amount as the low and no reward consonant compliance Ss, whereas the dissonant high reward Ss do ask more than twice as much than in the consonant high reward, the Ss of the no compliance staying again in medium rank order.

These subsidiary data, how ever weak the trends might be, do corroborate our *a posteriori* interpretation, which is helped by a rank ordering of the high reward conditions along a scale of "need for justification." The high reward was least justified for the consonant compliance Ss: they are almost unanimous to say that 500 BF is much too much. After all they received 500 BF for an extra favor to E which by all means was not difficult to role-play. Next are the no compliance Ss who received the same amount of money just for working one hour on a test they volunteered for. For the dissonant compliance Ss, the high reward was relatively most justified, although still disturbing and not just rewarding. Indeed, after a dull work, they had to tell that they had had a very good time.

Thus, on the basis of the two reward ratings mentioned, it makes sense to rank order the three high reward conditions from least to most justified as follows : consonant, no and dissonant compliance. And this is exactly the order of the observed attitude change in the high reward conditions. So, the less the reward is justified, the more the subject tries to deserve it by changing his attitude toward the tasks in a more negative direction.

We fully realize that this is not an experimentally verified hypothesis. The reader might however feel somewhat more confident when we tell him that the same interpretation sounds also most plausible for the results obtained in a similar experiment in which we gave the same high reward for writing a twenty-minute consonant essay.

CONCLUSION

We would like to stress the point that from the above discussion of results, we do not want to conclude with criticism of Festinger's cognitive dissonance theory. It is obvious that our interpretation offered for the high reward results perfectly fits into the broader conceptual framework of Festinger's theory. However, on the basis of the results of our critical replication, we propose a fundamental reinterpretation of the original Festinger and Carlsmith experiment.

It was indeed shown that it is very unlikely that the dissonant characteristic of the compliance was crucial for the interpretation of the low reward effect, and that the high reward might have been most dissonance creating. The results of the original experiment as well as those of our consonant and dissonant compliance design do support the interpretation that the small realistic reward does have a generalized reward effect, resulting in a positive attitude change toward the dull tasks, whereas the pure reward effect is suppressed in the high reward conditions. This is explained by the fact that the high embarrassing reward arouses the need for justification of the acceptance of the reward, which leads the S to try to deserve it more by accentuating the negative aspects of the experimental tasks. As a result there is no positive but rather a negative attitude change.

It is clear that the above reinterpretation of the Festinger and Carlsmith study also does imply a new definition of their manipulated independent variable. The very fact that we lack valid information on the meaning of the presumably manipulated variables makes the experimental foundation of cognitive dissonance theory very often unconvincing. Not much more convincing than the results of our replication. What do we know about the rewarding effect of money? It is very probable that, within the limits of our experimental situation, the relationship between the monetary size and the reward value is a curvilinear one. If one would force a subject to accept a .0001 dollar reward for any role-playing, consonant or dissonant, one certainly would not give him a pure low reward. All one would achieve is probably embarrassment for both subject and experimenter. If one goes to the opposite end of the continuum, one equally might not any more manipulate pure reward.

Furthermore, as shown in our replication, it is very unlikely that the reward manipulated was dynamically linked with the dissonance creating cognition of the role-playing. This fundamental supposition of the Festinger and Carlsmith interpretation could, we argued, have been checked by a better balanced design.

It is our conviction that the idea behind the original interpretation of the Festinger and Carlsmith experiment is a valid one. It must however, to say the least, be very difficult to manipulate a force which is "just barely sufficient" to elicit counter-attitudinal behavior. In our opinion, the experimental evidence that this variable was manipulated, has never been given.

The dissonance psychologists certainly have made a masterly step in trying to translate very interesting ideas into testable form. They have created real-life like and hence extremely complex situations in the laboratory. The very facts however that they never did succeed in producing "inter-ocular *traumata*," *i.e.* results which are so clear that they do hit right in between the eyes, and that even rigorous replication proves to be very difficult, should warn us to be cautious in identifying the variables operating.

12

An Experimental Analysis
of Self-Persuasion[1]

DARYL J. BEM

The radical behaviorism of B. F. Skinner has seldom been applied to social psychology in anything more than purely speculative fashion. It appears particularly inappropriate to the study of attitudes, which by definition centers upon concepts of intervening variables and internal processes whose importance Skinner explicitly denies. But both role playing and attitude assessment possess overt behavioral components; so Daryl Bem has essayed a Skinnerian approach to their study, with results which other attitude researchers have found provocative if not always convincing.

Bem has continued the line of reasoning presented here in several other papers (1967, 1968), and has applied it to areas other than role playing. Critical response to the approach can be found on pages 185–187 of this volume, and more extensively in the context of empirical studies by Jones, Linder, Kiesler, Zanna, and Brehm (1968) and by Cayley and Elms (1968).

This selection is excerpted from the Journal of Experimental Social Psychology, *1965, 1, 199–218, with permission of Academic Press Inc. and the author.*

Self-awareness, one's ability to respond differentially to his own behavior and its controlling variables, is a product of social interaction (Mead, 1934; Ryle, 1949; Skinner, 1953; Skinner, 1957). Among the responses that comprise self-awareness, verbal state-

[1] This research is drawn from part of a dissertation submitted to the Department of Psychology, University of Michigan, in partial fulfillment of the requirements for the degree of Doctor of Philosophy. The author is grateful to Harlan L. Lane and Theodore M. Newcomb who served as co-chairmen of the Doctoral Dissertation Committee.

ments that are self-descriptive are perhaps the most common, and the general procedures by which the socializing community teaches an individual to describe his own overt behavior would not seem to differ fundamentally from the methods used to teach him to describe other events in his environment. The community, however, faces a unique problem in training the individual to make statements describing internal stimuli to which only he has direct access, for the conditioning of the appropriate verbal responses must necessarily be based on the public stimuli and responses that often accompany or resemble these private events. Skinner (1953, 1957) has provided a detailed analysis of the limited resources available to the community for training its members thus to "know themselves," and he has described the inescapable inadequacies of the resulting knowledge.

One implication of Skinner's analysis is that many of the self-descriptive statements that appear to be exclusively under the discriminative control of private stimulation may, in fact, remain under the control of the same public events which members of the community themselves must use in "inferring" the individual's inner states. In our well-fed society, for example, it is not uncommon to find a man consulting his wrist watch to answer the question, "Are you hungry?" There is also direct experimental evidence that an individual relies on external cues for describing his emotional states (Schachter and Singer, 1962). Attitude statements may be similarly controlled. For example, when the answer to the question, "Do you like brown bread?" is, "I guess I do, I'm always eating it," it seems unnecessary to invoke a fount of privileged self-knowledge to account for the reply. In this example, it is clear that the discriminative stimuli controlling the attitude statement reside in the individual's overt behavior; indeed, the man's reply is functionally equivalent to the reply his wife might give for him: "I guess he does, he is always eating it."

It is the major thesis of this report, then, that an individual's belief and attitude statements and the beliefs and attitudes that an outside observer would attribute to him are often functionally equivalent in that both sets of statements are "inferences" from the same evidence: the public events that the socializing community originally employed in training the individual to make such self-descriptive statements. The three experiments reported below provide support for this hypothesis by demonstrating that an individual's belief and attitude statements may be predicted and controlled by manipulating his overt behavior and the stimulus conditions under which it occurs in ways that would lead an *outside* observer to infer that the individual held the "belief" or "attitude" we wish to obtain. The individual, in short, is regarded as an observer of his own behavior and its controlling variables; accordingly, his belief and attitude statements are viewed as "inferences" from his observations.

TACTS, MANDS, AND COMMUNICATOR CREDIBILITY

A descriptive statement, a verbal response that is under the discriminative control of some portion of the environment, is classified as a "tact" (Skinner, 1957). A speaker is trained to describe or "tact" his environment for the benefit of his listeners who provide generalized social reinforcement in return. An individual's belief and attitude statements are often tacts of stimuli arising from himself (e.g., "I am hungry"), his behavior (e.g., "I am generous"), or the effects of stimuli on him (e.g., "It gives me goosepimples"). Attitude statements in particular have the properties of tacts of the reinforcing effects of a stimulus situation on the individual (e.g., "I detest rainy weather," "I'd walk a mile for a Camel").

Verbal responses that are under the control of specific reinforcing contingencies are called "mands." A speaker who emits a mand is asking for, requesting, or "manding" a particular reinforcer (cf. de*mand*s, com*mand*s). Only a characteristic consequence will serve to reinforce the response, and often this reinforcer is specified explicitly by the response (e.g., "Please pass the milk"). Mands need not be verbal in the usual sense; for example, pointing to the milk pitcher may be functionally equivalent to the vocal request. Mands are often dsiguised as tacts as in "I believe you have the sports page" or as in the case of the television announcer who praises a product he is selling; his verbal behavior is a mand for the salary he receives and may not at all be under the actual discriminative control of the features of the product he appears to be tacting. A lie is often a mand for escape from aversive consequences; it, too, is a mand disguised as a tact. Any particular verbal response, then, may have both mand and tact characteristics in differing degrees. Thus, until the controlling circumstances are specified, it is not possible to determine the functional classification of a remark like "Darling, you look beautiful tonight"; the probabilities are high that it is a subtle blend of mand and tact.

It is clear, then, that in attempting to infer a speaker's "true" beliefs and attitudes, the listener must often discriminate the mand-tact characteristics of the communication. This is, in fact, an important dimension of "communicator credibility." A communicator is credible to the extent that his communication is discriminated as a set of tacts, and his credibility is vitiated to the extent that he appears to be manding in the form of disguised tacts. Thus, a communication attributed to J. Robert Oppenheimer is more persuasive than the same communication attributed to *Pravda* (Hovland and Weiss, 1951); the white coat and stethoscope on the television announcer are intended to indicate to the viewer that the announcer is one whose verbal behavior is under discriminative control of the product, not one who is manding money. Not only is a credible communicator more likely to persuade his listeners, but to the extent that his verbal responses appear to be "pure" tacts, they will be judged, by definition, to be his own "true" beliefs and attitudes. We turn now to evidence that the beliefs and attitudes of the communicator himself may be viewed as self-judgments based partially upon his credibility as a communicator; and, to the extent that this is so, they will coincide with judgments of his beliefs and attitudes that outside observers would make.

In an experiment by Festinger and Carlsmith (1959), two experimental groups of 20 undergraduates were employed as subjects. In the $1 condition, the subject was first required to perform long repetitive laboratory tasks. He was then hired by the experimenter as an "assistant" and paid one dollar to tell a waiting fellow student that the tasks were enjoyable and interesting. In the $20 condition, the subjects were hired for $20 to do the same thing. A panel of judges, in a blind rating procedure, rated the $20 persuasive communications as slightly but insignificantly more persuasive than $1 communications. Attitude measurement showed that subjects paid $1 evaluated the tasks and the experiment *more* favorably than did $20 subjects. We may interpret these findings within the present framework by considering the viewpoint of an outside observer who hears the individual making favorable statements about the tasks, and who further knows that the individual was paid $1 or $20 to engage in this behavior. When asked to judge the "true" attitude of the communicator, an outside observer would almost certainly judge a $20 communication to be a mand, behavior not at all under the control of the actual features of the laboratory task the individual appears to be tacting. Although a $1 communication also has mand properties, an outside observer would be more likely to judge it than the $20 communication to be a set of tacts, and hence, by definition, to be the "true" attitudes of the individual. If one places our hypothetical outside observer and the communicator in the same skin, the findings obtained by Festinger and Carlsmith are the result.

Blind evaluations of the persuasive communications were an elegant control feature of the Festinger-Carlsmith design, and, as mentioned, showed $1 communications to be no more persuasive than $20 communications *when the mand-tact conditions under which the verbal behavior was emitted were not available to the observer*. But this is precisely the information which makes one communicator more credible than another.

Cohen (Brehm and Cohen, 1962, p. 73) performed an experiment similar to the Festinger-Carlsmith study in order to rule out the interpretation that the $20 payment in the latter study was so large that it engendered suspicion and resistance, leading subjects to think, "It must be bad if they're paying me so much for it." (See also, Rosenberg, 1965.) Since this alternative interpretation is not unlike the mand-tact conceptualization offered here, it is relevant to examine Cohen's subsequent experiment in some detail.

Cohen's subjects were offered $.50, $1, $5, or $10 to write an essay against their initial opinions on a current issue. The post-essay belief statements essentially duplicated the Festinger-Carlsmith results: the higher the inducement, the less the belief statement coincided with the view advocated in the essays. (The $5 and $10 conditions did not differ significantly from the control group who were simply asked their opinions on the issue.) The crux of Cohen's argument resides in the fact that significant differences in post-essay belief statements emerged between the $.50 and the $1 conditions, and between them and the control condition. Since these payments were small and close to one another, Cohen's argument implies, the mand-tact discrimination could not account for the results.

This is, of course, an empirical question. The following study was designed to answer it by demonstrating that the belief statements made by Cohen's subjects when they were asked for their "true" opinions may be viewed as judgments based on the mand-tact characteristics of their own behavior, that is, on their own credibility as communicators.

AN INTERPERSONAL REPLICATION OF THE ESSAY STUDY

If the suggested interpretation of Cohen's results is correct, then an external observer should be able to replicate the true belief statement of one of Cohen's subjects with an interpersonal judgment if this observer is told the behavior of the subject and the apparent controlling circumstances of that behavior.

The subjects in the present study thus served as external observers; each subject judged one—and only one—volunteer in one of Cohen's experimental conditions.

Method

Sixty undergraduates were randomly assigned to "$.50," "$1," and "control" conditions. The first two groups were given the following instructions on a single sheet of paper; it consists of a description of the experimental situation employed by Cohen:

In the Spring of 1959, there was a student "riot" at Yale University in which the New Haven Police intervened with resulting accusations of police brutality toward the students. The issue was a very bitter and emotional one, and a survey of student opinion showed most of the student body to be extremely negative toward the police and their actions and sympathetic toward the students.

As part of a research project, a student member of a research team from the Institute of Human Relations at Yale selected a student at random and asked him to write a strong, forceful essay entitled,

"Why the New Haven Police Actions Were Justified," an essay which was to be unequivocally in favor of the police side of the riots. The decision to write such an essay or not was entirely up to the student, and he was told that he would be paid the sum of $.50 [$1.00] if he would be willing to do so. The student who was asked agreed to do so, and wrote such an essay.

The scale shown below was used in the original poll of student opinion on the issue. From this description, estimate as well as you can the actual opinion of the student who was willing to write the essay. Indicate your estimate by drawing a line through the appropriate point on the scale.

"Considering the circumstances, how justified do you think the New Haven police actions were in the recent riot?"

NOT JUSTIFIED AT ALL	VERY LITTLE JUSTIFIED	LITTLE JUSTIFIED	SOMEWHAT JUSTIFIED	QUITE JUSTIFIED	VERY JUSTIFIED	COMPLETELY JUSTIFIED

The control Ss in the present study received the same instructions except that the entire second paragraph was deleted and the third paragraph was altered to read: "From this description, estimate as well as you can the actual opinion of a student selected at random on the Yale campus. . . ."

In Cohen's experiment the subjects first wrote the essay and were then asked to indicate their own opinions on the scale. The scale employed in the present study is identical to Cohen's. The "control" condition in the present study also provides a check on the adequacy with which the situation on the Yale campus has been described.

RESULTS AND DISCUSSION

Figure 1 shows the interpersonal judgments of Ss in the present experiment compared to the belief statements collected by Cohen. Two-tailed probability levels based on t tests are also shown. It is seen that Cohen's results are closely replicated.

These results show that the mand-tact interpretation of the general inverse relation between amount of payment and subsequent belief statements is still viable: the lower the payment, the less the mand properties of the observed behavior predominate in the eyes of both intra- and inter-personal observers. To the extent that the behavior has non-mand properties, it will be discrim-

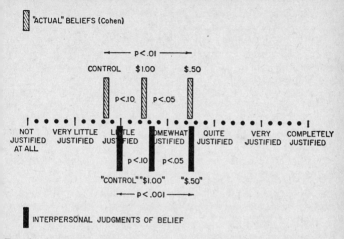

Fig. 1. A comparison of "actual" beliefs and interpersonal judgments of belief.

inated by an observer (including the individual himself) as indicating the "true" beliefs of that individual.

It should be noted that Ss in the experiment just presented did not actually read any of the essays written by Cohen's Ss. The successful interpersonal replication of his results, then, suggests that it may not have been necessary for his Ss to write the essays; that is, the behavior of *volunteering* may be the source of discriminative control over the beliefs. The "communication" may be contained in the commitment to write the essay, and it is the *commitment* that has the crucial mand or non-mand properties depending upon the payment offered. Brehm and Cohen (1962, pp. 115–116) cite a number of studies which, indeed, do demonstrate that commitment alone is sufficient; the essays themselves do not have to be written. . . .

Other studies from the literature are also amenable to the self-credibility interpretation. King and Janis (1956) compared improvised versus non-improvised role playing in producing belief change and found that subjects who read a communication and then played the role of a sincere advocate of the communication's point of view changed their beliefs more than those who read the fully prepared script aloud. It seems likely that the subjects who simply read the script clearly discriminated that their behavior was under the control of the text (cf., Skinner, 1957), whereas in the case of the subject who actually played out the role, every measure possible was taken to insure that he was surrounded by stimuli that would characteristically control the behaviors of an individual who "believed" the point of view. It should also be noted that subjects who were permitted to "improvise" would be expected to select precisely those arguments that had initial tact properties for themselves. It seems consonant with our analysis, then, to find that these subjects were more "persuasive" to themselves than the script readers.

In an experiment by Scott (1957), pairs of students were asked to debate different issues in front of a class; each student argued the position contrary to his initial beliefs. The experimenter manipulated the conditions so that a predetermined member of each pair "won" the debate. Later measurement of belief showed that the "winners" changed in the direction of the position that they had defended in the debate, but "losers" did not; in fact, "losers" shifted slightly toward the "winning" side. In a replication of the experiment in which a panel of judges rather than a class vote "decided" the winner of the debates, some of the debaters defended positions they actually held (Scott, 1959). Among these subjects, "winners" shifted still further in the direction of their arguments, and "losers" again shifted slightly in the direction of the "winning" side, a shift that was against the arguments they themselves presented *and* their initial beliefs.

Since the winners had been reinforced by winning and the losers had not, Scott interprets these results as showing that the reinforcement of overt verbal responses leads to a change in the beliefs. Such an interpretation, however, runs into difficulty in accounting for the results of the dissonance experiments previously described, which show an inverse relation between reinforcement and belief change. The present analysis suggests that the (falsified) class vote or judges' decision gave an additional tact property, or measure of credibility, to the beliefs stated in the "winning" argument; hence, the "winner" himself discriminated these beliefs as tacts, which is to say as his "true" beliefs. The fact that "losers" also shifted slightly toward the winning side is consistent with this interpretation. Further support for this interpretation comes from a study by Kelley and Woodruff (1956). College students who heard a recording of "prestigeful" members of their college group applaud a speech that opposed their initial beliefs changed their beliefs more than did a control group that was told that the applauding audience was a group of townspeople. These subjects thus based their credibility discriminations of the communicator on the judgment of other listeners, just as the debaters in the debate studies, it is suggested, based the credibility of their own communications on the decisions of the judges. The self-perception interpretation is thus consistent with the data from both the debate experiments and the dissonance theory experiments.

13

Role Playing, Incentive, and Dissonance[1]

ALAN C. ELMS

We cannot simply score each of the preceding papers as for or against dissonance theory, incentive theory, or some other alternative, and then total the points to see who wins. Each experiment usually raises more complex questions, and is less easily interpreted, than its authors originally intended; and the ultimate outcome of experimental controversies in psychology is seldom a clear "win" for anyone. More often, polarized positions are successively modified until some sort of rapprochement is reached. But one of the initial positions may still determine the larger part of what the rapprochement will finally be. This paper was written in an effort to show that, taking into account all of the relevant published material to the time of its writing, incentive theory still offered the most useful general framework for interpreting the bulk of role-play effects.

Since the paper first appeared, other experiments have been published which introduce further complications (see the two remaining selections in this book); and Janis (1968) has suggested elaborations of incentive theory—or, as he now calls it, conflict theory—which make a greater allowance for the commitment effects in role playing which have recently been stressed by dissonance theorists. It remains to be seen whether the modifications in Janis' original position will be any more persuasive to dissonance theorists, than their *efforts to allow for certain incentive effects (e.g., Carlsmith, 1968) have persuaded incentive/conflict theorists. But together, these modulatory trends should advance the eventual Day of Rapprochement.*

This selection is reprinted with abridgments from the Psycho-

[1] The author wishes to thank Irving L. Janis and Alvin J. North for their critical reading of an earlier version of this paper.

logical Bulletin, *1967, 68, 132–148, with permission of the American Psychological Association.*

Dissonance theory holds that the logic of the arguments for accepting a new attitude, or the consideration of needs which may be satisfied by adoption of the attitude, are relatively unimportant in most role-playing situations, except insofar as these factors may promote or impede dissonance reduction. The incentive theory position is that such factors are of central importance to the individual in ways besides dissonance reduction, for example, in satisfying various conscious and unconscous needs in addition to possible cognitive consistency needs. The incentive position also stresses psychological processes, such as anxiety, which may interfere with attitude change that might otherwise satisfy other needs (Janis, 1959). Dissonance theory, however, gains much of its distinctiveness as a theory by omitting consideration of such psychological complexities as biased scanning or affective reactions, basing its predictions instead largely on the ratio of consonant and dissonant elements in a situation and their relative importance, with dissonance and consonance defined in terms of the relationships between any two cognitive elements in a situation. The cognitive elements are considered alone, disregarding "the existence of all the other cognitive elements that are relevant to either or both of the two under consideration [Festinger, 1957, p. 13]."

This contrast between dissonance and incentive positions endows role-playing studies with a strategic theoretical significance. Dissonance theorists view extraneous rewards for role playing as dissonance-reducing elements, which diminish the necessity of changing one's attitudes to reduce the dissonance aroused by role playing. Incentive theorists view extraneous rewards either as incentives for the biased scanning of arguments which will lead to acceptance of the role-played attitude, or else as cues for the arousal of such interfering responses as suspicion of the rewarder's motives. Thus these two positions usually lead to opposite predictions about the effects of different levels of reward for role playing. In few other areas is the contrast between dissonance theory and incentive theory so clearly drawn. . . .

PRINCIPAL EXPERIMENTAL STUDIES

Initial Dissonance Evidence

Prior to Festinger and Carlsmith (1959), only Kelman (1953) had varied incentive levels in a role-playing study. He asked school-children to write essays (favoring certain comic-book heroes) which were, on the whole, opposed to the children's own opinions. One group ("low restriction") was told that five class members would get a free movie ticket for writing the counter-attitudinal essay; another group ("high restriction") was told that every member of the class would get the movie ticket as well as time off from class and a free book for writing the essay. After the essays were written, the low-restriction group showed greater attitude change in the direction of the role-played position.

One might think that a 100% chance to get a movie ticket *and* a book is of greater incentive value than a less than 10% chance to get a movie ticket alone. Festinger (1957, pp. 112–120) interpreted the study in just this way in his extensive reanalysis of Kelman's findings. Festinger did not even use Kelman's terms, low restriction and high restriction, to describe the experimental conditions; instead, he called them "low incentive" and "high incentive." Festinger concluded that the results were adequately explained by dissonance theory: high-incentive subjects' dissonance at counter-attitudinal role playing was reduced by "the knowledge of the rewards they were to get," while low-incentive subjects had no recourse to reduce their dissonance except through "a large amount of change in private opinion." Brehm (1960) also concluded that Kelman's results were "consistent with dissonance theory," as did Cohen (1964): "though he [Kelman] did not frame his research in terms of dissonance, the results seem to be well accounted for by dissonance theory [p. 85]."

However, Kelman had good reason to avoid the terms high incentive and low incentive in describing his experimental conditions. In what Festinger called the high-incentive group, everyone was promised a reward as long as he performed the role-playing task competently, and any suggestion of competition or intense effort was avoided: "Everyone here can do a job that will be good enough. Just try your best. I have enough passes for everyone in the class, and I am sure that everyone can get one." In what Festinger called the low-incentive group, competition was not overtly stressed but implied: "I think everyone here can do a good enough job. But, as I said, only five of you can get the passes." According to Kelman, the low-restriction subjects "seemed to interpret this as a competitive situation, in which attainment of the prize depended on the quality of their performance," and he further suggested that "in the Low Restriction group the incentive 'seemed' greater to the Ss because only five in a class could get the reward." Thus the stage was set for the low-restriction group to enter more enthusiastically into the role-playing assignment, to do not only a good enough job but a better job than nearly all their classmates. No investigation was made to find whether dissonance reduction or the competitive striving for a free movie ticket was uppermost in their minds at the time of the essay writing, but postexperiment ratings of essays, showing low-restriction subjects' superior performance, strongly suggested that they did indeed role-play with more enthusiasm or more care than the high-restriction subjects.

Further, the high-restriction group's instructions implied that everyone *must* write the essay opposed to personal opinion, or gain the displeasure of classmates: "If everyone here just tries his best to write good essays in which he favors jungle stories, then the whole class will get passes . . . and your whole class can go together." Such coercion could be interpreted as another element consonant with counter-attitudinal advocacy, serving to reduce dissonance further. The high-restriction subjects seemed to have felt it instead as an annoyance, since they later reported having felt significantly more interfering responses during the essay writing, and viewed the experimenter as significantly less friendly, than did low-restriction subjects.

The phenomena displayed here sound not as though the low-restriction subjects were striving for a prompt and efficient reduction of unpleasant dissonance, but rather as though the nature of the incentives presented to them elicited more of the attitude-change processes stressed by incentive theory, and fewer of the processes which interfere with attitude change, than did the incentives presented in the high-restriction condition. As Kelman (1953) himself suggested.

It seems justifiable to conclude that conditions favorable to change are those in which conformity [in writing the counter-attitudinal essay] is accompanied by implicit supporting responses, and conditions unfavorable to change are those in which conformity is accompanied by implicit interfering responses [p. 211].

Brehm (1960, p. 169) has noted that certain complications, such as subject self-selection in deciding whether to write the counter-attitudinal essay, weaken Kelman's study as support for any general theoretical position. But Festinger's reinterpretation appears unlikely, and an incentive interpretation (similar to Kelman's own) appears more satisfactory, when attention is directed to the competitive behavior elicited by the low-restriction incentive and the interfering responses elicited by the high-restriction incentive.

Festinger and Carlsmith's (1959) study is by now a familiar one. Male college students participated in an extremely boring task, and then they were temporarily "hired" for either $20 or $1 to dupe a female student into thinking the task would be interesting. The $1 condition elicited a significantly more positive attitude toward the boring task, postexperimentally, than did the $20 condition. In interpreting the results as favorable to dissonance theory, Festinger again (as in his reinterpretation of Kelman) viewed the connotations of a valuable reward rather narrowly: The greater the absolute value of the reward, the more consonant it appears in relation to any behavior a person does to get it, and the more dissonance reducing it therefore is. But money has additional implications in our culture, as might have been more obvious had Festinger rewarded subjects with one piece of silver versus thirty pieces of silver, rather than $1 versus $20.

Kelman (1953) suggested that subjects in his study's high-restriction condition (called high-incentive by Festinger) might have felt that the experimenter was bribing them for his own ends, or might have been suspicious that he "had something up his sleeve." Along similar lines, Janis and Gilmore (1965) have pointed out that

in the Festinger and Carlsmith experiment, the students were informed by the experimenter that he regularly does not tell the truth to his subjects about the purpose of his study and the role-playing task consisted of helping to perpetuate this type of deceit by lying to a fellow student who would be the next subject [p. 25].

Under such circumstances, according to Janis and Gilmore, a larger reward might

stimulate a considerable increase in suspiciousness, guilt, or other negative feelings to such an extent that the positive incentive value accruing to the increased financial reward could be outweighed and thus produce less attitude change than a lower amount of reward [p. 26].

These negative feelings would probably be increased further by the behavior of Festinger and Carlsmith's experimenter, described in the original paper as displaying "confusion," "uncertainty," and "a degree of embarrassment" in asking the subject to assist in the deception. Such confusion, uncertainty, and embarrassment might appear to be an academic psychologist's normal demeanor to the subject promised $1, but the same behavior could assume sinister overtones when accompanied by a $20 bill.

Thus the results of the Festinger and Carlsmith study, presented as clear support for a nonobvious dissonance theory prediction (the higher the reward, the less attitude change), may be readily explained by an incentive theory approach, assuming that subjects interpreted the large reward in any of the ways suggested above. At least two other explanations of Festinger and Carlsmith's result have been advanced, by Chapanis and Chapanis (1964) and by Rosenberg (1965).

Chapanis and Chapanis stressed possible reactions of incredulity to the $20 reward, causing subjects to view the entire situation as implausible. (Another balance theory of attitude change, Osgood and Tannenbaum's 1955 congruity theory, includes a built-in correction for certain incredulity reactions. Such a correction is not made explicit in dissonance theory.) Festinger and Carlsmith did tell subjects that the reward obligated them to be on call in case of later need, but the terms of obligation were so ambiguous that rather than making the $20 more plausible, they could have been interpreted by subjects as implying additional $20 rewards for further 2-minute performances. Unfortunately, subjects were not questioned on this point.

Cohen (Brehm & Cohen, 1962, pp. 73–78) attempted to vitiate the incredulity criticism by lowering the size of the reward in a similar experiment. In asking students to write an essay supporting a police force accused of brutality toward students, he offered a range of rewards from $.50 to $10. Significant differences were found in subsequent attitudes even between $.50 and $1 conditions, with the $.50 reward inducing more favorable attitudes than the $1 reward, as per dissonance theory predictions. It does seem unlikely that a $1 reward would arouse feelings of incredulity among Yale undergraduates. However, Brehm and Cohen (1962) used these findings to discount not only incredulity effects, but other types of emotional interference as well:

The idea that at high incentive levels, subjects might feel that something is "wrong," and that the suspicion they experience could reflect itself in resistance against changing their attitudes, is not relevant for a comparison between, for example, $1.00 and $.50 conditions. No more suspicion can be attached to a $1.00 offer than to a $.50 offer [p. 77].

It could as well be said that no more dissonance-reducing properties can be attached to a $1 offer than to a $.50 offer, in which case Brehm and Cohen would have no explanation for Cohen's results. If *any* differential implications can be attached to a $.50 reward versus a $1 reward, as Brehm and Cohen did when they speculated that the $1 reward was more dissonance reducing, then it is likely that the $1 reward could induce more suspicion of the experimenter's motives, more guilt at "selling out" one's fellow students, or more of various other interfering responses than the $.50 reward, as long as the experimental situation presents opportunities for the arousal of guilt, suspicion, or other negative affects. Conditions for the arousal of negative affects were amply provided by the experimenter's identification of himself as a "member of a research team from the Institute of Human Relations," which was "concerned with the recent riots" that prompted police to rough up students; his mention that "the University administration and the public are very concerned with the issue"; and his statement in this context that he wanted essays favoring the police side, since "we think we know pretty much how you feel about the students' rights in this matter." It seems entirely possible that students whose suspicions were aroused even slightly would wonder from these statements whether or not the experimenter's main purpose was to whitewash the police, and a $1 reward could make such suspicions more salient than a $.50 reward. Thus, although Chapanis and Chapanis' incredulity explanation (which still may account, at least in part, for Festinger and Carlsmith's results) does not seem to apply to Cohen's findings, the incentive theory approach remains quite applicable.

Alternative Experimental Evidence

Rosenberg (1965) was also concerned with the effects of suspicion and guilt, as well as the effects of general concern about being psychologically evaluated, in the variable-incentive role-playing situation. But he felt that the effect of the negative feelings aroused by a high reward is likely to be expressed most directly through subjects' conscious distortion of attitudes at the time of the post-manipulation attitude measure (to show the experimenter they cannot be bribed, or to wreck his study), rather than through interference with the attitude-change process during role playing. He applied this interpretation to Cohen's results, and suggested that it may apply to Festinger and Carlsmith's results as well, although in their study a different person than the experimenter measured postmanipulation attitudes. Rosenberg conducted an experiment similar to Cohen's (involving students' writing counter-attitudinal essays in favor of an unpopular faculty decision on athletics), but was careful to have subjects' postessay attitudes measured by someone who appeared considerably more unconnected with the role-playing task than was the case in either Cohen's or Festinger and Carlsmith's study. This separation of experimenter and attitude measurer would presumably diminish the effects of evaluation apprehension and negative affect directed at the experimenter, and would allow the different monetary incentives to work straightforwardly in promoting the consideration and stabilization of new attitudes. Rosenberg's findings supported his hypotheses: As monetary incentive increased, attitudes became significantly more favorable to the role-played position.

The positions of Chapanis and Chapanis, Rosenberg, and Janis and his collaborators need not be mutually exclusive. Incredulity and evaluation apprehension are both interfering affects within

the terms of incentive theory. Incentive theory emphasizes interference during the *process* of role playing, essentially without the
subject's control, rather than during the *measurement* of role-
playing effects through the conscious reactions of the subject;
but it is entirely possible that conscious distortion of expressed
attitudes has contributed further to the measured lack of attitude
change in at least some high-incentive role-playing conditions.
(Rosenberg, 1966, has himself noted the similarities between his
and Janis' position, though he continues to emphasize conscious
reactions to measurement.) On the other hand, modifications
made by Rosenberg in Cohen's procedure suggest an interpretation of Rosenberg's results in incentive theory terms alone.
Though Rosenberg gave subjects an explanation of the purpose of
their role playing "modeled word-for-word upon that used in the
earlier experiment," his study was conducted in a more innocuous
context (an education graduate student doing a "little experiment") than Cohen's, and at a considerably greater distance in
time from the controversy around which the role playing cen-
tered. Both these circumstances are likely to have reduced interfering responses during the role playing itself.

Rosenberg's suggestions also strengthen the incentive interpretation of previous studies in that he stressed the disturbing
aspects for many individuals of *any* psychological experiment or
similar experience. In such situations, again, the presentation of
a reward may well have unpleasant implications. This would
probably be particularly true in a counter-attitudinal role-playing
situation, where subjects are asked to perform a peculiar and
possibly anxiety-provoking behavior: arguing strongly against
their own personal beliefs. Care must be taken to avoid introduc-
ing other disturbing elements into the situation or to offset those
already present, and this has not been done in most such studies.

Two experiments have been designed specifically to test incentive theory formulations about role playing—Janis and Gilmore
(1965) and Elms and Janis (1965). Their general design was
similar: Students were asked to role-play counter-attitudinally in
return for either a high or a low monetary reward. Some subjects
were told that the sponsor of the role playing was an organization
to which students might react negatively, while other subjects
were told that the sponsor was an organization to which students
might react positively. An attitude measure was given by the

experimenter immediately after the role-playing task was completed. In Elms and Janis' study, a pre-role-playing measure of attitude was given as well. In other words, these studies were designed to vary experimentally the opportunity for arousal of interfering responses by monetary reward, a variable which had not been controlled experimentally in dissonance-oriented studies.

In Janis and Gilmore's study, subjects were asked to write essays in favor of adding an unpopular science and math requirement to the undergraduate curriculum. The positive sponsor was a national research organization "working on behalf of a number of the leading universities in the United States," and the negative sponsor was "a new publishing company . . . trying to build up the market for its science textbooks." Reward levels were $1 and $20. The positive-sponsorship condition yielded significantly more positive attitudes than the negative-sponsorship condition, thus tending to support incentive theory rather than dissonance theory (since the latter condition should have generated more dissonance), but the variations in reward yielded no clear results. The lack of differences between attitudes at different reward levels may have been a function of student views of the sponsors: A textbook firm interested in making money, though regarded less favorably than "the leading universities," may not have been a clearly negative, guilt- or suspicion-arousing sponsor among most undergraduates, and the consortium of universities may not have been an altogether positive sponsor. Janis and Gilmore did find from subject interviews that the high reward in both sponsorship conditions was not perceived as unambiguously consonant with subjects' role-playing behavior but was "a source of vague suspicions, guilt, or conflict" for some subjects (though it was a strong positive incentive for others).

Elms and Janis (1965) used sponsorship variables whose positive and negative qualities were probably more sharply differentiated than those in Janis and Gilmore's study. Subjects were asked to write essays in favor of sending American students to study "the Soviet system of government and the history of communism" in a Russian university for 4 years. In the negative-sponsorship condition, the Soviet Embassy was said to be the sponsor of the essay writing; in the positive-sponsorship condition, the sponsor was said to be the United States State Department. Rewards ranged from $.50 to $10. In the positive-sponsorship condition, high-reward role players showed significantly greater positive attitude change than low-reward role players; in the negative-sponsorship condition, low-reward role players showed more (though not significantly more) positive attitude change than high-reward role players. Here the incentive theory prediction appears clearly supported, and the dissonance theory prediction contradicted: When rewards are presented under circumstances where they do not arouse emotional responses which interfere with attitude-change processes, highly rewarded role playing produces *more* attitude change than when the rewards are low. This finding suggests that previous instances where rewards appeared to work in an opposite direction may be viewed as similar to the negative-sponsorship condition of the Elms and Janis study.

Brehm (1965) has criticized the Elms and Janis study as an unfair test of dissonance theory, but, interestingly, he said nothing at all about the positive-sponsorship condition, which presents the major contradiction to dissonance theory. He felt that the negative-sponsorship condition offered an unfair test of dissonance predictions because the position of the essay was so distasteful, and the negative sponsorship made it even more so, that subjects would have been reluctant to change their attitudes as a means of reducing the dissonance aroused by their essay-writing behavior; instead, they might have reduced dissonance in all sorts of other ways, such as admitting that they were "wrong to write the essay." This resort to alternative ways of reducing dissonance, the choice of which cannot be predicted but only guessed post hoc, would of course make it possible for Brehm to dismiss any and all disconfirmations of dissonance theory. It is not even necessary in this case, since Brehm uses it only against the negative-sponsorship results, where the direction of the attitude-change differences can be explained by *either* dissonance theory or the incentive theory hypothesis that a large reward in a negatively toned situation may impede attitude change more than a small reward. The results of the positive-sponsorship condition, however, apparently cannot be accounted for easily by dissonance theory, and Brehm simply did not mention the results of this condition. Brehm's other major criticism of the Elms and Janis study was that persons who are not dissonance theorists may not be able to appreciate the theory's subtleties sufficiently to devise adequate tests of it:

Perhaps in practice the person best equipped to disprove a dissonance hypothesis is one who has been successful in supporting it. When such a person designs a test, he is more likely to do so in a sensitive and adequate way and is thus in a position to produce and to recognize disconfirming evidence when it appears [p. 64].

It need hardly be said that this criticism is in itself invalid. It is to be hoped that advocates of dissonance theory (or any other theory) can make their hypotheses and assumptions sufficiently explicit to permit independent tests by other interested researchers.

Experimentally Based Dissonance Reinterpretations

Nuttin (1966) has also raised the possibility that high monetary rewards may introduce a disturbing element into the role-playing situation, but he interpreted such effects within a somewhat revised dissonance-theory framework. Nuttin had subjects perform a boring task, and then asked some subjects to convince a stooge that the task was interesting ("dissonant compliance"), as in Festinger and Carlsmith's study. Other subjects were asked to convince the stooge that the task was boring and time wasting ("consonant compliance"). Subjects were given no reward, a small reward, or a large reward for so arguing. An individual supposedly not connected with the study measured postexperiment attitudes. In the dissonant-compliance condition, low-reward subjects reported finding the task more enjoyable than did high-reward subjects. The difference was not significant, but was in the same direction as Festinger and Carlsmith's results. In the consonant-compliance condition, low-reward subjects showed even more favorable attitudes than high-reward subjects. Nuttin discounted any influence of the role playing on these attitudinal differences, and suggested instead that the high reward was itself dissonant with the small effort exerted to get it. To reduce this dissonance, high-reward subjects in both dissonant-compliance and consonant-compliance conditions presumably changed their attitudes to make the experimental task more unpleasant in recollection and thus more deserving of reward.

This dissonance-oriented explanation of Nuttin's results is certainly a possibility, though it is rather different from Festinger and Carlsmith's explanation of their own results. However, it apparently cannot account for such findings as the greater attitude change in Elms and Janis' (1965) high-reward positive-sponsorship condition. On the other hand, if one notes how Nuttin's results relate to the content of his role-playing variations, the results in high- and low-reward conditions are strikingly similar to the pattern which would be predicted by incentive theory: Dissonant-compliance subjects, told that the experimenter frequently lies to his subjects and asked to assist in the lying themselves, endorse their role-played position *less,* the more money they are given. Consonant-compliance subjects, told that the experimenter often warns his subjects of how boring the experimental task will be and asked to help him warn other subjects, endorse their role-played position *more*, the more money they are given. As in Elms and Janis' study, a higher reward seemed to promote role-playing-induced attitude change in benevolent circumstances but apparently interfered with such change when it was associated with suspicious or deceitful manipulations. (Not all of Nuttin's results, however, can be as readily explained by incentive theory; no-reward subjects' attitudes do not obviously fit either an incentive theory or a dissonance theory pattern.)

Carlsmith, Collins, and Helmreich (1966) have attempted to maintain a dissonance theory approach to role-playing effects in a rather different way than Nuttin. They argued that perhaps since in such studies as Elms and Janis and Janis and Gilmore the role-playing task was written rather than spoken and was anonymous, subjects did not feel committed and thus did not experience dissonance. This is a rather drastic criticism, since it eliminates both the Cohen (Brehm & Cohen, 1962) and Kelman (1953) studies as support for dissonance theory (though Carlsmith et al. continue to claim the Cohen study as strong support), as well as most of the dissonance studies using different levels of "justification" for role playing, to be discussed briefly later. Only a very small number of studies using face-to-face communication, such as Festinger and Carlsmith's, would be left standing.

It is difficult to determine whether any experimental situation arouses dissonance, since dissonance theorists have so far failed to develop a means to measure the presence or intensity of dissonance, independent of the dissonance-reducing behavior which follows its occurrence. But Carlsmith et al.'s criticism does not distinguish such studies as Elms and Janis from a variety of studies in which the dissonance theorists themselves have claimed the arousal of dissonance. In the Elms and Janis study, subjects were not simply asked whether they had "the intellectual ability to see some arguments on the opposite side of the issue," as Carlsmith et al. suggested. Subjects were explicitly informed that "the arguments you write down will almost certainly be included" in a pamphlet to be distributed to college students all over the United States. The effect of their essays would thus be to persuade large numbers of students to support a plan which the subjects themselves did not support, to send American students to Russia to be fed Communist propaganda for 4 years. Once subjects began writing the role-played essays, they were committed to an anonymous but undeniable form of support for this plan, which was dissonant with their own beliefs; they could not stop manufacture or distribution of the pamphlets once they had written the essays. Even Brehm (1965) stated,

It is likely that dissonance was aroused, as Elms and Janis endeavored to show, because it seems that Ss in the unfavorable sponsorship condition were resistant to writing the essay and were quite uncomfortable about doing so [p. 62].

Brehm did not discuss the question of dissonance arousal in the favorable-sponsorship condition, but there, too, the writing of an essay against one's own beliefs, to be used in opposition to one's beliefs in a persuasive pamphlet directed at millions of college students, seems to fall under every definition of dissonance published up to the date of Carlsmith et al.'s paper.

Having postulated a qualitative difference between face-to-face and written role playing, Carlsmith et al. set out to verify it empirically. Again, subjects were asked to do a boring task for an hour, then to argue convincingly that the task was really interesting. Subjects were paid $.50, $1.50, or $5, and role-played either by face-to-face verbal communication or by essay writing. However, Carlsmith et al. did not simply ask some subjects to deliver a brief spoken persuasive communication face-to-face to another subject and ask other subjects to spend the same amount of time in writing an anonymous persuasive communication to be used for the same purpose in the same situation. Instead, they had the face-to-face role players deliver a *2-minute* persuasive statement to a *female subject* (a confederate; all true subjects were males) under *urgent* time pressure, with the confederate quoting a friend's direct *contradiction* of the subject's role-played position. After 2 minutes, the subject's performance was *interrupted* by the experimenter. Essay role players, on the other hand, were asked to write a *5–10-minute* essay (they were actually allowed up to 17 minutes), which would never be read by *any other subjects* (female or male), but would be read some time later by the experimenters "briefly to get some ideas and phrases for an essay which we, the experimenters, will write." The subject was allowed to *choose his own* termination time for the task, unless he went over 15 minutes. The authors themselves acknowledged that their face-to-face role players "performed under somewhat more 'hectic' or crisis circumstances" than essay role players. What Carlsmith et al. may actually have established was not a simple contrast between face-to-face oral and anonymous written role playing, but a contrast between a condition which offered many instigations for the development of negative affect (guilt, suspicion, hostility), and a condition which offered few instigations for the arousal of negative affect. They accomplished this by varying the behavioral context of role playing, rather than by varying the sponsorship of the role playing as in Elms and Janis or Janis and Gilmore, but the effect on subjects may have been quite similar. It is thus unsurprising that their results were similar to those of Elms and Janis: Attitudes became more positive with increasing reward level in the condition presenting few instigations for negative affect arousal (essay writing), and became more negative with increasing reward level in the condition presenting more instigations for negative affect arousal (face-to-face).

Carlsmith et al. preferred a straight dissonance theory explanation of the face-to-face role-playing results and were reluctant to accept an incentive theory explanation even of the essay-writing condition's results, for which they could provide no dissonance theory interpretation. They suggested that the incentive interpretation is inadequate because it should involve superior performance in the high-incentive conditions and such superior performance did not appear in their performance measures. Unfortunately, as they themselves indicated, it is difficult to measure quality of performance meaningfully when the important behavior may occur internally. The biased scanning emphasized in incentive theory as being crucial to role playing presumably includes not only direct compliance with role-playing instructions but also "open-minded cognitive exploration" of the incentive value of improvised arguments (Elms & Janis, 1965). Detection of the latter may necessitate the use of considerably more subtle performance measures than any which have so far been employed in role-playing studies. (That it is possible to write good essays while rejecting their content is indicated by Collins and Helmreich's 1966 study, where "consequence" subjects wrote significantly better essays than "process" subjects but much more frequently indicated that they personally did not believe the statements they had written.) The relatively crude performance measures which have been used so far have not supported either dissonance theory or incentive theory consistently (cf. Brehm & Cohen, 1962, pp. 117–121; Collins & Helmreich, 1966, pp. 21–23; Elms & Janis, 1965, pp. 58–59).

Carlsmith et al. suggested instead that the essay role players' good mood, engendered by being paid, "generalized to the task they had been doing," though the same presumably did not happen to face-to-face role players, who had all that damnable dissonance to deal with. However, the only measure of mood came after all role playing had been completed, and at that time the face-to-face role players' mood was virtually identical with the essay role players' mood, in the $.50 and $5 conditions. (Face-to-face control subjects, who presumably had no dissonance to reduce, showed a noticeably fouler mood than essay controls; the same was true in the $1.50 experimental conditions.) It is difficult to say what this measure of current mood, in a different situation and at a later time than the role playing, signifies; but it does not seem to provide a substantial alternative to an incentive theory explanation of the essay role-playing results.

Collins and Helmreich (1966) have noted that dissonance

theory discussions of role playing generally emphasize the *consequences* of the behavior, such as the subject's perception of the impression he has fostered upon his audience, while incentive theory discussions usually emphasize the *process* of role playing, involving such activities as biased scanning, in which the subject's internal responses while role playing act to change his attitudes. Collins and Helmreich conducted an experiment in which the experimenter's emphasis on the process or the consequences of role playing was varied along with monetary reward for role playing. Subjects were asked to taste a bitter liquid and evaluate its taste, then to write an essay on the liquid's positive attributes, then to taste a presumably different but actually identical liquid and evaluate *its* taste. The essay instructions emphasized either thinking carefully about the positive aspects of the liquid (process instructions) or writing a persuasive essay (consequence instructions). The variation in payment for the essay yielded no significant differences in attitude change, although these results were in the direction of either a dissonance theory or an interfering-negative-affect (incentive theory) interpretation. The major difference occurred between the consequence and process conditions: The latter yielded significantly greater attitude change than the former, in the direction of the role-played position. In fact, the consequence instructions yielded negative change, the process instructions positive change. (The mean in neither condition was, however, significantly different from the control mean of zero.)

Collins and Helmreich interpreted these results, buttressed by an internal analysis of essay quality, to mean that "the subject's *behavior* (what he actually does in the compliance situation) is related to the amount of attitude change which is produced," although they felt that perception of one's own dissonant stance may also elicit attitude change under some circumstances. Their conclusion may be counted as substantially in support of the incentive theory position concerning the importance of biased scanning. However, the consequence instructions may also have increased the likelihood of interfering emotional responses more than the process instructions, and this would alter the interpretation of the results somewhat. In the consequence instructions, the subject was told that the essay she was to write would be used to deceive someone else about the taste of the liquid samples. In the process instructions, the essays were said to be useful in getting ideas for future studies. In both conditions, subjects were told that the essay writing "isn't really what you signed up to do, but rather something extra that's really involved with a future experiment," and were paid $2 or $.50 for 10 minutes of essay writing, though they were paid only $1 for their total participation time of 45 minutes. Thus, the $2 reward might seem somewhat suspicious in both the process and the consequence conditions. It is likely to have been particularly effective in arousing negative affect in the consequence condition, and the attitude-change scores reflect this likelihood. Nonetheless, Collins and Helmreich's study is valuable in calling attention to a troublesome tendency in dissonance theory: the emphasis on a few end-products of role playing to the virtual exclusion of the internal processes without which overt role-playing behavior would be meaningless.

Collins and Helmreich's findings are complicated by a further study (Collins, 1966) using essentially the same design, but substituting electronic music for quinine water and emphasizing to subjects the truth versus the persuasiveness of the role-played essay, rather than the process versus the consequences of role playing. As Collins suggested, one might expect the emphasis on truth to yield results similar to the earlier process instructions and the emphasis on persuasiveness to yield results similar to consequence instructions, but the results were actually the reverse. For subjects run singly, "true" subjects showed slightly (but not significantly) more positive attitude change in the low- than in the high-incentive condition; "persuasive" subjects showed significantly more positive change in the high- than in the low-incentive condition. The basis for this result is not clear. It may simply have been that "persuasive" subjects felt less restricted in entertaining a variety of different positive arguments than the "true" subjects, who had to be careful to think only about true arguments. That is, Collins' "persuasive" instructions may have encouraged freer biased scanning than his "true" instructions.

The emphasis upon consequences rather than process was carried to its ultimate in a study by Bem (1965). His position was based on Skinner's analysis of verbal behavior rather than on dissonance theory, but the basic assumption was similar: The role player changes his attitudes not as a result of any internal process of reviewing the logic of arguments or anticipating the rewards that adoption of a particular attitude may bring, but rather as a result of seeing himself mouthing a particular position and bringing his concept of his internal attitudes into consonance with this external behavior. According to Festinger, the person role playing for a high reward should show little attitude change because the dissonance aroused in role playing is relieved by the $20, which is highly consonant with his role-playing behavior. According to Bem, this role player shows little attitude change because he perceives his role playing as *manding* behavior, aimed at getting the $20, rather than *tacting* behavior, aimed at giving an accurate description of his own feelings.

Bem felt that an outside observer should be as adept as the role player himself in analyzing the presence of tacting or manding in role-playing situations, since the outside observer and the role player both presumably depend only on the role player's external behavior for their assessment of his internal attitudes. To test this hypothesis, Bem presented subjects with a written description of Cohen's (Brehm & Cohen, 1962) general experimental procedure and asked them to guess the attitude of a single student participant in one condition of the experiment. As he had predicted, Bem's results were very similar to Cohen's and might therefore be claimed by dissonance theorists as additional support for their position (though the results do call into question the "nonobviousness" of dissonance theory predictions).

The same criticisms cannot be made of Bem's study as were made earlier of Cohen's, since Bem did not mention any of Cohen's stated "justifications" for the role playing except that it was part of a research project for the Institute of Human Relations. (This omission by itself makes comparison with Cohen's study difficult.) An obvious alternative to Bem's own explanation of his results comes from Bem's stress on having each of his subjects judge "one—and only one—volunteer in one of Cohen's experimental conditions." After telling his subjects that "most of the student body" at Yale was "extremely negative toward the police and their actions," Bem said that the experimenter in Cohen's study "selected a student at random" and asked him to write a pro-police essay for either $.50 or $1. "The student who was asked agreed to do so, and wrote such an essay." Bem's subjects were then asked, "From this description, estimate as well as you can the actual opinion of the student who was willing to write the essay." From all this, Bem's subjects might well have concluded that the student in Cohen's study favored the New Haven police *before* participating in the study, but just happened to be chosen at random from a generally anti-police student body. If many of Bem's subjects reached this conclusion, it would seriously weaken the usefulness of his results as support for either a Skinnerian or a dissonance approach to attitude change, since it does not involve attitude change at all—only an inference by his subjects of biased sampling. That a number of Bem's subjects may have indeed reasoned in this way is suggested not only by his use of statements involving a single student, who agreed to write the essay for apparently no good reason (particularly in the $.50 condition), but also by Bem's instructions to estimate "the actual opinion of the student who was willing to write the essay"—not necessarily his opinion *after* writing this essay, but simply his opinion, perhaps before, perhaps after, perhaps always.

Since Bem did not provide any data on his subjects' reasons for assigning a particular attitude to the Cohen subject, it is not possible to accept the biased-sampling explanation for his results with any certainty. However, the results of a study by Cayley and Elms (1968) suggest that Bem's results may have been determined at least partially by this factor. Cayley and Elms, using Bem's general procedure, asked subjects to predict the opinion of subjects in Rosenberg's (1965) study. Subjects were then asked why they thought the Rosenberg subjects would hold this particular attitude. Subjects were asked to predict the average of a number of students' opinions, rather than only one student's opinion, and this may have lowered the number of subjects who reasoned that the sample was biased. Nonetheless, considerably more subjects predicting the results of Rosenberg's no-reward and $1 conditions than those predicting his $5 condition results said his role-playing subjects must have been in favor of the role-played position before writing the essay, since otherwise they would not have written it. (Most other subjects stated that the process of role playing, for example, consideration of opposing arguments, changed the students' opinions favorably; only three reasoned similarly to Bem or Festinger.)

ADDITIONAL EVIDENCE

Several other studies, which for one reason or another do not bear directly on the adequacy of dissonance theory versus incentive theory in explaining the effects of variable rewards on role playing, are sufficiently relevant to be discussed briefly.

Scott (1957, 1959) used a competitive debate setting to study the effects of reinforcement on role-played opinions. His first study cannot be applied to the present discussion, since the "reinforcement" he used was a class vote for the winner of a debate; the vote could be interpreted as exerting pressure for conformity, or serving as consensual validation for the role players' opinion statements, rather than as being a social reward. In Scott's second study, however, debaters were promised $20 for winning a series of three debates and nothing for losing, and this contrast between a $20 reward and a zero reward for role playing resembles conditions in several of the studies already discussed. Winners of the first debate round were determined randomly; winning increased the chance of getting the $20, while losing eliminated that chance completely.

Scott found that among role players who were assigned to debate against their own position, debate winners showed significantly more attitude change toward the role-played position than did losers. This finding is in the direction of incentive theory formulations and opposite to dissonance theory hypotheses. (Neither the assignment to debate a position different from one's own nor the promised $20 prize should have aroused suspicion or similar negative responses since neither is unusual in college debating contests. Nor should the stated purpose of the debates, "to see how well people can present opinions they don't actually hold, and how well their opponents can judge their own true attitudes.") However, these results cannot be claimed as clear-cut support for incentive theory. First, it might be argued that since participants were not allowed to choose a position on the debate topic, they would feel little dissonance at debating against their own positions. This is unlikely since they did have the choice of participating or not, and even skilled intercollegiate debaters often feel "dissonance" when debating against their own position. A more serious drawback to Scott's study is that in addition to rendering a win-loss verdict, the three judges of each debate made comments about each debater's performance, in support of their decision. Although they did not comment on the content of the debates, their statements may again have been perceived by winners as social support for the views they had advocated; and thus the incentive variable may have been confounded with other variables which do not relate directly to the problem at hand.

That this criticism by judges of one's performance can have an important effect on one's opinions, independent of material rewards, was indicated by Wallace's (1966) debating study. Wallace had a two-person audience present false judgments to debaters concerning their speech content and performance. Those who spoke against their own position and then were praised only for their performance showed significantly greater attitude change toward the role-played position than those who were praised only for their content or for neither content nor performance. Wallace noted several possible explanations, none entirely satisfactory, for his results, but the results do suggest that studies such as Scott's involve more than response reinforcement alone.

Greenbaum (1966) had subjects improvise a counter-attitudinal speech on civil defense and varied reinforcement level by having a tape-recorded "speech professor" give the speech a rating, ranging from "strong negative" to "strong positive," with reasons supplied for the ratings. Greenbaum found no significant effect of this kind of "reinforcement" on attitudes. He tentatively attributed the significant relationships between attitude change and reinforcement in other role-playing studies to social psychology's current bête noire, demand characteristics: Subjects wish "to appear consistent to the experimenter who had 'rewarded' them," so they report their own attitude as similar to the attitude they have role-played. Greenbaum felt that he had controlled such demand characteristics by separating attitude measurement from the role-playing situation. However, most other experimenters in this area have done likewise to a greater or lesser extent. If demand characteristics have contaminated the results of very many of the studies reviewed here, it is unlikely that they have done so in the simple fashion suggested by Greenbaum.

Goldstein and McGinnies (1964) attempted to vary social reinforcement for role playing by having prochurch subjects read an antichurch essay to a small audience, whose members then discussed the essay with the role player. The audience was instructed to act either prochurch, neutral, or antichurch. Role players with an antichurch audience showed significantly greater attitude change in an antichurch direction than did those having a prochurch audience. Goldstein and McGinnies interpreted these results as showing the positive influence of social reinforcement on role-played attitudes. The study could thus be counted as support for an incentive position, though it could also be argued that the antichurch audience aroused more dissonance concerning the subject's own beliefs, which he reduced by changing his opinions. However, a simpler explanation than either of these is that the audience, during the post-role-playing discussion, delivered additional persuasive messages to the role player, or advanced pressure for conformity, which in the antichurch-audience condition supported the role-played position.

Sarbin and Allen (1964) had an audience give positive "social reinforcement" (e.g., smiles) or negative "social reinforcement" (e.g., frowns) while subjects spoke against their own positions. Sarbin and Allen found no significant differences between the two conditions, though role players receiving negative reinforcement showed slightly more attitude change toward the role-played position than did those receiving positive reinforcement. This might be taken as weak support for dissonance theory, but Sarbin and Allen suggested instead that the results occurred as they did because role players felt more highly motivated to convince a negative audience than a positive one, "seemed to be *more involved* and to engage in more improvisation"—attitude-change-producing processes emphasized by incentive theory rather than dissonance theory.

Bostrum, Vlandis, and Rosenbaum (1961) assigned high or low grades randomly to students for writing an essay opposed to their own position. Students receiving an A changed significantly more toward the position advocated by the essay than did those receiving a D—again, a result apparently harder to explain from a dissonance standpoint than from an incentive standpoint. However, a D has rather different implications for most students than a low money reward. The D students may have been showing their resentment toward their instructor on the attitude posttest, and the A students their pleasure, rather than evincing any real differences in attitude change. . . .

CONCLUSION

In analyzing these studies, incentive theory appears to be adequate to explain most attitude-change results in role-playing experiments where varying rewards or incentives were used. Although dissonance theory also appears to offer a cogent explanation for some results, its special assumptions seem generally unnecessary and often unuseful in dealing with this particular body of data. This is not to say that dissonance theory is of no use at all, or to dismiss it completely. No doubt many people develop a sensitivity to dissonance or inconsistency and feel a need to reduce or eliminate it as a result of various experiences where consistency has been rewarded and inconsistency punished. Dissonance reduction itself can thus be subsumed under incentive theory (although the reverse cannot be easily argued). Janis has developed this point in more detail in his discussion of the "illusion of commitment" as a basis for incentive effects under certain conditions (Janis, 1968). It seems doubtful, however, that this acquired drive toward consistency dominates the attitude-change processes of most individuals; attitudes serve a variety of needs, some of them presumably more important than a need to be consistent (cf. Katz, 1960; Smith, Bruner, & White, 1956). Dissonance reduction may occasionally account for attitude change in a role-playing experiment, but the available evidence does not support the idea that this frequently or always happens. The more cautious claims about dissonance theory's broad applicability (Aronson, 1966; Brehm, 1965; Carlsmith et al., 1966) seem also to be more realistic.

It should be clear, however, that the experimentation done to date cannot support *any* theoretical position unequivocally. Too often have extraneous variables confounded experimental results; too often have experimenters failed to collect all the information needed to evaluate their hypotheses. It should not be necessary to warn future experimenters to control for the possibility that money or other rewards may possess multiple connotations which can influence attitude change in unexpected directions. It seems desirable that even dissonance theorists or behaviorists who do not feel that the silent review of arguments is crucial to attitude change through role playing should question subjects closely about their own perceptions of what happened to them during the role-playing process. It would also be very helpful if someone were to develop a good measure for the occurrence of dissonance, so that both dissonance theorists and incentive theorists could know to what degree they had either aroused dissonance or avoided it in any particular experimental condition. The competing claims of incentive theory, dissonance theory, and other theories which may appear relevant cannot be completely evaluated until additional research using such procedures is performed.

The appeal of the dissonance explanation for incentive effects on role playing is not surprising; it is simple, and it appears to contradict common sense as well as attitude-change theories based on a major theoretical tradition in psychology. But when one considers the ultimate implications of the dissonance position—that we are most likely to retain a temporarily adopted attitude when it is least supportive of our personal interests, and most likely to reject a new attitude when it would be most functional (except when it performs the function of reducing dissonance)—it may be reassuring to find that situations complying with the dissonance formulation are few, and that most such attitude-change situations conform adequately to the tenets of incentive theory.

14

Decision Freedom as a Determinant of the Role of Incentive Magnitude in Attitude Change[1]

Darwyn E. Linder, Joel Cooper, and
Edward E. Jones

According to one writer (Insko, 1967), the findings reported here are "the best news that the supporters of dissonance theory have heard in some time." Specifically, the authors have reexamined some of the conditions presumably necessary for dissonance arousal and have shown that a lack of such conditions in certain previous studies could have accounted for results apparently contradictory to dissonance theory. Linder, Cooper, and Jones still have proposed no way to measure dissonance arousal directly, so their conclusions remain somewhat inferential; but the methods they use to support their inferences are worthy of attention in future research. (An introductory summary of several studies included in this volume is omitted.)

This selection is reprinted with abridgments from the Journal of Personality and Social Psychology, *1967, 6, 245–254, with permission of the senior author and the American Psychological Association.*

The major focus of these studies has been the relationship between the amount of incentive offered and subsequent attitude change, but a clear prediction from dissonance theory cannot be made unless the subject makes his decision to comply *after* con-

[1] This experiment was facilitated by National Science Foundation Grant 8857. We are indebted to H. B. Gerard for his valuable suggestions.

sidering the incentive magnitude. The incentive must be one of the conditions potentially affecting the decision to comply rather than a reward for having already so decided.

Both Cohen (1962) and Rosenberg (1965) reported that they took care to assure subjects that the decision to write the essay was entirely their own. It may be argued, however, that Rosenberg's major alteration of Cohen's procedure, the separation of the compliant-behavior setting from the attitude-measurement setting to eliminate evaluation apprehension, reduced his subjects' freedom not to comply. When Rosenberg's subjects arrived for the experiment, they found him busily engaged and were given the option of waiting for "15 or 20 minutes" or, as an afterthought, participating in "another little experiment some graduate student in education is doing." Professing to know little about this other experiment except that it "has to do with attitudes" and "I gather they have some research funds," Rosenberg did not pressure the subject into a decision, but let him decide for himself whether he wanted to participate or wait. Having made the decision to participate, each subject further strengthened his commitment by walking to the location of the second experiment. The choice then offered by the second experimenter was considerably less than a free one. Being already effectively committed, the subject would be more likely to treat the subsequent monetary offering as a bonus for prior compliance than as one of the conditions to be considered in making a free choice.

If the preceding argument is correct, Rosenberg's findings cannot be compared with Cohen's because different conditions prevailed in the two experiments when the counterattitudinal essays were written. Rosenberg inadvertently made it difficult for subjects not to comply and found that degree of attitude change was positively related to incentive magnitude, in support of a reinforcement position or an affective-cognitive consistency model (Rosenberg, 1960). In contrast to this, Cohen's procedure presented the choice not to comply as a more viable alternative and found that attitude change was inversely related to incentive magnitude, in support of a derivation from dissonance theory. A meaningful resolution of these discrepant findings would be to show that the effects of incentive magnitude on attitude change are either direct or inverse, depending on the presence or absence of freedom not to comply. Th first experiment to follow was conducted as a direct test of the role of such freedom to choose not to engage in counter-attitudinal behavior.

EXPERIMENT I

Method

Attitude issue and subjects. At the time of the first experiment a rather heated controversy was raging in the state of North Carolina concerning the wisdom of a law that forbade Communists and Fifth Amendment pleaders from speaking at state-supported institutions. On the basis of informal opinion sampling, fortified by the plausible expectation that students deplore implied restrictions on their own freedom to listen, we assumed that college-student subjects would be strongly opposed to speaker-ban legislation. The issue thus seemed comparable to "the actions of the New Haven police" (Cohen, 1962) and to a ban on Ohio State's participation in the Rose Bowl (Rosenberg, 1965).

Fifty-five introductory psychology students at Duke University served as subjects in the experiment. Forty subjects (15 males and 25 females) were randomly assigned to four experimental conditions[2]; 13 were subsequently assigned to a control condition. All experimental subjects were asked to write a "forceful and convincing essay" in favor of the speaker-ban law. After writing the essay, each subject was asked to indicate his opinion about the speaker-ban law by checking a point on a 31-point scale comparable to Cohen's (1962) and Rosenberg's (1965) measure. The scale read, "In my opinion the Speaker Ban Law of North Carolina is . . . ," followed by 31 horizontal dots with seven labels ranging from "not justified at all" to "completely justified." Subjects in the control condition merely filled out the scale without having previously written a pro-speaker-ban essay.

Procedure and Design

The basic procedure was closely modeled after that of Cohen (1962) except that the subjects were recruited from the intro-

[2] Two more experimental subjects were actually run whose data were not analyzed. One of these was obviously in favor of the speaker-ban law at the outset, and the other was the victim of experimenter error in presenting instructions.

ductory psychology course and came individually to the laboratory, rather than being approached in their dormitory rooms. The experimenter introduced himself as a graduate student in psychology. In the *free-decision condition* he immediately said, "I want to explain to you what this task is all about. I want to make it clear, though, that the decision to perform the task will be entirely your own." In the *no-choice condition* he merely said, "I want to explain to you what this task that you have volunteered for is all about." He then proceeded in both conditions to provide the following rationale for the essay-writing task:

The Association of Private Colleges of the Southeast, of which Duke is a member, is considering the adoption of a uniform speaker policy that would be binding on its member schools. Before they can decide what kind of policy to adopt, if indeed they decide to adopt one, they have undertaken a large scale research program in order to help them understand what the issues really are. This study is part of that program. The APCSE is working through the Department of Psychology here at Duke and through the departments of psychology at other private schools in the area because of the access which the department has to a wide cross-section of students such as yourself who must participate in psychological experiments and because of the number of graduate students that are available to conduct research. We have found, from past experience, that one of the best ways to get relevant arguments on both sides of the issue is to ask people to write essays favoring only one side. We think we know pretty much how you feel about the student's rights in this matter. [Here the experimenter paused and waited for a comment that would confirm the subject's initial opinion opposing the speaker-ban law. Only one subject expressed a favoring opinion at this point; see Footnote 2.] Nonetheless, what we need now are essays favoring the speaker ban.

At this point, the free-decision and no-choice conditions again diverged. In the free-decision condition the subjects were told that the APCSE was paying $.50 (low incentive) or $2.50 (high incentive) in addition to the standard experimental credit given to all subjects. The experimenter again stressed that the decision to write the essay was entirely up to the subject and that he would receive experimental credit in any case. In the no-choice condition the experimenter acted as if, naturally, the subject in volunteering for the experiment had committed himself to its requirements. He simply pointed out that the experiment involved writing a strong and forceful essay favoring the speaker-ban law. After the subject was handed a pencil and some paper, but before he began to write, the experimenter broke in: "Oh yes, I almost forgot to tell you. . . . The APCSE is paying all participants $.50 [or $2.50] for their time."

In all conditions subjects were paid, *before* they wrote the essay, the amount of money promised them. The experimenter then left the room and allowed the subject 20 minutes to complete his essay. When he returned, the experimenter collected the essay, administered the brief attitude scale, and interviewed the subject concerning his perceptions of the experiment. No subject indicated any suspicion regarding the true purpose of the experiment. The purpose was then explained to each in detail, and all deceptions were revealed. None of the subjects recalled having any doubts about the existence of the fictitious APCSE. Each subject was ultimately allowed to keep $1.50. Because they were made to realize that they were assigned by chance to the high-inducement condition, those who had initially received $2.50 were quite agreeable when asked to return $1 of their money. Subjects in the low-inducement condition were delighted to learn of their good fortune—that they would receive $1 more than they had bargained for.

Results

Before the results bearing on the central hypothesis are presented, it is of interest to note the difference in decision time in the two free-decision conditions. After the experimenter began to notice that *free-decision* subjects in the low-incentive condition took much longer to make up their minds about writing the essay than *free-decision* subjects in the high-incentive condition, he started to record decision times with a hidden stop-watch. The last seven subjects in the low-incentive condition took an average of 25.29 seconds to reach a decision; the comparable mean for the last seven subjects in the high-incentive condition was 11.00 seconds. In spite of the reduced n, this difference is significant ($p < .025$, U test). This evidence strongly suggests that there was greater predecisional conflict in the low-incentive condition, and thus the conditions are appropriate for testing the dissonance hypothesis: since predecisional conflict leads to postdecisional dissonance (Festinger, 1964), more dissonance and hence more attitude change should occur in the free-decision–low-incentive condition.

After establishing that the means for female and male subjects were nearly identical ($t = .18$), the posttreatment attitude scores were placed in a simple 2 (for Degree of Decision Freedom) $\times$ 2 (for Level of Incentive) factorial design. The means for each condition are presented in Table 1. Scale values could range from

TABLE 1

Attitude-Scale Means Obtained in the Five Conditions: Experiment I

	Incentive	
	$.50	$2.50
No choice	1.66[a]	2.34
Free decision	2.96	1.64
Control[b]	1.71	

Note.—$n = 10$ under both incentives for free-choice and free-decision conditions. For the control condition, $n = 13$.

[a] The higher the number, the more the speaker-ban law was considered to be justified.

[b] Since subjects in the control condition were all run after the main experiment was completed, the mean for this condition is presented only as an estimate of student opinion toward the issue in the absence of dissonance or incentive effects. The data from the control condition were not included in the statistical analysis.

1.0 (antispeaker ban) to 7.0 (prospeaker ban). Table 2 summarizes the analysis of variance and appropriate orthogonal comparisons. The prediction that the amount of inferred attitude change would relate positively to inducement level in the no-choice conditions and negatively in the free-decision conditions is clearly confirmed ($F_{1, 36} = 8.70$; $p < .01$). The dissonance effect in the free-decision condition was itself significant; the reinforcement effect in the prior-commitment condition was not. The control subjects, who checked the scale without writing an essay, were about as much against the speaker ban as subjects in the conditions where little or no change was predicted.

In an effort to shed light on possible mechanisms underlying these findings, the essays themselves were examined. The average number of words per essay was 192.3, and there were no significant differences among the four conditions in essay length. The essays were evaluated in a manner similar to that described by Rosenberg (1965). Two independent raters, blind as to the sub-

TABLE 2

Summary of Analysis of Variance: Experiment I

Source of variation	MS	F
Choice (A)	0.90	<1
Incentive (B)	1.02	<1
A × B	10.00	8.70****
Error	1.15	
Low incentive vs. high incentive within free-decision conditions	8.71	7.57****
Low incentive vs. high incentive within no-choice conditions	2.31	2.01*

Note.—Two-way analysis of experimental conditions.
* $p < .20$, $df = 1/36$.
**** $p < .01$, $df = 1/36$.

ject's condition, rated the essays in terms of the degree of organization manifested and the degree of "intent to persuade." Each of these ratings was made in terms of a 5-point scale. The judges agreed or were 1 point discrepant in 72% of the organization ratings and 85% of the persuasiveness ratings. These percentages of agreement were comparable to those obtained by Rosenberg (1965), but two independent judges using 5-point rating scales should, by chance, be no more than 1 point discrepant on more than 50% of their ratings. When a more traditional estimate of the reliability of the ratings was calculated (Winer, 1962, pp. 124 ff.), it was found that the reliability coefficient for the ratings of degree of organization was .54, and the coefficient for the ratings of persuasiveness was .55. These coefficients estimate the reliability of the ratings that result from averaging over the two judges. When these ratings were submitted to an analysis of variance, there were no differences among conditions in either organization or persuasiveness.

Since the reliability of the ratings discussed above was quite low, an attempt was made to obtain ratings of acceptably high reliability. Two varsity debate partners agreed to rate the essays. General criteria to be used in determining the ratings were discussed, but the ratings were made independently. Each essay was rated for the persuasiveness of the presentation on a 7-point scale. Sixty percent of these ratings were no more than 1 point discrepant; the reliability coefficient was .48. (The chance percentage for agreements or 1-point discrepancies is 39% when a 7-point scale is used by two independent judges.) There were again no differences among the conditions in the rating received. Also, no between-condition differences appeared on the ratings made by any individual judge.

Discussion

The major purpose of the present experiment was achieved: to show that dissonance and reinforcement effects can be obtained within the same forced-compliance paradigm by varying the degree to which the subject is committed to comply before learning about the monetary incentive. Subjects who commit themselves after weighing the unpleasantness of the essay-writing task against the amount of incentive offered show the effects predicted by dissonance theory. The decision-time data strongly suggest that the subjects do in fact consider the essay-writing task unpleasant. Subjects who are not free to decide against compliance and then learn about a financial "bonus" produce results in line with reinforcement theory (that which is associated with something of value itself takes on value) or in line with the more complex affective-cognitive consistency model espoused by Rosenberg.

The present study was stimulated by Rosenberg's (1965) experiment, but the relevance of the results to a critique of Rosenberg's conclusions rests on the claim that his way of removing evaluation apprehension precommitted the subject to an unpleasant task before he had a chance to weigh the incentive for compliance. If this criticism is valid, then it should be possible to reproduce Rosenberg's results by closely replicating his procedures, and to obtain the converse of these results (confirming the dissonance prediction) by insuring that the subject does not commit himself before being confronted with the incentive for compliance. A second experiment was planned in an attempt to do precisely this.

EXPERIMENT II

Method

Attitude issue. As we prepared to run the second experiment, certain paternalistic policies of the Duke University administration were being challenged by the undergraduates, and there was a movement toward liberalization of *in loco parentis* social regulations. It was assumed, therefore, that undergraduates who were induced to write forceful and convincing essays in support of strict enforcement of *in loco parentis* policies would be performing a counterattitudinal task.

Subjects. Fifty-nine male introductory psychology students volunteered to participate for experimental credit in a study described as an "Attitude Survey." The data of 50 of these students, who were randomly assigned to the four experimental conditions and the control condition, were used in the reported analysis. Six subjects were eliminated because they did not complete the experimental procedure. Usually, they chose to read or study while waiting for the first experimenter rather than go to the second experimenter. Another subject was eliminated because he was initially in favor of strict *in loco parentis* policies, and writing the essay would not have been counterattitudinal for him.

Only two subjects who had completed the procedure were eliminated from the analysis. The first of these was excluded when it was discovered during the final interview that he had misinterpreted the attitude questionnaire. The second was eliminated because he accurately perceived the true purpose of the experiment. Both subjects had been assigned to the *free-decision-high-incentive condition*. The results of the study are not changed if these two subjects are included in the analysis.

Procedure and design. The procedure was a close approximation to that used by Rosenberg (1965). All subjects reported to the office of the first experimenter (E_1) where they found E_1 engaged in conversation with another student and were told, "I'm sorry, but I'm running late on my schedule today, and I'll have to keep you waiting for about 15 or 20 minutes. Is that all right?" All subjects agreed to wait.

Each experimental subject was then told:

Oh, I've just thought of something; while you're waiting you could participate in another little experiment that some graduate student in education is doing. This fellow called me the other day and said he needed volunteers in a hurry for some sort of study he's doing— I don't know what it's about exactly except that it has to do with attitudes and that's why he called me, because my research is in a similar area as you'll see later. Of course, he can't give you any credit but I gather they have some research funds and they are paying people instead. So, if you care to do that, you can.

At this point, one-half of the experimental subjects (*prior-commitment condition*) were allowed to leave for the second experiment without further comment by E_1. Since it was believed that Rosenberg's procedure restricted subjects' freedom not to comply with the task of the "little experiment," it was decided to manipulate degree of choice by removing this restriction. Thus, for subjects in the *free-decision* condition, after the subject had agreed to participate in the second experiment, E_1 added:

All I told this fellow was that I would send him some subjects if it was convenient but that I couldn't obligate my subjects in any way. So, when you get up there, listen to what he has to say and feel free to decide from there.

All experimental subjects then reported to the second experimenter (E_2). To control for the effects of experimenter bias, E_2 was not informed whether the subject was in the prior-commitment condition or the free-decision condition. E_2 presented himself as a graduate student in the Department of Education and introduced the essay-writing task using a procedure that, as in Experiment I, very closely approximated Cohen's (1962).

Rather than the free-decision versus no-choice manipulation of Experiment I, E_2 began by saying to all subjects, "At the present time, Duke University is beginning to question the wisdom of assuming the role of 'substitute parent' to its students." From that point, the instructions paralleled those of Experiment I with the substitution of *in loco parentis* regulations for the speaker-ban law. After confirming that the subject held an opinion opposed to rigid *in loco parentis* regulations, E_2 concluded:

What we need now are essays favoring a strict enforcement of *in loco parentis*. So, what we would like you to do—if you are willing[3]— is to write the strongest, most forceful and most convincing essay that you can in favor of a strict enforcement of the substitute parent concept here at Duke.

It was then explained that the sponsoring agency was offering either $.50 (*low-incentive* conditions) or $2.50 (*high-incentive* conditions) for participation in the study. When the subject agreed to write the essay, he was paid the money promised to him and then began the task.

After completing the essay and being thanked and dismissed by E_2, all experimental subjects returned to E_1's office. To introduce the dependent measure, E_1 explained:

What I had wanted you to do was participate in a continuing study I carry on every semester as a sort of Gallup poll to keep a check on opinion patterns on different University issues. I'd like you to fill out this questionnaire as an objective indication of your opinions and when you've finished I'd like to chat for a while about various issues on campus. OK?

E_1 was not informed of the amount of money the subject had received, and in no case did he find out until after the subject had completed the dependent measure.

The dependent measure consisted of an eight-item questionnaire dealing with various university issues. The critical item read, "How justified is the University's policy of assuming parental responsibilities for its students?" and was accompanied by the familiar 31-point scale. When the subject had completed the questionnaire, E_1 put it aside (without looking at the responses) and began a structured interview that included probes for suspicion and checks on perceptions of the manipulations. When E_1 was satisfied that the subject had not perceived the true purpose of the experiment, he revealed the deceptions and explained the

[3] This vague statement of choice was given to all subjects in order to keep the instructions constant across experimental groups and to enable E_2 to remain "blind" as to the condition of each subject. It was assumed that the crucial manipulation of free decision versus prior commitment had already been accomplished by E_1.

necessity for them. As in Experiment I, all experimental subjects agreed to accept $1.50 for their time.

Subjects assigned to the control condition also found E_1 engaged in conversation and were asked if they could return in 15 or 20 minutes. Upon their return they were treated exactly as experimental subjects.

These procedures resulted in five conditions: two levels of incentive magnitude under a condition of free decision, the same two levels under a condition of prior commitment, and the control condition.

Results

The mean attitude-scale scores on the critical item for each of the five conditions are presented in Table 3. It can be seen that

TABLE 3

Attitude-Scale Means Obtained in the Five Conditions: Experiment II

	Incentive	
	$.50	$2.50
Prior commitment	2.68[a]	3.46
Free decision	3.64	2.72
Control	2.56	

Note.—$n = 10$ in all conditions.
[a] The higher the number, the more strict application of *in loco parentis* regulations was considered justified.

the results are very similar to those of Experiment I. The data were submitted to a one-way analysis of variance, summarized in Table 4. The overall treatment effect was significant ($F_{4, 45} = 4.02$; $p < .01$). The two comparisons reflecting the hypotheses of this study were also significant: Within the free-decision conditions a low incentive produced more inferred attitude change than a high incentive ($F_{1, 45} = 6.82$; $p < .025$). Within the prior-commitment conditions this effect was reversed, and a high incentive produced more inferred attitude change than a low incentive ($F_{1, 45} = 4.90$; $p < .05$). The position of the control group indicates that differences between the experimental conditions

TABLE 4

Summary of Analysis of Variance: Experiment II

Source of variation[a]	MS	F
Treatment	2.49	4.02****
Error	.62	
Low incentive vs. high incentive free-decision conditions	4.23	6.82***
Low incentive vs. high incentive prior-commitment conditions	3.04	4.90**

Note.—One-way analysis of five conditions.
[a] The control condition differs significantly from both the prior-commitment–high-incentive and the free-decision–low-incentive conditions.
** $p < .05$, $df = 1/45$.
*** $p < .025$, $df = 1/45$.
**** $p < .01$, $df = 4/45$.

resulted from positive attitude change rather than a combination of positive and negative changes.

Once again we attempted to investigate the possibility that these effects were mediated by some aspect of the counterattitudinal performance. Two raters, working independently and without knowledge of the experimental conditions, rated each essay on 7-point scales for the extremity of attitudinal position advocated, the persuasiveness of the essay, and its degree of organization. The two raters agreed or were within 1 point of each other for 65% of the essays when estimating the attitudinal position, 60% when rating them for persuasiveness, and 52.5% when rating them for organization. The reliability coefficient for the estimated attitudinal position (Winer, 1962, pp. 124 ff.) was .67, the coefficient for the persuasiveness ratings was .51, and the coefficient for the organization ratings was .38. There were no differences among conditions on any of these ratings. The essays were then rated for the persuasiveness of the presentation on a 7-point scale by the same varsity debaters as had rated the essays from Experiment I. The debaters agreed or were within 1 point of each other for 65% of the essays, and the reliability coefficient was a somewhat more acceptable .71. Again, however, there were no differences among conditions on these ratings, whether the judges' ratings were averaged or each judge's ratings were examined separately. In a final attempt to find a performance difference among the conditions the number of words in each essay was counted; the conditions were compared on this measure of performance and were found not to differ from one another.

Discussion

The results of Experiment II support the argument that Rosenberg's (1965) procedure for the elimination of evaluation apprehension committed his subjects to perform the essay-writing task before they learned of the nature of the task and the amount of reward offered. The positive relationship between incentive magnitude and attitude change in the prior-commitment conditions of the present experiment replicates the no-choice results of Experiment I and the relationship found by Rosenberg (1965). It could be argued on this basis alone that such procedures as Rosenberg's have the same effect as allowing the subject no choice concerning performance of the counterattitudinal act. The argument becomes much more convincing, however, if it can be shown that appropriate alteration of Rosenberg's procedure, reducing the prior commitment of the subject, leads to an *inverse* relationship between incentive magnitude and attitude change. The free-decision conditions of Experiment II demonstrate precisely this point: when the subject does not feel that he has previously committed himself to performance of the counterattitudinal action requested by E_2, attitude change is an inverse function of incentive magnitude.

It should be noted here that a "balanced replication" (Aronson, 1966) of Rosenberg's (1965) study was required. Had Experiment II included only the free-decision conditions it would be possible to argue that our procedure was not successful in eliminating evaluation apprehension and that the results reflected once again the effect of this contaminant in research on forced compliance. The results of the prior-commitment conditions of Experiment II, however, counter this criticism. A persistent critic might still argue that the free-decision manipulation reintroduced evaluation apprehension. Perhaps the comment added to create the free-decision condition in some way increased the chances that subjects would see the experiments as related. However, the structured interview conducted by E_1 revealed no differential level of suspicion between the prior-commitment and free-decision conditions. In the absence of a reliable and valid measure of evaluation apprehension, we can do no more than contend that our interview was sensitive enough to detect suspicion and that we found no indication of differential suspicion among the conditions.

The results of the two studies reported above imply that the discrepancy between Cohen's (1962) findings and the results of Rosenberg's (1965) experiment may indeed be resolved in the manner indicated earlier in this paper. For Cohen's subjects the decision not to comply was a viable alternative at the time they were confronted with the essay-writing task and offered an incentive of certain value. Under such conditions dissonance will be induced whenever the incentive is not large enough to justify performance of the task, and incentive magnitude will be inversely related to subsequent attitude change. However, if a subject's freedom not to comply has been restricted before he is confronted with the task and with a clear description of the incentive, dissonance cannot be induced by an incentive of insufficient magnitude. Under these conditions, the reinforcing properties of the incentives will lead to a positive relationship between incentive magnitude and attitude change. Although Rosenberg (1965) demonstrated such a relationship, his assertion that it may be obscured by failure to remove evaluation apprehension seems no longer tenable. No attempt was made in the procedure of Experiment I to remove evaluation apprehension, and yet the results are very similar to the results of Experiment II.

Rosenberg (1966) has more recently advanced two additional hypotheses intended to resolve discrepancies in the forced-compliance literature. The first of these is that we must distinguish counterattitudinal actions that are simple and overt from those featuring the elaboration of a set of arguments. Supposedly a performance of the former kind (e.g., eating a disliked food) will lead to the inverse relationship between attitude change and incentive magnitude, while an act of the latter kind (e.g., writing a counterattitudinal essay) will result in a positive relationship. The second hypothesis is that we must distinguish between two kinds of counterattitudinal performances: (a) those carried out under instructions that lead the subject to believe his performance will be used to deceive others, and (b) those following from instructions to elaborate, for some reasonable and legitimate purpose, a set of arguments opposite to his private opinion. It is hypothesized that even if the actual task is the same, say essay writing, the first type of instruction will lead to an inverse relationship between incentive magnitude and attitude change, and the second type of instruction will lead to a positive relationship.

In the studies reported above the subject's task was presented with no hint that his performance would be used to deceive anyone, and the task in all cases was to elaborate a set of arguments opposite to his own opinion. It follows from the two hypotheses suggested by Rosenberg (1966) and presented above that we should not have been able to obtain the inverse relationship between incentive magnitude and attitude change using our procedures. However, in both experiments, we obtained the positive *and* the inverse relationship. We are forced to conclude that neither the "simple versus complex" hypothesis nor the "duplicity versus legitimate" hypothesis can account for the present results.

In place of these hypotheses we conclude that at least some of the discrepancies in the forced-compliance literature may be resolved by closer attention to the role of decision freedom at the time the incentive is offered. A barely sufficient incentive for making counterattitudinal statements *does* result in dissonance and subsequent attitude change if the subject feels he is quite free not to comply. When the freedom not to comply is removed or markedly decreased, on the other hand, attitude change is greater the greater the incentive for compliance.

15

The Effect of Monetary Inducements on the Amount of Attitude Change Produced by Forced Compliance[1]

BARRY E. COLLINS

The fertility of role playing as a topic and technique for attitude change studies is vividly illustrated in the work of Barry Collins. Not strongly committed to any one theoretical orientation, he has produced enough tests of role-play hypotheses to give pause, stimulate thought, and renew interest among researchers of a variety of outlooks. Several of his studies still await publication, but in the following paper (adapted by Dr. Collins especially for this volume), he reviews the entirety of his research on role playing. It seems quite fitting to end the book with this paper, which suggests that possibilities for research on role playing remain open-ended, that many problems remain to be solved, and that their experimental resolution will continue to contribute much that is useful for the general understanding of attitude change. (Examples of other recent contributions are the research reported by Nel, Helmreich, and Aronson, 1968, supporting a dissonance approach, and the research reported by Heslin and Rotton, 1968, supporting an incentive approach.)

Festinger and Carlsmith (1959) describe a study in which subjects, after working approximately an hour on a very dull task, were enticed to tell an attractive female accomplice that the

[1] A version of this paper was read at a symposium at the New York meeting of the American Association for the Advancement of Science in December of 1967. The research in this paper was supported by National Science Foundation Grant NSF GS-492 and NSF GS-1194 and a grant from the Advanced Research Projects Agency of the Defense Department through Grant No. AF-AFOSR-1200-67.

task was, in fact, interesting. Subjects paid $20.00 for this coun-terattitudinal act showed less attitude change than those paid $1.00. I have argued elsewhere (Collins, 1968a) that there are a number of alternative explanations for this negative relationship between financial inducement and attitude change. But in this paper, I shall attempt to analyze the original dissonance theory prediction for the Festinger and Carlsmith experiment and to suggest some possible revisions to the original theoretical for-mulation which are necessary if dissonance theory is to account for subsequent data.

As originally formulated (Festinger, 1957; Festinger & Carl-smith, 1959), dissonance theory appeared to state that dissonance would be aroused whenever a person *thinks* one thing and *says* the opposite. Although there have been subsequent revisions to the theory including such prerequisites as "choice" (Linder, Cooper, & Jones, 1967) and "commitment" (Aronson, 1966), Festinger originally applied the theory to situations where very little choice or commitment was involved (e.g., Janis & King, 1954; King & Janis, 1956). As originally formulated, the theory specifies that dissonance will be aroused whenever a person thinks one thing and says the opposite. This original version of dissonance theory was considerably embarrassed by several studies which reported an anti-dissonance, positive relationship between financial inducement and attitude change (e.g., Rosen-berg, 1965; Carlsmith, Collins, & Helmreich, 1966; Elms & Janis, 1965). The original formulations of dissonance theory, quite clearly, must predict a negative relationship between finan-cial inducement and attitude change in these studies.

What, then is wrong with the original formulation of disso-nance theory? The trouble probably lies in our intuitive notions about what is dissonant with what. For instance, why is it incon-sistent to know, on the one hand, "I personally *think* the task is very dull" and also to know, on the other hand, "I *told* that attractive female coed that the task was fun and interesting?" There are, I think, two reasons why most people find these cogni-tions intuitively inconsistent.

(1) *Moral transgression.* First, the overt statement may consti-tute a moral transgression. In our Judeo-Christian culture, at least, it's sinful to tell a falsehood. The two cognitions may pro-duce a cognitive dilemma—not because they are inconsistent in

and of themselves—but because they lead the subject to the conclusion that he has told a lie. If this is the mechanism by which dissonance is aroused, dissonance would be very similar to guilt.

(2) *Inconsistency in thought and action.* Second, many of us may find the Festinger-Carlsmith cognitions inconsistent because of our theories about the relation between thought and action. Many of us hold a theory, implicitly at least, that the human organism is wired in such a way that it is difficult for him to *say* one thing and *think* another. Thus, it would be an unusual, dissonant, or inconsistent situation if an individual were induced to generate a response inconsistent with his private convictions. It might be that the physiological make-up of man is such that he has trouble behaving one way and thinking another; or it might be that children in our society are rewarded for consistency between thought and action. In either event, I suspect that it is one of these first two sources of dissonance which Festinger and Carlsmith actually used to make their original prediction in 1959.

Unfortunately, these first two mechanisms apply equally to the Festinger and Carlsmith face-to-face confrontation and the Rosenberg essay-writing counterattitudinal task where positive, anti-dissonance relationships are reported. It is just as morally wrong to lie verbally as it is to lie in writing; and there is just as much sin in a lie to an unseen reader as in a lie to an immediate audience. Similarly, if it is the act of saying one thing while thinking another which generates the cognitive dilemma, there should be dissonance in the Rosenberg and Carlsmith, et al. studies. It should not matter whether the act is public or private, nor should it matter whether the act is oral or written; it's still difficult to say one thing and think another. Both of these first two mechanisms apply equally to the anonymous essay-writing task and to the Festinger and Carlsmith task. It would appear that the subject must do something more than merely tell a small lie or make statements inconsistent with his private opinions in order to experience dissonance. Something has been added to the simple counterattitudinal act itself in the face-to-face confrontation—and this "something else" appears to be necessary before the two cognitions are dissonant or inconsistent.

As I think about the crucial difference between the essay writing and face-to-face confrontation conditions of Carlsmith, Collins, & Helmreich (and as I read the arguments of others), I can discern at least three possible sources of dissonance in addition to the two listed above.

(3) *Social retaliation.* It might be, for instance, that the subject is concerned about the social consequences to himself. The subject may be concerned about meeting his audience outside the experimental situation. The attractive, female age-peer might very well think the less of the male subject—either because the subject had expressed a ridiculous and absurd opinion about the task or because she had been deceived by the subject.

If social consequences to self are the source of dissonance, the crucial cognitions in the Festinger and Carlsmith experiment would be different from those previously mentioned. The dissonance would be between the cognitions "That girl is likely to make fun of me or say bad things about me to my friends" and "I don't like people to make fun of me or say bad things to my friends." Thus, not only would the source of dissonance be different from that originally specified by Festinger, the cognitions involved in the dissonance would be different.

A crucial manipulation for this source of dissonance is, of course, anonymity. According to this third mechanism, the subject is concerned that his counterattitudinal behavior will be attributed to him outside the laboratory. If the audience for the counterattitudinal behavior is unable to identify the source, the audience will be unable to make fun of the subject or say bad things about him to his friends. Isolating the subject from his audience should also eliminate the dissonance.

(4) *Consequences to self-esteem.* Fourth, on the other hand, it might be that the subject is concerned about the consequences of the counterattitudinal act for *his self-esteem.* The subject may experience dissonance whenever he, the subject, feels that he has made a fool out of himself. Is the public-private variable relevant to this source of dissonance? I suspect that an individual in our culture is not much concerned with the silly and foolish things he does while locked in a dark closet. Thus, there may have to be an audience for the counterattitudinal behavior before the act has serious consequences for the subject's self-esteem. But the members of the audience would not have to retaliate directly. If they did not know the subject or his friends and thus could not

chastise him directly, the counterattitudinal act might still damage the subject's self-esteem. Knowing that the members of your
audience would chastise you, if they could, is probably sufficient
to damage the self-esteem of anyone in our culture. Thus,
anonymity, *per se,* probably does not prevent a counterattitudinal
act from damaging one's self-esteem. Publicness might, however,
exaggerate the threat to self-esteem.

(5) *Aversive consequences.* Finally, an individual may experience dissonance if his overt act produces objective negative consequences for himself or his audience. The subject in the Festinger and Carlsmith experiment, for instance, might have been
concerned that he persuaded the experimental accomplice to
participate in a dull and boring experiment—after she had been
well advised by her friend to avoid the whole thing. This latter
mechanism is particularly helpful in understanding results of a
number of essay-writing studies which find the dissonance predicted, negative relationship between financial inducement and
attitude change (Cohen, 1962; Linder, Cooper, & Jones, 1967).
In these studies, the "audience" for the essays was a policy-
making agency which made policies directly affecting the subject.
If this "audience" were persuaded by the subject's essays, it
would make policies inconsistent with the subject's self-interest.

The extent to which the subject felt he had choice in deciding
to make the counterattitudinal response could affect the extent
to which he feels *personally* responsible for the consequences of
his behavior. Similarly, subjects in the essay conditions of Carlsmith, Collins, and Helmreich were told that their essays would
never be used as such. The experimenter would use a few ideas
and phrases for an essay which he, *the experimenter,* would
write. Thus it might be that there was no dissonance produced
in those conditions because subjects felt that the experimenter
was responsible for any aversive consequences which might be
produced. This fifth source of dissonance, then, produces dissonance because the subject feels personally responsible for some
deleterious consequence of his behavior.

SOME EXPERIMENTS ON SOCIAL RETALIATION

Since the summer of 1964, when Carlsmith, Helmreich, and I
conducted the anonymous essay vs. face-to-face confrontation

study, Studies in Forced Compliance I, my associates and I have completed approximately fifteen additional studies which explore the problem further. My own strategy has been almost entirely empirical. I have attempted to break down the complex stimulus manipulation used in Study I into simpler, more unidimensional, manipulations. For a number of reasons, the face-to-face confrontation paradigm is a difficult and expensive one to handle experimentally. The roles of experimenter and experimental accomplice require an unusual degree of experimental sophistication and acting skill. Furthermore, the paradigm requires four separate people (the experimenter, a secretary, the experimental accomplice, and a posttester) to run a single subject. Almost entirely for these practical reasons, I chose to work largely within the essay-writing paradigm.

For me at least, the most compelling difference between the face-to-face and essay-writing conditions had been the public-private dimension. Although the distinctions I mentioned above were developed after the fact, it would now appear that I, along with most of the others who reacted to the original study, intuited that the subject was concerned about negative social feedback he might receive from his audience. By dissociating the subject from his essay (in the audience's eyes, not in the subject's) the audience would not be able to retaliate directly.

In Studies in Forced Compliance II (Collins & Helmreich, in press) Bob Helmreich and I induced nursing-school students to write essays stating that a very bitter solution tasted pleasant. One-half of the subjects were told, "We'll understand that you're not writing down your total impression. Write your essay on this sheet, *and don't bother to sign your name; no one but the experimenters will ever read it*. We're just looking for ideas to use in future studies." In an effort to create an essay-writing task similar to the face-to-face confrontation situation, the other half of the subjects were told, "Remember, only say positive things about the samples, because the whole purpose is to persuade someone that they will taste good. . . . *Write on this sheet, and put your name and address where it says to. The essays will be used in an experiment next semester*." One-half of the subjects were paid $.50 and one-half $2.00 as an inducement to write the essay. Although people writing the private essay showed more attitude change than those writing the public essay, the financial inducement seemed to have no effect. The experimenter did report that these nursing-school students seemed bothered by the money in a context where they had expected none, and this may provide one explanation. There are some other interesting results in the study but, for our purposes here, it is sufficient to note that we were unable to produce a negative relationship with the public, signed essays.

Studies in Forced Compliance IV (Collins, 1968c) attempted to correct two faults in the second study. In the first place, the public-private instructions were shortened to create a simpler manipulation. Secondly, subjects were recruited to participate in an experiment "for pay." Hopefully this increased the plausibility of an "extra monetary incentive" introduced in the middle of the experiment. After approximately 20 minutes of rating dull and uninteresting slides with randomly arranged lines (Munsinger & Kessen, 1964) subjects were asked to describe the pictures as exciting, interesting, and good works of art—a decidedly coun-terattitudinal stance. Public subjects were told "Other students from the New Haven high schools will actually read your de-scriptions. They will sign up for a study like you did, and then we will give them your descriptions to read before they rate the pictures." When subjects agreed to write the essays, they were given a sheet which contained spaces for their name and other identifying information. Subjects in the private condition were told, "No one other than the experimenters will read your de-scriptions. We will look at your descriptions in order to get ideas and phrases which we will use to help us write up a description. Only this final description, which we will write up, will be shown to the subjects." These private subjects were *not* asked to sign their names.

Subjects receiving the high financial inducement showed more attitude change than those receiving the low financial induce-ment. Even when subjects were told that their signed essays would be presented to fellow students as sincere testimonials, there was more attitude change under high inducement than low inducement. As always, speculations are available which would save the original hypothesis—i.e., to keep alive the hypothesis that dissonance is produced because the subject fears social retal-iation from his audience. Subjects actually received their request to write the essays in groups of five; and they actually wrote their essays in a much larger room containing approximately sixty subjects—many of whom were also writing essays. The sight of all these other subjects writing essays may have reassured our public subjects so that they did not feel any dissonance or inconsistency. Although the script carefully and explicitly stressed that subjects had a choice to write or not to write the "description," some of the dissonant information was not introduced until after the choice was made. Furthermore, the manipulation was only one or two sentences in the midst of a great deal of new and novel stimulation. Even though the verbally-induced manipulation was reinforced by having the subjects either sign or not sign their written product, it's possible that the manipulation was not seen as very potent by the subjects.

So, we decided to try again. In Studies in Forced Compliance VIII (Collins, 1968b), we tried to make the public condition more public, the private condition more private, and we ran subjects individually. Choice was again stressed, and all dissonant information was introduced before the choice was made. Again, subjects were recruited initially by advertising $1.50 for an hour's work. After listening to a number of selections of electronic music—specially chosen to be exceptionally dull—they were induced to write an essay stating that the electronic music is fun to listen to, that people will like it, and that it is better than popular music. The favorable comparison with popular music, in particular, was decidedly counterattitudinal for these teenage subjects. Public subjects were told, "Now, if you write this description, it will be shown to several students in your high school. So, since the description will have your name on it, these students in your high school will recognize your name. That'll make the description more believable to them. In other words, we'll have a description written by a student, [point to subject] you, but more important, the students reading the description will know you." Subjects signed their name and provided other identifying information.

Private subjects were assured that not even the experimenter would see their essays, that they, along with other subjects, would mail their unsigned essay directly to a professor in another town—who, of course, would not be able to identify them personally. Again, subjects who were offered an additional $1.50 as an inducement to write the essay showed more attitude change than those paid $.25. Again, there was an anti-dissonance, *positive* relationship between inducement and attitude change. Even subjects who were told that their signed essay would definitely be used to deceive a personal acquaintance showed more attitude change with high inducement than with low inducement.

Before the data from this study were completely analyzed, Fred Hornbeck (1967, Studies in Forced Compliance IX) began a study which, among other things, included public-private and financial-inducement manipulations. Public subjects were told ". . . Your paper will also be used as a part of a display in the main hall near the principal's office so that those students not included in this survey can see what you wrote about electronic music. . . . Your paper will also be used on the bulletin board display after Mr. Collins reads it." After the subject had agreed to write the essay, the experimenter said: "Please sign your name right away." Private subjects were told that ". . . Only Mr. Collins, who won't know who you are, will read your paper. No one else will see it. All the material which we are gathering in this study is simply for research purposes and will under no circumstances be used for anything else." Again, even under the public conditions, there is no sign of a dissonance, or negative relationship between financial inducement and attitude change. In fact, for three of the five dependent variables used, there is significantly more attitude change in the high-inducement condition: a *positive* relationship between attitude change and inducements.

After these three follow-up studies, we had concluded that the public-private dimension of the face-to-face confrontation vs. essay-writing study was not the crucial dimension separating the conditions. But—again, and as always—it is possible to save the social-retaliation hypothesis. Perhaps subjects anticipate avoiding retaliation by explaining—at the time of confrontation—why they "really wrote the essay."

In Studies in Forced Compliance X (Ashmore & Collins, 1968) we attempted to induce the subjects to make a counter-attitudinal statement in the lab—and then live up to it in confrontations *outside* the laboratory. Subjects compared bad selections of electronic music favorably to both classical music and popular music by recording a statement into a tape recorder. Public subjects gave their name and other identifying personal information. Public subjects also signed official-looking "re-leases" in which they pledged to maintain their position outside the laboratory for a period of three months if they were con-fronted by a member of their audience.

The inducement manipulation had no effect in either condi-tion. One must always be careful about interpreting this last "no difference" finding; but one must admit the results from these five studies are consistent in one respect. In none of these five experiments following up Study 1 (the face-to-face confrontation vs. anonymous essay-writing experiment) has the low inducement condition produced more attitude change than the high induce-ment condition. Each of the preceding five studies is subject to a number of criticisms individually. But the combined results lead me to abandon the notion that the public-private dimension is the crucial one for the production of a dissonance, negative relation-ship between financial inducement and attitude change.

Before I discuss alternative explanations, let me describe a study just recently completed in collaboration with Robert Helm-reich in the fall of 1967 (Helmreich & Collins, 1968). In the light of our previous unhappy experience with the essay-writing task, Studies in Forced Compliance XIV was designed to model more closely the face-to-face confrontation condition of Study I. Some subjects were asked to record a counterattitudinal presentation on video tape. They were told that their tapes would be used as stimulus material in an attitude change experiment to be con-ducted in a large psychology class. To insure that subjects were fully aware of what they had done, their presentations were re-played to them. In the condition designed to maximize disso-nance, subjects were not allowed to explain their behavior at the end of the experimental session and—since the experiment in-volved a delayed posttest—they expected to stand by their counterattitudinal position for the next three months.

A second video-tape condition was designed to eliminate some of the features of the first condition which, on an *a priori* basis, seemed to contribute to the arousal of dissonance. Subjects were assured that they would be able to explain the reasons for their counterattitudinal position at the end of the experimental session. They were, in fact, asked to record their own explanation and were promised that the explanation would be played at the end of the one-hour experimental session. Since these subjects were

allowed to "undo" or "take back" their counterattitudinal behavior, since their audience would be deceived only for a short
period of time, and since these "take back" subjects would not
have to maintain their counterattitudinal position in a face-to-
face confrontation outside the laboratory, less dissonance should
be produced.

In a third condition, subjects made an anonymous audio tape.
Unlike the preceding conditions, subjects did not identify themselves on the tape. Furthermore, the recording was audio only,
so it is unlikely that a member of the audience would recognize
the subject outside the laboratory.

In the video, no-takeback condition, the $.50 condition pro-
duces significantly more attitude change than the $2.50 condition
with a probability less than one in a thousand (with only 11 subjects in each cell). This is the strongest dissonance, negative
relation between attitude change and financial inducement yet
reported in the literature.

Surprisingly, however, the negative relation in the take-back
condition is almost as strong. Even though subjects were allowed
to head off social retaliation by recanting and explaining their
own behavior at the end of the experimental session, they still
experienced dissonance. These lines are almost parallel. This
result casts even further doubt on the social retaliation hypothesis
since subjects should have been able to avoid retaliation by
"taking back" their act. While the increase in the anonymous
audio condition is not significant, the slope of that line is significantly more positive from the slope of the line in each of the
other two conditions.

SOME SPECULATIONS ABOUT THE ROOTS
OF INCONSISTENCY OR DISSONANCE

We have, then, some data which argue against the first three
of our five sources of dissonance. It seems unlikely that the
dissonance produced by counterattitudinal advocacy is produced
by guilt over a moral transgression. Similarly, it seems unlikely
that the dissonance is produced because human beings are wired
in such a way that they have difficulty saying one thing and
thinking another. If either of these two alternatives was the root

of dissonance and inconsistency, then the dissonance or negative relationship between attitude change and financial inducement should occur with private as well as public counterattitudinal overt acts. I have just detailed the chain of events which has cost me my enthusiasm for the social-retaliation hypothesis.

That leaves us with two other sources of dissonance—both of which lie in the *consequences* of the counterattitudinal overt act. The first of these two remaining sources of dissonance (No. 4 on our list of 5) speculates that dissonance may be produced when an overt act has negative implications for the subject's self-esteem—i.e., when this behavior makes him feel foolish. The last of our list of 5 speculates that dissonance may be produced when a counterattitudinal act produces objectively negative consequences either for the subject himself or for his audience.

In conclusion, I would speculate that subjects are bothered—i.e., feel dissonance or inconsistency—to the extent that their overt actions have aversive consequences for them. I would speculate that it is not important whether the act is counterattitudinal or pro-attitudinal; the important thing is that the act has negative consequences. Whether these speculations are correct or not, at least two conclusions are justified by the data. (1) First, the original version of dissonance theory (Festinger, 1957; Festinger & Carlsmith, 1959) must be significantly revised so that it does not predict a negative relationship between financial inducement and attitude change in all situations. (2) The social retaliation hypothesis does not appear to be a satisfactory revision of dissonance theory or a satisfactory explanation of the Carlsmith, Collins, and Helmreich (1966) results.

APPENDIX

When one manipulates a variable which has theoretical significance, no matter which way it comes out—such as financial inducement—one's *a priori* hypotheses entitle him to do a two-tailed *t* test between high and low inducement for each possible comparison in large factorials. But one's *a priori* notions don't prevent approximately one in every twenty comparisons from being significant at the .05 level by chance. For this reason, I have numbered all the studies conducted since the face-to-face confrontation vs. anonymous essay-writing Studies in Forced Compliance I. By numbering each study, whether successful or unsuccessful, a record is provided of the number of times the null hypothesis has been rejected in relation to the number of times it has been accepted. Since the studies were numbered in the order in which they were conducted and analyzed—rather than the order in which they were written up and published—write-ups of the early studies are not yet available. It's possible that some of the "no difference" studies will never be written up in full form.

In the first part of this paper, I did review all the studies which contained a public-private and financial-inducement manipulation. There are, however, six additional studies which were not reviewed above. I mention them briefly here in order to make public the total number of two-tailed tests between high and low inducements which have been made.

In Studies in Forced Compliance: III (SFC III, Collins, 1968b) I investigated the effect of running the subjects in pairs as opposed to running them alone. Some subjects were instructed to write true essays; others were instructed to write persuasive essays. Half received low financial inducements and half high—creating a standard $2 \times 2 \times 2$ factorial experiment. For subjects run in pairs, all four means are close together. For subjects run individually, there is a significant interaction between true-persuasive instructions and low-high inducement. Subjects instructed to write persuasive essays show a significant positive relationship between attitude change and financial inducement. Subjects instructed to write true essays show a non-significant negative relationship between financial inducement and attitude change.

SFC V was an incomplete replication of SFC IV with non-significant results. SFC VI was conducted within the context of a debate study in a New England high school. Each subject participated in two rounds of debates—one "practice" round in which there was a chance of winning a $5.00 prize and one "competitive" round in which there was a chance of winning a savings bond. The degree of discrepancy between the subject's own opinion and the debate position was also varied; some moderate subjects debated an extreme position with which they agreed slightly, other subjects debated a position either moderately or extremely different from their own opinion. There are several significant positive and several significant negative relations; but all of these are part of significant higher-order interactions—which typically include an interaction with the particular topic being debated.

SFC VII was a replication of Kelman's (1953) study in which junior high school students were induced to write counterattitudinal essays in favor of jungle comic books. In an effort to simplify Kelman's complex inducement manipulation, ⅓ of the subjects were offered no extra inducement to write in favor of jungle comic books, ⅓ were offered a low inducement, and ⅓ were offered a high inducement. An attempt was made to keep the inducements for jungle comic books low enough so that a certain percentage of subjects in each condition would refuse to comply and write in favor of fantastic-hero comic books.

Unfortunately, nearly all subjects in the high-inducement condition wrote the counterattitudinal pro-jungle comic book essays. A comparison parallel to Kelman's experiment is possible, however, in the control and low-incentive conditions. There were significantly more subjects writing counterattitudinal essays in the low-inducement than in the no-inducement conditions; but there were enough non-compliers in the low-incentive condition to allow statistical analyses. As in Kelman's study, the introduction of an incentive increased attitude change among non-compliers. In direct contradiction to Kelman's results (and in contradiction to Festinger's, 1957, interpretation of that study) there was also a positive relationship between incentive and attitude change among subjects who did write the counterattitudinal, pro-jungle-comic-book essays.

SFC XI was a relatively straightforward replication of Festinger and Carlsmith (1959), except that the subject matter of the face-to-face confrontation was a favorable statement of electronic music rather than a favorable statement about the dull task. For one-half of the subjects, the experimental accomplice omitted the comment in which she says: "But my friend was in this study and he gave me the impression that he really didn't like the electronic music." The results have not been completely analyzed, but the Festinger-Carlsmith study is not replicated.

SFC XIII (Ashmore, Collins, Hornbeck, & Whitney, 1968) consisted of a series of three, two-cell experiments designed to produce the dissonance, negative relationship between attitude change and financial inducement. All three involved a blend of Linder, Cooper, and Jones' (1967) two-experimenter, high-choice procedure with the Festinger and Carlsmith (1959) dull-task, face-to-face confrontation procedure. The three studies found either no difference or a slight positive relationship.

SFC XV (Collins & Ashmore, 1968) reports three studies, each of which contains a replication of Linder, Cooper, and Jones (1967). Of the five comparisons between high and low financial inducement, one comparison replicates the dissonance effect, three are not significant, and one represents a significant positive relation between inducement and attitude change. Of the three comparisons which are close replications of Linder, Cooper, and Jones (1967), Study 1 replicated their results, Study 2 failed to replicate, and Study 3 produced significant results in the opposite direction. The implications of Studies 2 and 3 for the "consequences" argument (Collins, 1967) is ambiguous. It was theorized that the Linder, et al. (1967) subjects thought the experimenter might use their essays to present an improper view of student opinion. Thus the essays would have negative consequences. Rating of the experimenter and experimental situation confirm these theoretical speculations. The significant interaction in Study 3 for attitude change, however, is directly opposite to that predicted by the "consequence" interpretation of the forced compliance data.

Bibliography

ARONSON, E. The psychology of insufficient justification: An analysis of some conflicting data. In S. Feldman (Ed.), *Cognitive consistency.* New York: Academic Press, 1966.

ARONSON, E., & CARLSMITH, J. M. Effect of the severity of threat on the devaluation of forbidden behavior. *Journal of Abnormal and Social Psychology,* 1963, 66, 584–588.

ASHMORE, R. D., & COLLINS, B. E. Studies in forced compliance: X. Attitude change and commitment to maintain publicly a counter-attitudinal position. *Psychological Reports,* 1968, 22, 1229–1234.

ASHMORE, R. D., COLLINS, B. E., HORNBECK, F. W., & WHITNEY, R. E. Studies in forced compliance: XIII. In search of a dissonance producing forced compliance paradigm. Unpublished mimeographed paper, U.C.L.A., 1968.

BAVELAS, A. Role-playing and management training. *Sociatry,* 1947, 1, 183–191.

BEM, D. J. An experimental analysis of self-persuasion. *Journal of Experimental Social Psychology,* 1965, 1, 199–218.

BEM, D. J. Self-perception: An alternative interpretation of cognitive dissonance phenomena. *Psychological Review,* 1967, 74, 183–200.

BEM, D. J. The epistemological status of interpersonal simulations: A reply to Jones, Linder, Kiesler, Zanna, & Brehm. *Journal of Experimental Social Psychology,* 1968, 4, 270–274.

BIRCH, H. G. The effect of socially disapproved labelling upon well-structured attitudes. *Journal of Abnormal and Social Psychology,* 1945, 40, 301–310.

BOSTROM, R. N., VLANDIS, J. W., & ROSENBAUM, M. E. Grades as reinforcing contingencies and attitude change. *Journal of Educational Psychology,* 1961, 52, 112–115.

BREHM, J. W. Comment on "Counter-norm attitudes induced by consonant versus dissonant conditions of role-playing." *Journal of Experimental Research in Personality,* 1965, 1, 61–64.

BREHM, J. W., & COHEN, A. R. *Explorations in Cognitive Dissonance.* New York: Wiley, 1962.

BURDICK, H. A. The relationship of attraction, need achievement, and certainty to conformity under conditions of a simulated group atmosphere. *Dissertation Abstracts,* 1956, 16, 1518–1519.

CAMPBELL, D. T. *A Study of Leadership among Submarine Officers.* Columbus: Ohio State University, Personnel Research Board, 1953.

CAMPBELL, D. T., & FISKE, D. W. Convergent and discriminant validation by the multitrait-multimethod matrix. *Psychological Bulletin,* 1959, *56,* 81–105.

CARLSMITH, J. M. Varieties of counter-attitudinal behavior. In R. Abelson, E. Aronson, W. McGuire, T. Newcomb, M. Rosenberg, & P. Tannenbaum (Eds.), *Theories of Cognitive Consistency: A Sourcebook.* Chicago: Rand McNally, 1968.

CARLSMITH, J. M., COLLINS, B. E., & HELMREICH, R. L. Studies in forced compliance: I. The effect of pressure for compliance on attitude change produced by face-to-face role playing and anonymous essay writing. *Journal of Personality and Social Psychology,* 1966, *4,* 1–13.

CARLSON, E. R. Attitude change through modification of attitude structure. *Journal of Abnormal and Social Psychology,* 1956, *52,* 256–261.

CAYLEY, W. E., & ELMS, A. C. "Interpersonal replication": A failure to replicate. Unpublished manuscript, Southern Methodist University, 1968.

CHAPANIS, N. P., & CHAPANIS, A. C. Cognitive dissonance: Five years later. *Psychological Bulletin,* 1964, *61,* 1–22.

COHEN, A. R. An experiment on small rewards for discrepant compliance and attitude change. In J. W. Brehm & A. R. Cohen, *Explorations in Cognitive Dissonance,* 73–78. New York: Wiley, 1962.

COHEN, A. R., BREHM, J. W., & FLEMING, W. H. Attitude change and justification for compliance. *Journal of Abnormal and Social Psychology,* 1958, *56,* 276–278.

COLLINS, B. E. Studies in forced compliance: III. Attitude change produced by "truthful" as opposed to "persuasive" essays. Unpublished manuscript, Yale University, 1966.

COLLINS, B. E. The effect of monetary inducements on the amount of attitude change induced by forced compliance. Paper presented at the meeting of American Association for the Advancement of Science, New York, December, 1967.

COLLINS, B. E. Counterattitudinal behavior. In R. Abelson, E. Aronson, W. McGuire, T. Newcomb, M. Rosenberg, & P. Tannenbaum (Eds.), *Theories of Cognitive Consistency: A Sourcebook.* Chicago: Rand McNally, 1968a.

COLLINS, B. E. Studies in forced compliance: III and VIII. The effect of true-persuasive instructions, public-private essays and financial inducement on attitude change produced by forced compliance. Unpublished mimeographed paper, U.C.L.A., 1968b.

COLLINS, B. E. Studies in forced compliance: IV. The failure of public, high commitment counterattitudinal essays to produce dissonance. Unpublished mimeographed paper, U.C.L.A., 1968c.

COLLINS, B. E., & ASHMORE, R. D. Studies in forced compliance: XV. Further search for a dissonance producing forced compliance paradigm. Unpublished mimeographed paper, U.C.L.A., 1968.

COLLINS, B. E., & HELMREICH, R. K. Studies in forced compliance: II. Mechanisms of attitude change. Unpublished manuscript, Yale University, 1966.

COLLINS, B. E., & HELMREICH, R. L. Studies in forced compliance: II. Contrasting mechanisms of attitude change produced by public-persuasive and private-true essays. *Journal of Social Psychology*, 1968, in press.

CRAWFORD, C. E. Some experimental studies of the results of college note taking. *Journal of Educational Research*, 1925, *12*, 379–386.

CROWNE, D. P., & MARLOWE, D. A new scale of social desirability independent of psychopathology. *Journal of Consulting Psychology*, 1960, *24*, 349–354.

CULBERTSON, F. M. Modification of an emotionally held attitude through role playing. *Journal of Abnormal and Social Psychology*, 1957, *54*, 230–233.

DOOB, L. W. The behavior of attitudes. *Psychological Review*, 1947, *54*, 135–156.

EDWARDS, A. L. *The Social Desirability Variable in Personality Assessment and Research*. New York: Dryden Press, 1957.

EDWARDS, A. L. *Experimental Design in Psychological Research*. New York: Holt, Rinehart, & Winston, 1960.

ELMS, A. C. Influence of fantasy ability on attitude change through role playing. *Journal of Personality and Social Psychology*, 1966, *4*, 36–43.

ELMS, A. C. Role playing, incentive, and dissonance. *Psychological Bulletin*, 1967, *68*, 132–148.

ELMS, A. C., & JANIS, I. L. Counter-norm attitudes induced by consonant versus dissonant conditions of role-playing. *Journal of Experimental Research in Personality*, 1965, *1*, 50–60.

FESTINGER, L. *A Theory of Cognitive Dissonance*. Evanston, Ill.: Row, Peterson, 1957.

FESTINGER, L. *Conflict, Decision, and Dissonance*. Stanford: Stanford University Press, 1964.

FESTINGER, L., & ARONSON, E. The arousal and reduction of dissonance in social contexts. In D. Cartwright & A. Zander (Eds.), *Group Dynamics*. Evanston, Ill.: Row, Peterson, 1960.

FESTINGER, L., & CARLSMITH, J. M. Cognitive consequences of forced compliance. *Journal of Abnormal and Social Psychology*, 1959, *58*, 203–210.

FREEDMAN, J. L. Attitudinal effects of inadequate justification. *Journal of Personality*, 1963, *31*, 371–385.

FREEDMAN, J. L. Long-term behavior effects of cognitive dissonance. *Journal of Experimental Social Psychology*, 1965, *1*, 145–155.

GOLDSTEIN, I., & McGINNIES, E. Compliance and attitude change under conditions of differential social reinforcement. *Journal of Abnormal and Social Psychology*, 1964, *68*, 567–570.

GREENBAUM, C. W. Effect of situational and personality variables on improvisation and attitude change. *Journal of Personality and Social Psychology*, 1966, *4*, 260–269.

HARVEY, O., & BEVERLY, G. Some personality correlates of concept change through role playing. *Journal of Abnormal and Social Psychology*, 1961, *63*, 125–130.

HELMREICH, R. L., & COLLINS, B. E. Studies in forced compliance: Commitment and magnitude of inducement to comply as determinants of opinion change. *Journal of Personality and Social Psychology*, 1968, *10*, 75–81.

HESLIN, R., & ROTTON, J. Studies in counterattitudinal advocacy: I. Commitment, reward and attitude change. Unpublished manuscript, Purdue University, 1968.

HOCHBAUM, G. M. The relation between group members' self-confidence and their reactions to group pressures to uniformity. *American Sociological Review*, 1954, *19*, 678–687.

HORNBECK, F. W. Studies in forced compliance: IX. The effects of deception, commitment, and incentive on attitude change produced by the writing of a counterattitudinal essay. Paper presented at the meeting of the Western Psychological Association, San Francisco, May 1967.

HOVLAND, C., JANIS, I., & KELLEY, H. *Communication and Persuasion.* New Haven: Yale University Press, 1953.

HOVLAND, C. I., LUMSDAINE, A. A., & SHEFFIELD, F. D. *Experiments on Mass Communication.* Princeton: Princeton University Press, 1949.

HOVLAND, C. I., & WEISS, W. The influence of source credibility on communication effectiveness. *Public Opinion Quarterly*, 1951, *15*, 635–650.

INSKO, C. A. *Theories of Attitude Change.* New York: Appleton-Century-Crofts, 1967.

JANIS, I. Motivational factors in the resolution of decisional conflicts. In M. R. Jones (Ed.), *Nebraska symposium on motivation, 1959.* Lincoln: University of Nebraska Press, 1959.

JANIS, I. L. Attitude change via role playing. In R. Abelson, E. Aronson, W. McGuire, T. Newcomb, M. Rosenberg, & P. Tannenbaum

(Eds.), *Theories of Cognitive Consistency: A Sourcebook*. Chicago: Rand McNally, 1968.

JANIS, I. L., & GILMORE, J. B. The influence of incentive conditions on the success of role playing in modifying attitudes. *Journal of Personality and Social Psychology*, 1965, *1*, 17–27.

JANIS, I. L., & KING, B. T. The influence of role playing on opinion change. *Journal of Abnormal and Social Psychology*, 1954, *49*, 211–218.

JANIS, I. L., & MANN, L. Effectiveness of emotional role-playing in modifying smoking habits and attitudes. *Journal of Experimental Research in Personality*, 1965, *1*, 84–90.

JONES, R. A., LINDER, D. E., KIESLER, C. A., ZANNA, M., & BREHM, J. W. Internal states or external stimuli: Observers' attitude judgments and the dissonance theory—self-persuasion controversy. *Journal of Experimental Social Psychology*, 1968, *4*, 247–269.

KATZ, D. The functional approach to the study of attitudes. *Public Opinion Quarterly*, 1960, *24*, 163–204.

KELLEY, H. H., & WOODRUFF, CHRISTINE L. Members' reactions to apparent group approval of a counternorm communication. *Journal of Abnormal and Social Psychology*, 1956, *52*, 67–74.

KELMAN, H. C. Attitude change as a function of response restriction. *Human Relations*, 1953, *6*, 185–214.

KELMAN, H. C. The induction of action and attitude change. In *Proceedings of the XIV International Congress of Applied Psychology*. Copenhagen: Munksgaard, 1961.

KELMAN, H. C. Discrepant action and attitude change: A functional analysis. Unpublished paper (dittoed), University of Michigan, 1967.

KELMAN, H. C., & BARON, R. M. Inconsistency as a psychological signal. In R. Abelson, E. Aronson, W. McGuire, T. Newcomb, M. Rosenberg, & P. Tannenbaum (Eds.), *Theories of Cognitive Consistency: A Sourcebook*. Chicago: Rand McNally, 1968.

KING, B. T., & JANIS, I. L. Comparison of the effectiveness of improvised versus non-improvised role-playing in producing opinion changes. *Human Relations*, 1956, *9*, 177–186.

LAWRENCE, D. H., & FESTINGER, L. *Deterrents and Reinforcement: The Psychology of Insufficient Reward*. Stanford: Stanford University Press, 1962.

LEVENTHAL, G. S. Reward magnitude, task attractiveness, and liking for instrumental activity. *Journal of Abnormal and Social Psychology*, 1964, *68*, 460–463.

LIFTON, R. *Thought Reform and the Psychology of Totalism*. New York: Norton, 1961.

LINDER, D. E., COOPER, J., & JONES, E. E. Decision freedom as a determinant of the role of incentive magnitude in attitude change. *Journal of Personality and Social Psychology*, 1967, *6*, 245–254.

LIPPITT, R. The psychodrama in leadership training. *Sociometry*, 1943, *6*, 286–292.

MAIER, N. R. F. *Principles of Human Relations*. New York: Wiley, 1952.

MEAD, G. H. *Mind, Self, and Society*. Chicago: University of Chicago Press, 1934.

MORENO, J. L. *Psychodrama*. Vol. 1. New York: Beacon House, 1946.

MOSTELLER, F., & BUSH, R. R. Selected quantitative techniques. In G. Lindzey (Ed.), *Handbook of Social Psychology*. Vol. 1. *Theory and Method*. Cambridge, Mass.: Addison-Wesley, 1954.

MUNSINGER, H., & KESSEN, W. Uncertainty structure and preference. *Psychological Monographs*, 1964, *78*, 9, Whole No. 586.

MYERS, G. C. Control of conduct by suggestion: An experiment in Americanization. *Journal of Applied Psychology*, 1921, *5*, 26–31.

NEL, E., HELMREICH, R., & ARONSON, E. Opinion change in the advocate as a function of the persuasibility of his audience: A clarification of the meaning of dissonance. Technical Report No. 8, University of Texas at Austin, 1968.

NUTTIN, J. M., JR. Dissonant evidence about dissonance theory. Paper read at Second Conference of Experimental Social Psychologists in Europe, Frascati, Italy, 1964.

NUTTIN, J. M., JR. Attitude change after rewarded dissonant and consonant "forced compliance": A critical replication of the Festinger and Carlsmith experiment. *International Journal of Psychology*, 1966, *1*, 39–57.

ORNE, M. T. On the social psychology of the psychological experiment: With particular reference to demand characteristics and their implications. *American Psychologist*, 1962, *17*, 776–783.

OSGOOD, C., & TANNENBAUM, P. H. The principle of congruity in the prediction of attitude change. *Psychological Review*, 1955, *62*, 42–55.

PEAK, HELEN. Attitude and motivation. In M. R. Jones (Ed.), *Nebraska Symposium on Motivation, 1955*. Lincoln: University of Nebraska Press, 1955.

RABBIE, J., BREHM, J., & COHEN, A. Verbalization and reactions to cognitive dissonance. *Journal of Personality*, 1959, *27*, 407–417.

RIECKEN, H. W. A program for research on experiments in social psychology. In N. F. Washburne (Ed.), *Decisions, Values, and Groups*. Vol. 2. New York: Pergamon Press, 1962.

ROSENBERG, M. J. Cognitive structure and attitudinal affect. *Journal of Abnormal and Social Psychology*, 1956, *53*, 367–372.

ROSENBERG, M. J. An analysis of affective-cognitive consistency. In C. I. Hovland & M. J. Rosenberg (Eds.), *Attitude Organization and Change*. New Haven: Yale University Press, 1960.

ROSENBERG, M. J. When dissonance fails: On eliminating evaluation apprehension from attitude measurement. *Journal of Personality and Social Psychology*, 1965, *1*, 28–42.

ROSENBERG, M. J. Some limits of dissonance: Toward a differentiated view of counter-attitudinal performance. In S. Feldman (Ed.), *Cognitive Consistency*. New York: Academic Press, 1966.

ROSENBERG, M. J. Hedonism, inauthenticity and other goads toward expansion of a consistency theory. In R. Abelson, E. Aronson, W. McGuire, T. Newcomb, M. Rosenberg, & P. Tannenbaum (Eds.), *Theories of Cognitive Consistency: A Sourcebook*. Chicago: Rand McNally, 1968.

ROSENTHAL, R. On the social psychology of the psychological experiment: The experimenter's hypothesis as unintended determinant of experimental results. *American Scientist*, 1963, *51*, 268–283.

RYLE, G. *The Concept of Mind*. London: Hutchinson, 1949.

SARBIN, T. R., & ALLEN, V. L. Role enactment, audience feedback, and attitude change. *Sociometry*, 1964, *27*, 183–193.

SCHACHTER, S., & SINGER, J. Cognitive, social, and physiological determinants of emotional state. *Psychological Review*, 1962, *69*, 379–399.

SCHEIN, E. The Chinese indoctrination program for prisoners of war: A study of attempted "brain washing." *Psychiatry*, 1956, *19*, 149–172.

SCOTT, W. A. Attitude change through reward of verbal behavior. *Journal of Abnormal and Social Psychology*, 1957, *55*, 72–75.

SCOTT, W. A. Rationality and non-rationality of international attitudes. *Conflict Resolution*, 1958, *2*, 8–16.

SCOTT, W. A. Cognitive consistency, response reinforcement, and attitude change. *Sociometry*, 1959, *22*, 219–229.

SCOTT, W. A. Attitude change by response reinforcement: Replication and extension. *Sociometry*, 1959, *22*, 328–335.

SILVERMAN, I. In defense of dissonance theory: Reply to Chapanis & Chapanis. *Psychological Bulletin*, 1964, *62*, 205–209.

SKINNER, B. F. *Science and Human Behavior*. New York: Macmillan, 1953.

SKINNER, B. F. *Verbal Behavior*. New York: Appleton-Century-Crofts, 1957.

SMITH, M. B., BRUNER, J. S., & WHITE, R. W. *Opinions and Personality*. New York: Wiley, 1956.

STANLEY, J. C., & KLAUSMEIER, H. J. Opinion constancy after formal role playing. *Journal of Social Psychology*, 1957, *46*, 11–18.

TURNER, E. A., & WRIGHT, J. C. Effects of severity of threat and perceived availability on the attractiveness of objects. *Journal of Personality and Social Psychology*, 1965, *2*, 128–132.

VON CRANACH, MARIO L. Meinungsänderung durch eigenes Handeln. *Psychologische Forschung*, 1965, *28*, 89–152.

WALLACE, J. Role reward and dissonance reduction. *Journal of Personality and Social Psychology*, 1966, *3*, 305–312.

WINER, B. J. *Statistical Principles in Experimental Design*. New York: McGraw-Hill, 1962.

ZANDER, A., & LIPPITT, R. Reality-practice as educational method. *Sociometry*, 1944, *7*, 129–151.

ZIMBARDO, P. G. The effect of effort and improvisation on self-persuasion produced by role-playing. *Journal of Experimental Social Psychology*, 1965, *1*, 103–120.

*Note

By the Editors of the Series

In the field of psychology we believe that the student ought to get the "feel" of experimentation by reading original source materials. In this way he can acquire a better understanding of the discipline by seeing scientific ideas grow and change. However, one of the main problems in teaching is the limited availability of these sources, which communicate most effectively the personality of the author and the excitement of ongoing research.

For these reasons we have decided to edit several books,* each devoted to a particular problem in psychology. In every case we attempt to select problems that have been and are controversial —that have been and still are alive. We intend to present these problems as a set of selected original articles, arranged in historical order and in order of progress in the field. We believe that it is important for the student to see that theories and researches build on what has gone before; that one study leads to another, that theory leads to research and then to revision of theory. We believe that *telling* the student this does not make the same kind of impression as letting him see it happen in actuality. The idea is for the student to read and build ideas for himself.

Suggestions for Use—These readings books can be used by the student in either of two ways. They are organized so that, with the help of the instructor (or of the students if used in seminars), a topic can be covered at length and in depth. This would necessitate lectures or discussions on articles not covered in the series to fill in the gaps. On the other hand, each book taken alone will give a student a good idea of the problem being covered and its historical background as well as its present state and the direction it seems to be taking.

* (Pub. note: a sub-series within the Insight Book Series.)